100 Treasures of
Windsor Castle

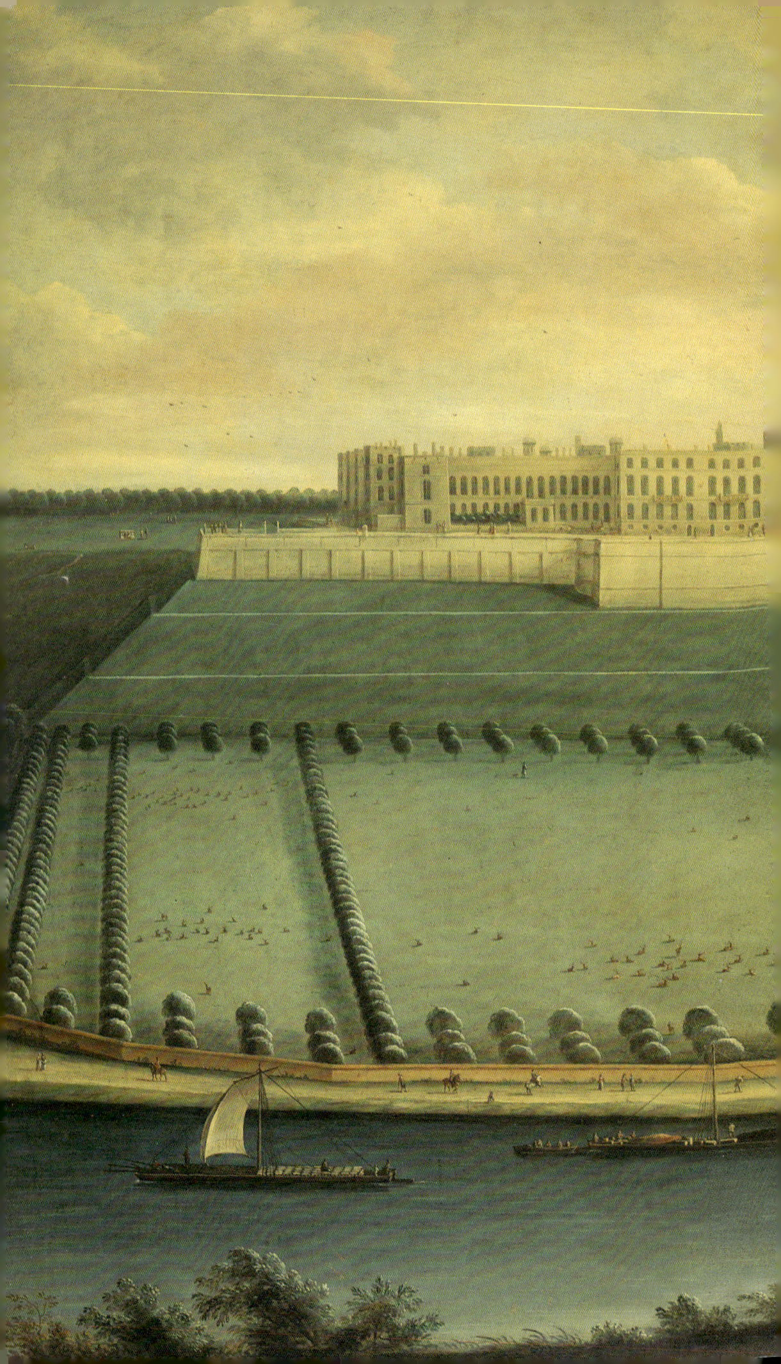

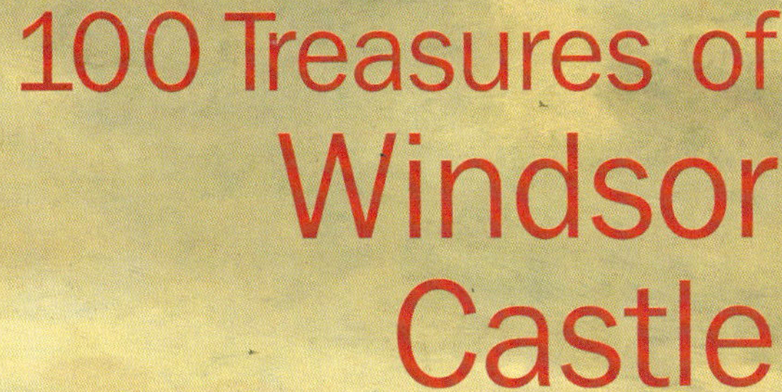

100 Treasures of Windsor Castle

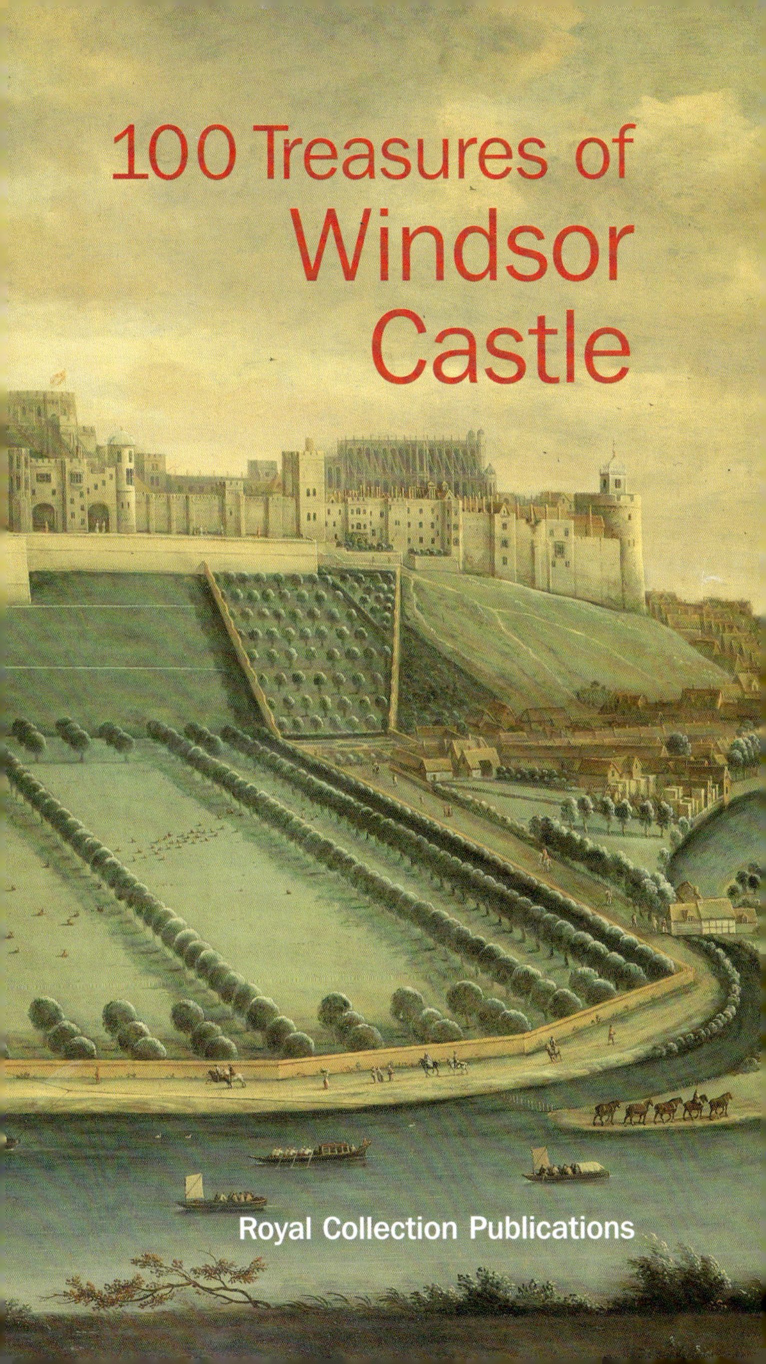

Royal Collection Publications

Contents

Foreword

The works of art illustrated in this book are among the finest of their kind. They form part of the Royal Collection, which is owned by The Queen as Sovereign and held in trust for her successors and the nation.

The Royal Collection contains paintings, drawings, furniture, porcelain, silver, sculpture, jewellery, books, arms and armour, and textiles. Most of it is on display or in use at the principal royal residences, which include Buckingham Palace, Windsor Castle, the Palace of Holyroodhouse, St James's Palace, the Tower of London, Hampton Court Palace, the Banqueting House in Whitehall, Sandringham House, Balmoral Castle and Osborne House.

Since 1993, a charitable trust, the Royal Collection Trust, has been responsible for the care and conservation of the Collection. The Trust is funded solely by income from visitors to the official residences of The Queen (Buckingham Palace, Windsor Castle and the Palace of Holyroodhouse).

One of the chief aims of the Royal Collection Trust, of which The Prince of Wales is Chairman, is to ensure that the works of art are presented in ways that will enhance the visitor's understanding and appreciation. A wide-ranging programme of publications, now including *100 Treasures of Windsor Castle*, supports this important objective.

Introduction

Windsor Castle is the oldest of the British royal residences, having been in more or less continuous occupation since its foundation by William the Conqueror in the eleventh century. Originally built to guard the western approaches to London, it occupies a key strategic hilltop position overlooking the Thames valley. Of almost equal importance for sovereigns down the ages, the Castle lay next to Windsor forest, which served as the ideal location for the royal hunt.

The massive stone walls, covering a site of some 10.5 hectares (26 acres), enclose buildings of the greatest architectural significance, including St George's Chapel, the Round Tower and the State Apartments. The latter, which stand in the north-eastern area of the Castle and until the nineteenth century were used regularly by the Sovereign, contain some of the finest works of art in the Royal Collection and are open to visitors throughout the year.

The selection of treasures from Windsor included in this publication covers the whole range of British royal patronage and collecting. As well as unique architectural features of the Castle buildings from the medieval period, the choice includes paintings, drawings, furniture, metalwork, porcelain, clocks and sculpture, ranging in date from the Renaissance to the twentieth century.

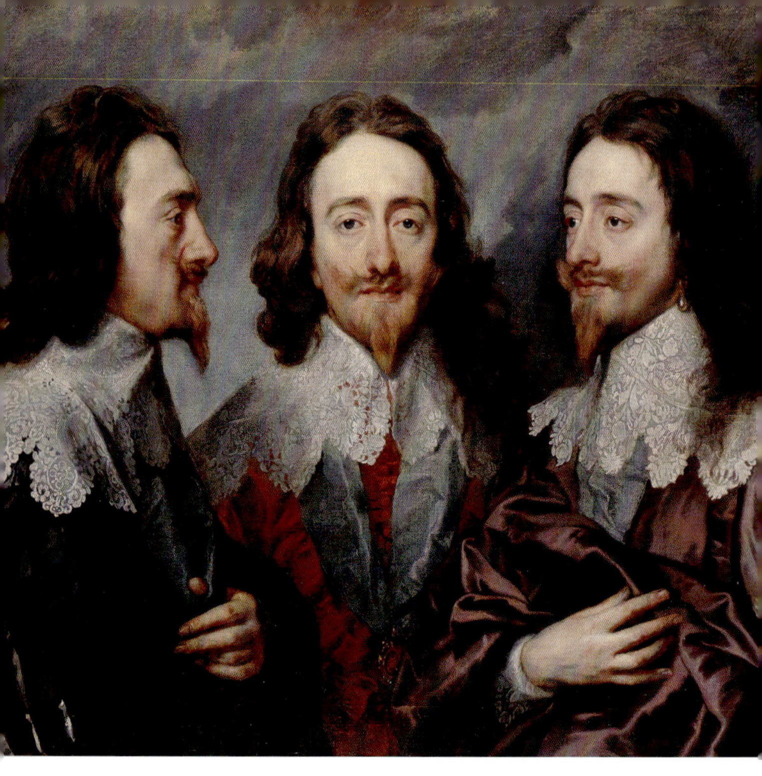

ANTHONY VAN DYCK, *Charles I in Three Positions* (1635)

The principal collectors represented include Henry VIII, the founder of the modern Royal Collection; Charles I, the first great royal collector of European (particularly Italian) paintings; Charles II, who rebuilt the royal apartments at Windsor in the 1670s and 1680s; Frederick, Prince of Wales and his son, George III, avid collectors of paintings and drawings in the eighteenth century; and, above all, George IV. As Prince of Wales, Regent and King, George IV was an obsessive collector on a grand scale. Over a

50-year period until his death in 1830, he assembled superb examples of French and English furniture and clocks, silver, porcelain and sculpture, and Old Master and contemporary paintings, at a rate and of a quality which has seldom been equalled and never surpassed. His niece Victoria, Queen from 1837 to 1901, also added substantially to the Royal Collection, especially during the lifetime of her husband and principal artistic adviser, Prince Albert (d.1861). In modern times, the emphasis has been on the conservation and display of the collection, a process only interrupted by the major fire at Windsor in 1992. The restoration of the Castle took five years and in the process of reconstruction several new architectural features have been introduced, some of which have themselves become objects of interest and significance for visitors.

Notes for the Visitor

The commentaries on the works of art in this guide are designed to follow the visitor route through the State and Semi-State Apartments. The name of each room is given at the foot of each page of text, with an arrow ➤ indicating when the last object in a room has been reached.

As the State Apartments are used regularly for entertaining and public ceremonies, and many loans from the Royal Collection are made to external exhibitions, individual objects may occasionally be relocated or removed.

The Semi-State Apartments are included in the visitor route during the winter period from October to March.

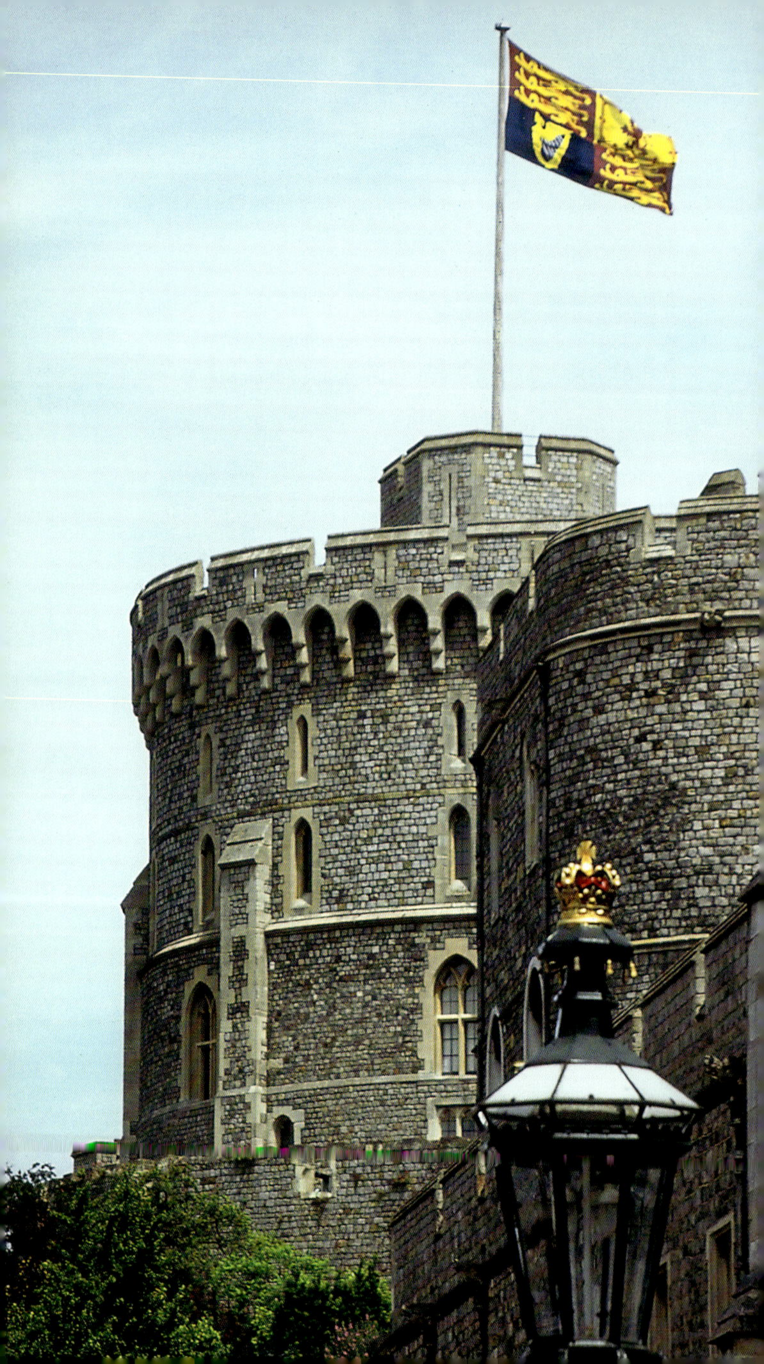

The Round Tower

late twelfth century and later

The Round Tower dominates the famous skyline of Windsor. Rising to a height of 41 metres (134 feet), it stands in the middle of the Castle on a chalk mound surrounded by a dry moat, and from above its battlements the Royal Standard flies whenever the Sovereign is in residence. The first tower, or keep, built entirely of wood, was erected here by William the Conqueror in the 1080s as the principal defensive point of the Castle. A hundred years later, Henry II rebuilt it in stone, and in the fourteenth century Edward III created within its hollow walls a royal lodging, which later became the residence of the Constable of the Castle.

Its present appearance is due to Sir Jeffry Wyatville, George IV's architect at Windsor, who was commissioned to give the Castle the romantic and picturesque Gothic form we see today. A major feature of Wyatville's great project, which began in the mid-1820s and was finally completed 20 years later, was the doubling of the height of the Round Tower. The resulting massive increase in weight eventually caused the foundations of the Tower to begin to slip, and in the late 1980s an extensive programme of underpinning was carried out to ensure the long-term survival of this unique structure. At the same time additional storage space was created within the walls for the Royal Archives, which have been housed in the Round Tower since the early twentieth century.

The Gilebertus Doors

c.1250

The magnificent gilded ironwork on these doors is signed 'GILEBERTUS' in three places, but unfortunately nothing is known of the medieval smith who so unusually and boldly signed his work. Costly metal enrichments of this kind were invariably reserved for buildings of high importance, and very little work of this date and on this scale has survived intact. This survival may be due as much as anything to the fact that the significance of the doors themselves is now much less obvious than when they were first made in the thirteenth century. Due to the adjacent construction in the late fifteenth century of the new St George's Chapel, what was originally built in the 1240s as the principal west portal of Henry III's chapel dedicated to St Edward, and entered through these doors, has become a dark and enclosed backwater, now used only when the Sovereign attends St George's Chapel.

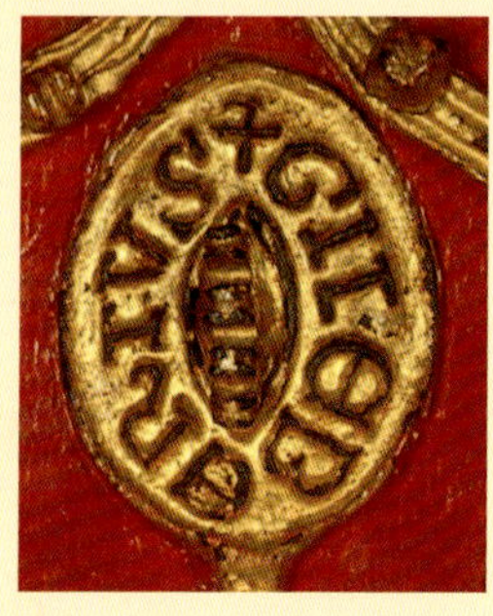

Very little else of Henry III's work in this part of the Castle survives, and St Edward's Chapel itself was rebuilt by Henry VII in the 1490s as a Lady Chapel and Royal Tomb House. After numerous further changes, the Lady Chapel re-emerged in its present elaborate High Victorian dress as the Albert Memorial Chapel, dedicated to the memory of the Prince Consort, who died in 1861.

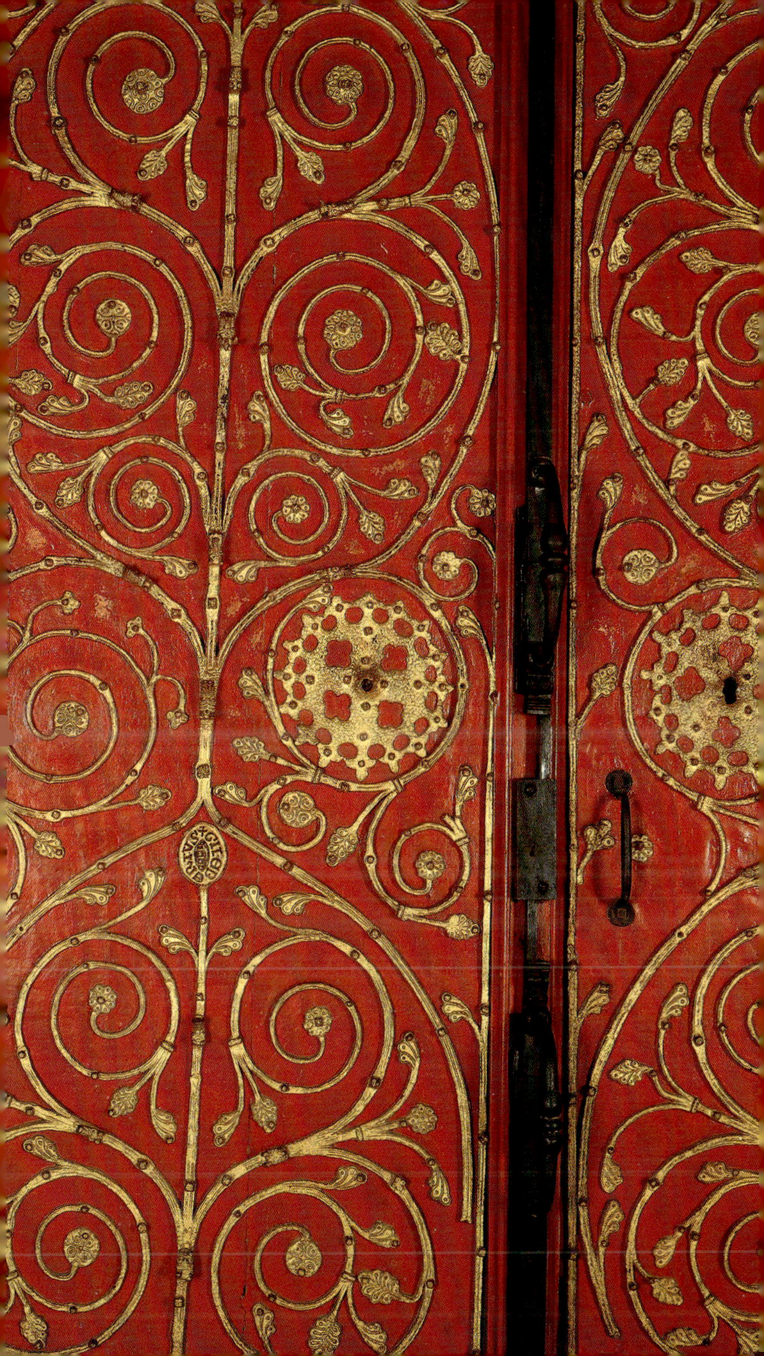

Princess Charlotte's Tomb

Matthew Cotes Wyatt (1777–1862)

completed 1824

Unlike her father the Prince Regent, Princess Charlotte Augusta of Wales (1796–1817) enjoyed great popularity and was held up as a model of cultivation and charity. Her marriage in April 1816 to Prince Leopold of Saxe-Coburg-Saalfeld was widely celebrated, and her death in childbirth in November of the following year was seen as a national disaster, marked by extraordinary scenes of collective public grief. Wyatt's spectacular monument, extravagant in its use of marble, was paid for by public subscription, limited to one shilling per donor. The universal response to the tragedy is reflected in the fact that the monument is completely uninscribed.

The soul of the Princess is represented rising heavenwards from a curtained tomb, accompanied by angels, one of whom cradles her stillborn infant. Below, on an altar-like block, lies the draped corpse, enveloped by a sheet from which the fingers of one hand protrude. To each side, the kneeling forms of four female mourning figures can be discerned beneath drapery, contributing a sense of exhaustion and desolation. The composition has few parallels in English churches, where such emotional imagery was discouraged. When first completed, the monument was lit from each side by yellow and violet stained glass.

Matthew Cotes Wyatt was the son of James Wyatt, Surveyor of the Fabric of Windsor Castle. Before securing this commission, he was employed by George III on ceiling paintings throughout the State Apartments.

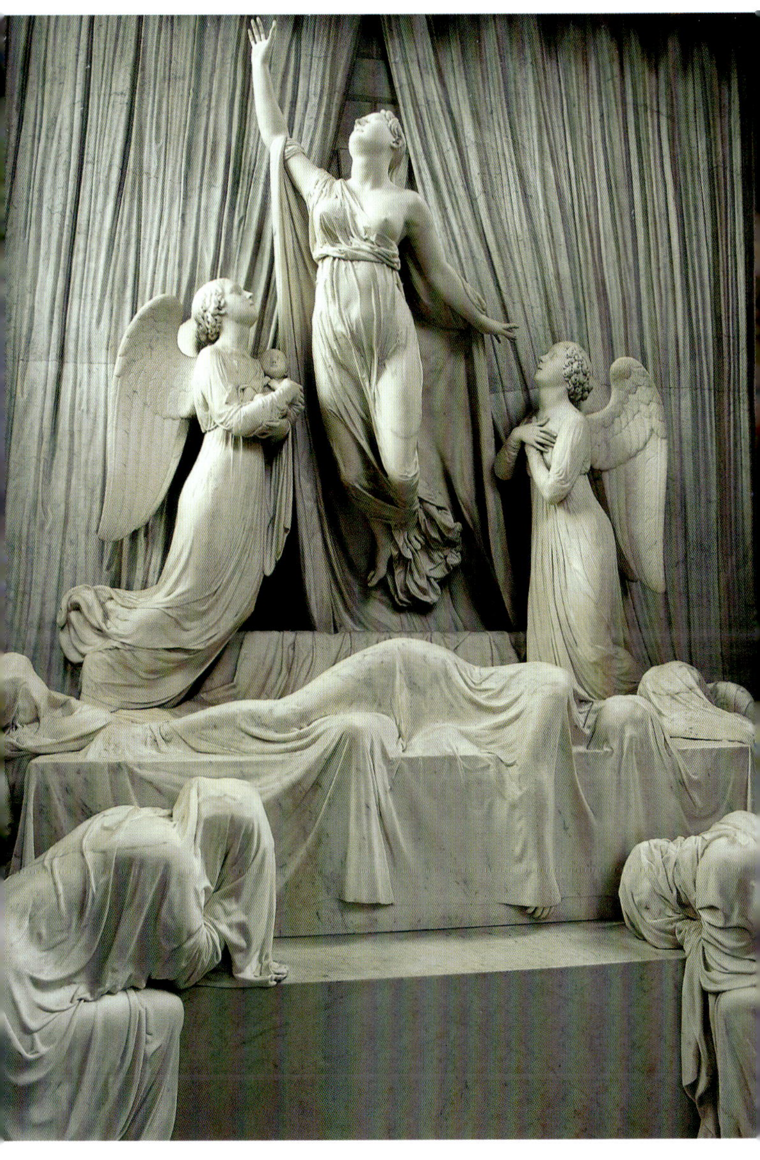

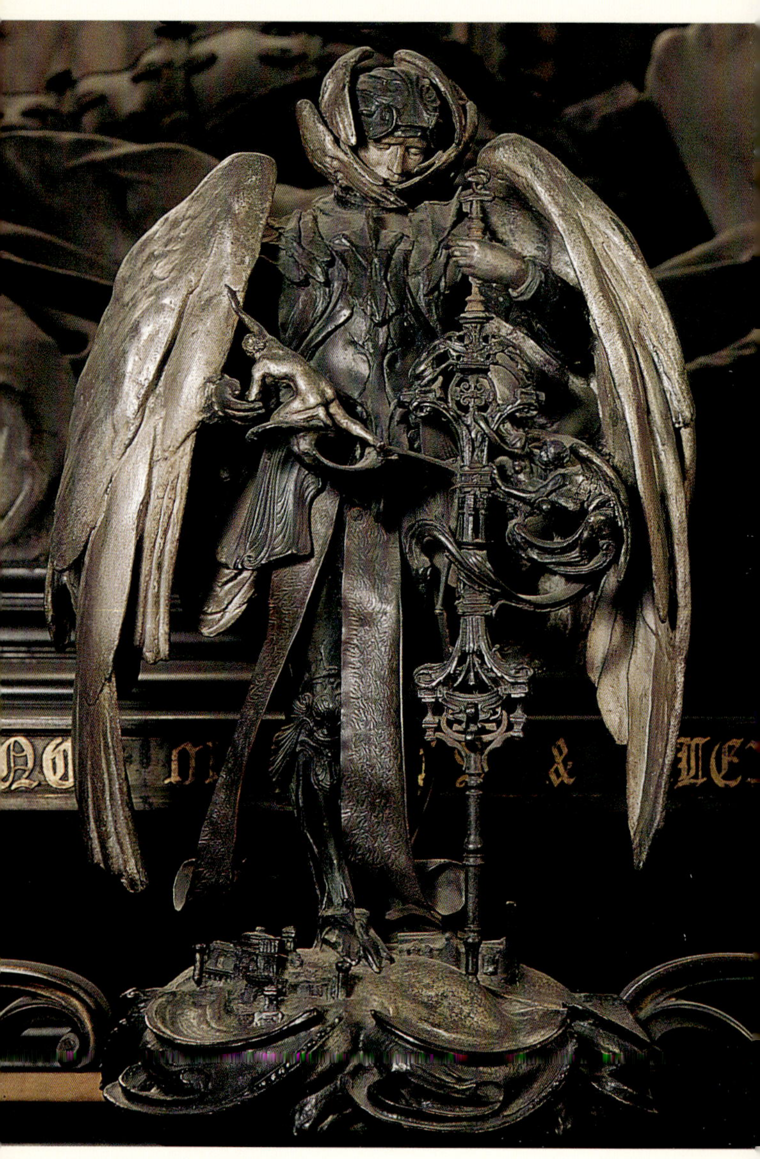

Tomb of the Duke of Clarence

Alfred Gilbert (1854–1934)

1892–9, with additions 1926–8

Although dedicated by Queen Victoria to the memory of her husband, the Albert Memorial Chapel is dominated by the tomb of their grandson, Albert Victor, Duke of Clarence and Avondale (1864–92), who died of influenza in January 1892, at the age of 27. Prince Albert Victor was the eldest son of Albert Edward and Alexandra, Prince and Princess of Wales, the future King Edward VII and Queen Alexandra.

Alfred Gilbert saw in this commission the opportunity to create his masterpiece, a work of unparalleled complexity, worthy of comparison with the greatest of medieval royal tombs and with that of Henry VII by Torrigiani at Westminster. Although it was installed in the chapel in 1898, the tomb took a further 30 years to complete. The recumbent effigy of the Prince in hussars' uniform is barely visible, facing the heavens. Most of the work on the tomb is cast in bronze, but the Prince's head and hands are of white marble, and his voluminous mantle (like the crowning angel above the Prince's head) is of aluminium, the material of Gilbert's most famous statue, *Eros* (Piccadilly Circus, London). Following the pattern of earlier royal tombs, the central chest is surrounded by a grille, but Gilbert's is like no other: it is punctuated by a dozen figures of guardian saints (as shown opposite), standing on torch-like columns, held by paired angels with vaned wings.

Queen Mary's Dolls' House

Sir Edwin Lutyens (1869–1944)

1921–4

Probably the most famous dolls' house in the world, this is a magnetic attraction for visitors of all ages. It was the brainchild of Princess Marie-Louise, granddaughter of Queen Victoria and childhood friend of Queen Mary. The Princess persuaded the celebrated architect Sir Edwin Lutyens to design the house, which was intended as a gesture of thanks and loyalty to King George V and Queen Mary for their leadership during the First World War. Lutyens wanted to create something that would enable future generations to see how a grand English house was furnished and occupied in the early 1920s, and to provide a showcase for all that was best in British craftsmanship and design of that era. Nearly 1,500 artists, authors and craftsmen were involved in supplying the contents, all made to the overall scale of 1 to 12. Among the specially commissioned contents are musical scores by Delius and Holst, books by Conan Doyle, Kipling and Conrad, Rolls-Royce and Daimler motor cars, and sporting guns by Purdey.

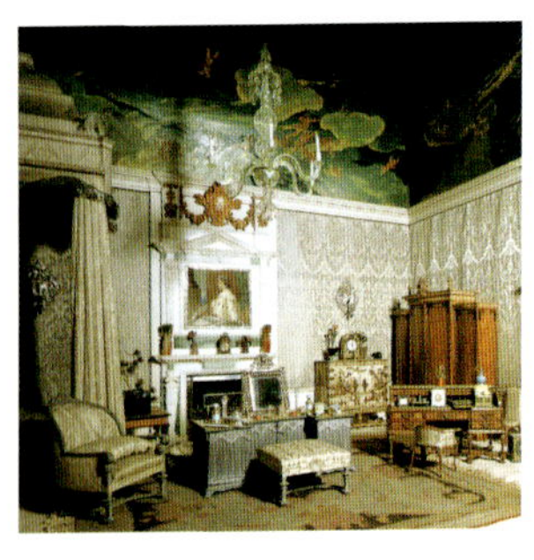

The Queen agreed that the Dolls' House should first be shown to the public in aid of her charities at the British Empire Exhibition at Wembley in 1924, and subsequently at the Ideal Home Exhibition at Olympia in 1925. Since then it has never moved from Windsor, where it is shown in the setting designed for it by Lutyens.

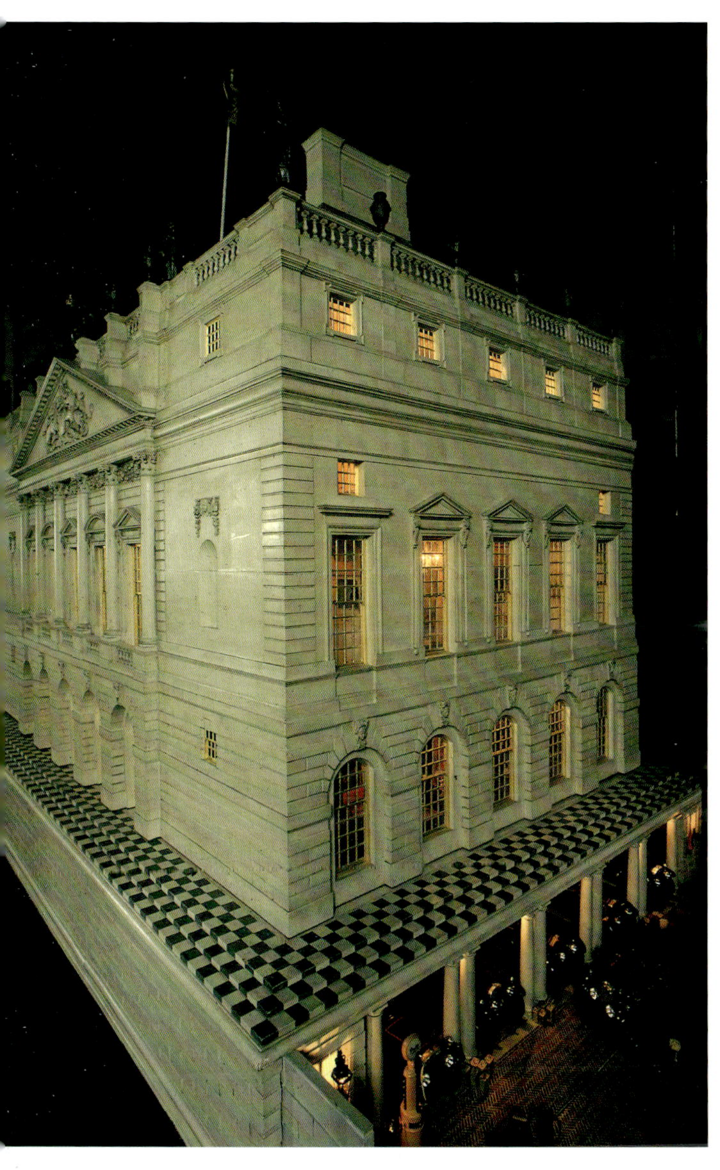

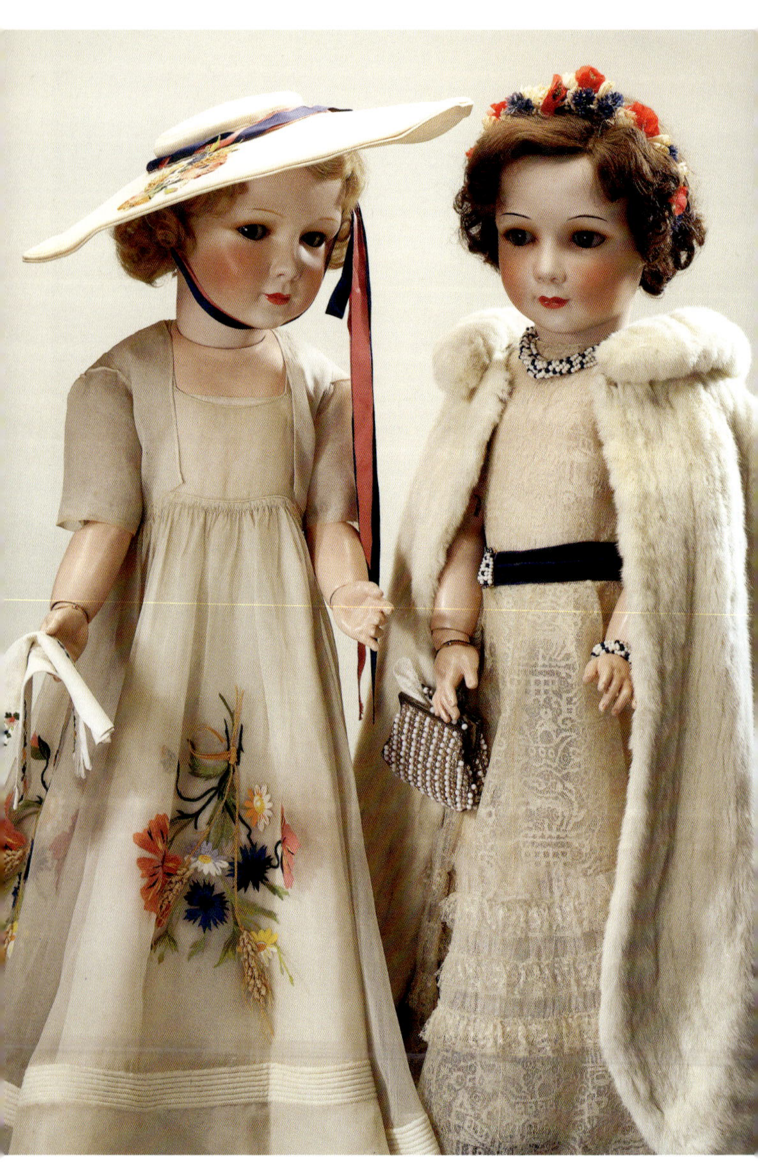

France and Marianne

Paris

1938

Gifts between rulers have been a commonplace of international diplomacy for hundreds of years, but the presentation of these two dolls – France, the brown-eyed blonde, and Marianne, the blue-eyed brunette – with their extensive trousseaux, marked a watershed in this process: never before had dolls played such a significant (if indirect) part in the affairs of two nations. France and Marianne were given in the name of the Children of France to the young Princesses Elizabeth and Margaret Rose, on the occasion of the State Visit paid by their parents, King George VI and Queen Elizabeth, to Paris in July 1938. The visit itself came at a time of heightened international tension, and was designed to strengthen the ties between Britain and her nearest ally, France. No effort was spared to provide the English Princesses with dolls that would exceed in quality and range of accessories anything seen before.

The dolls themselves were made by the famous firm of Jumeau, and their wardrobes were filled with dresses, hats, gloves, shoes, handbags and lingerie for every occasion, made by the leading couturiers of the day – Lanvin, Worth, Patou and Rochas among them. Their accessories were equally sophisticated: scent by Guerlain, jewellery by Cartier, fans by Duvelleroy, porcelain from Sèvres, luggage by Vuitton, and even model cars by Citroën.

From September 1940 to September 1941 the dolls toured Canada to raise funds for the Canadian National Committee on Refugees, returning to England after the end of the Second World War. They are now displayed with a selection of items from their wardrobes, next to Queen Mary's Dolls' House.

Sir Thomas More

Hans Holbein the Younger (1497/8–1543)

c.1527

Hans Holbein the Younger was born in Germany but worked for two periods in England, from 1526 to 1528 and from 1532 until his death. His inventiveness and technical accomplishment transformed the arts in England. The 80 portrait drawings by Holbein in the Royal Library were probably acquired on the artist's death by King Henry VIII, who employed Holbein intermittently as his court artist. The drawings are life studies for the painted portraits that were Holbein's chief activity during his years in England.

This is a study of Sir Thomas More (1476–1535), author of *Utopia*, Speaker of the House of Commons and later Lord Chancellor, who was executed for his opposition to Henry VIII's religious reforms. Holbein probably lodged at More's house in Chelsea during his first stay in England.

The Royal Library at Windsor Castle houses one of the world's finest collections of Old Master drawings, including unsurpassed groups by Leonardo da Vinci, Holbein, Canaletto, Poussin and many other artists. For reasons of conservation, works on paper cannot be on permanent display, so a changing selection of these drawings is shown in the Drawings Gallery.

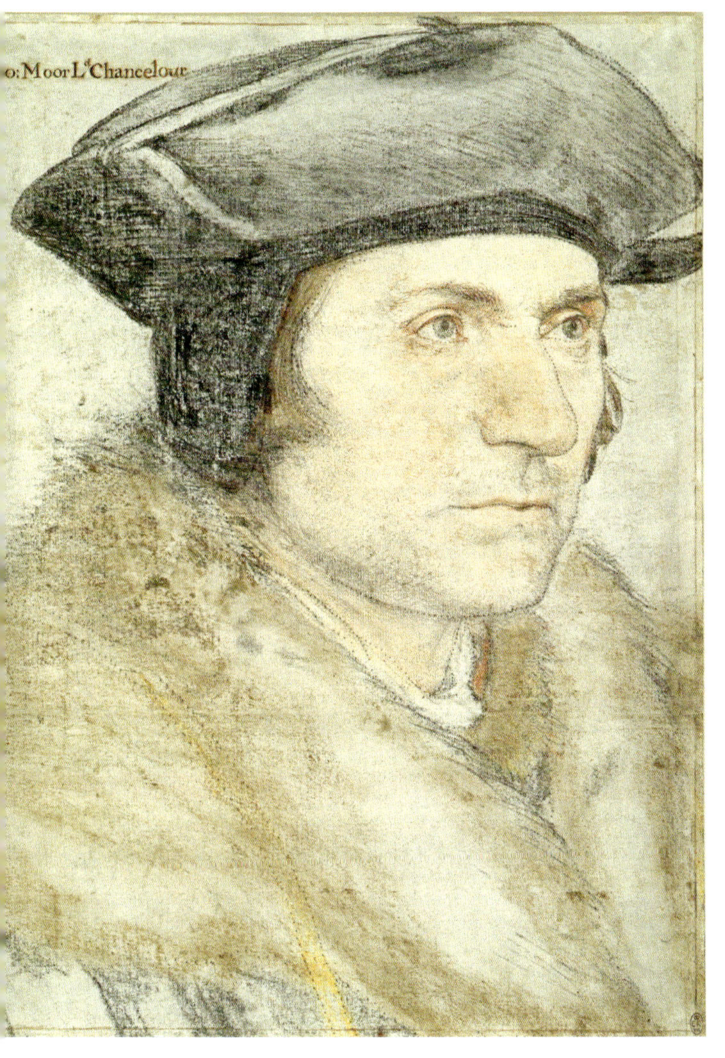
o: Moor Ld Chancelour

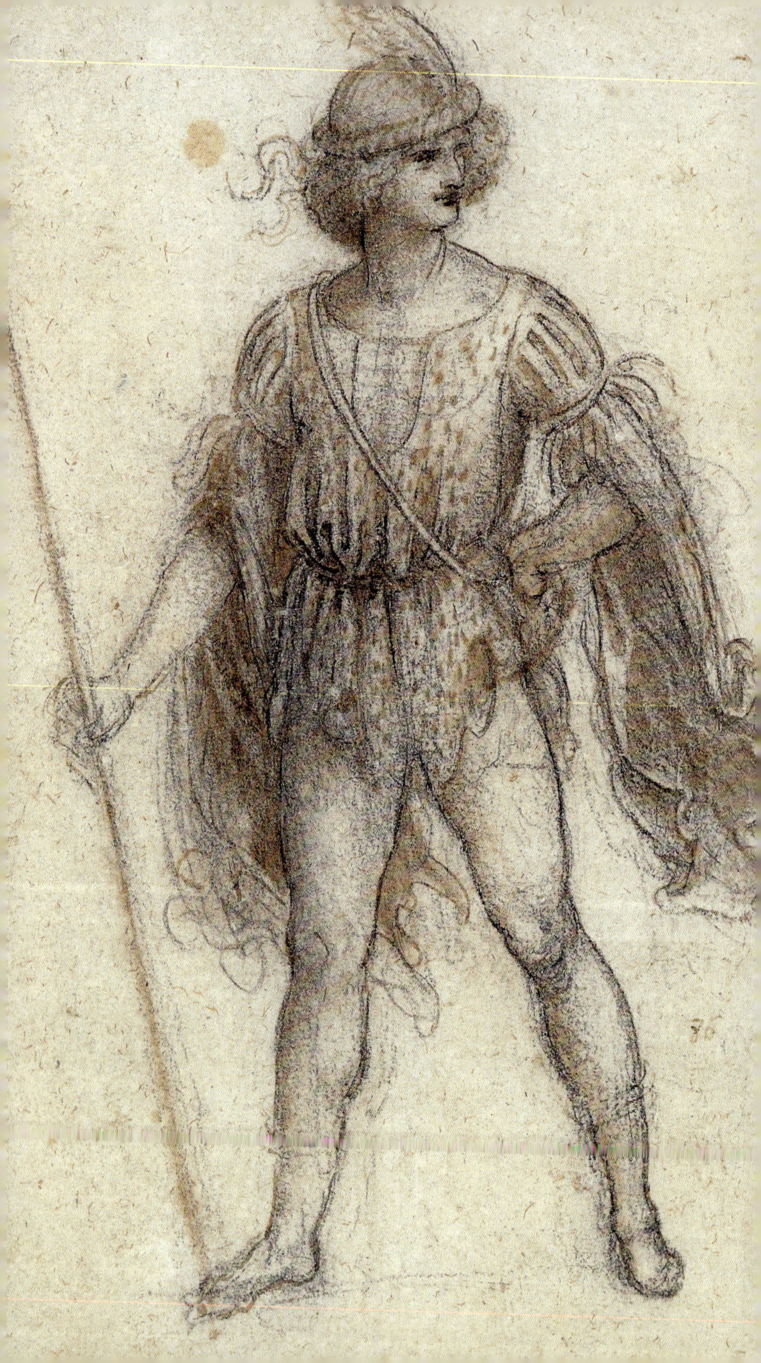

A Masquerader

Leonardo da Vinci (1452–1519)

*c.*1517–18

The 600 drawings by Leonardo da Vinci are the greatest treasure of the Royal Library. They illuminate all aspects of the archetypal Renaissance man's life – not only as a painter, sculptor and architect, but also as an engineer, musician, anatomist, geologist and botanist. Indeed, many of Leonardo's activities are known only through these drawings.

For over half his career Leonardo was employed as a court artist, in Milan, in Rome and, at the end of his life, in France. In addition to his artistic duties, he was required to advise on architecture and fortifications, and to devise entertainments – theatrical productions, costumes for processions, and so on. This drawing seems to have been a design for a costume to be worn by the young Federico Gonzaga of Mantua, at a ball held in his honour by the King of France in January 1518.

The drawings by Leonardo have been kept together as a group since the artist's death, and were probably acquired for the Royal Collection by Charles II.

The Etruscan Service

Royal Neapolitan factory

1785–7

The Etruscan style, inspired by ornaments and figures from ancient vases, was one of the most enduringly popular variants of the neoclassical style of the late eighteenth century, and perhaps nowhere more so than in ceramics. Josiah Wedgwood rechristened his Staffordshire factory 'Etruria' in 1769, and his competitors in France and Germany exploited much the same source material, especially following the completion, in 1776, of a magnificent set of printed volumes illustrating the vase collection formed by Sir William Hamilton, British Ambassador at Naples.

The Etruscan Service was commissioned in 1783 by King Ferdinand IV of the Two Sicilies from his own factory at Naples (known as the Real Fabbrica Ferdinandea), as a gift for George III. Originally comprising 282 pieces, it was the ceramic equivalent of Hamilton's printed volumes, illustrating the King's own collection of vases. Some are represented in the central reserves of the plates and bowls, while the functional pieces, such as tureens and wine-bottle coolers, are ingenious modern adaptations of the ancient shapes themselves.

The service was brought to England by the chief modeller and painter of the factory in two warships of the Neapolitan navy, whose crew had been instructed to make use of their visit by reporting back on the strength and disposition of the English fleet and the naval dockyards.

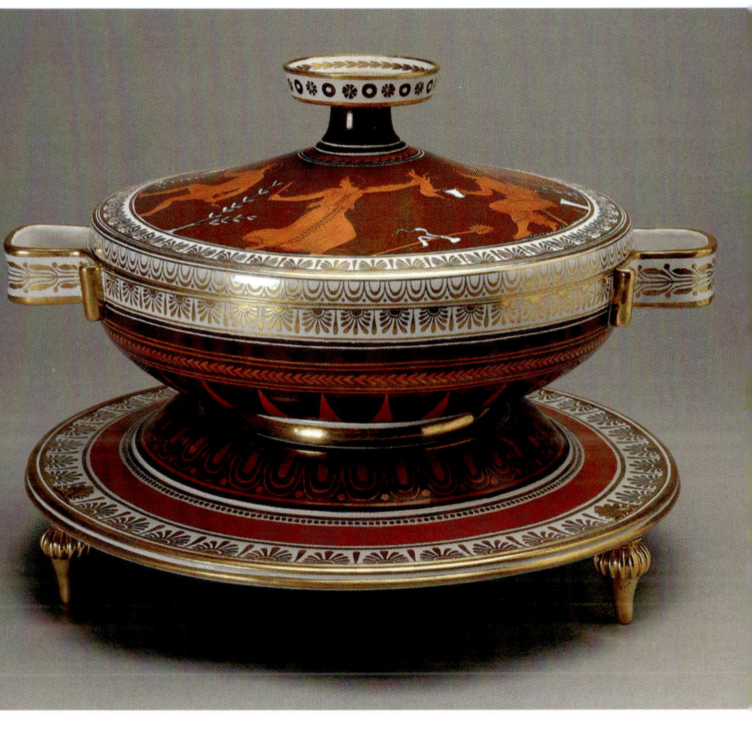

The Fürstenberg Service

Northern Germany

c.1773

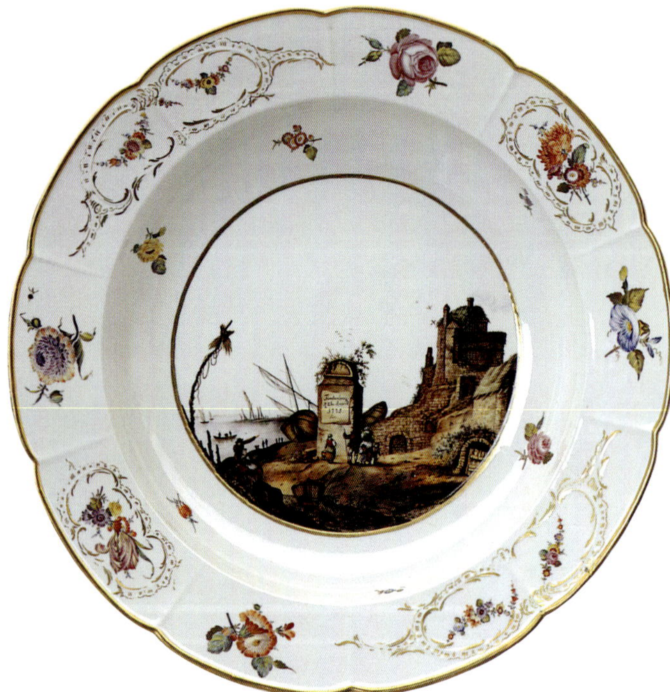

Like the Etruscan Service, this is an example of a porcelain service conceived for a purpose normally reserved for printed books or sets of engravings. Though painted on porcelain, the landscapes depicting the Harz Mountains and Weserbergland in the Duchy of Brunswick in northern Germany constitute a sort of picture gallery in miniature.

Most of the scenes were painted by P.J.F. Weitsch, a versatile artist who served in the Brunswick army and taught himself to paint landscapes by studying the work of seventeenth-century Dutch painters such as Jan Both and Nicolaes Berchem. Weitsch's landscape vignettes were worked up from his own topographical drawings, but there are also scenes in Italy, France and Switzerland which may have been copied from prints. This is certainly true of the harbour scene on the large circular bowl, which is copied from a print by F.E. Weirotter and bears the date 1773. The very distinctive outline of the landscapes, framed with rockwork and roots – sometimes resembling lumps of earth pulled from the ground – was frequently (though not uniquely) used by Weitsch.

The Fürstenberg porcelain factory was founded by Duke Charles I of Brunswick in 1747, at Fürstenberg Castle on the river Weser.

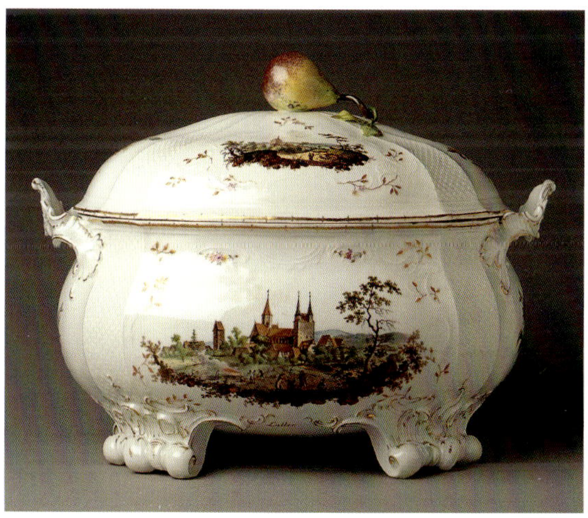

The Rockingham Service

Brameld Brothers

1830–37

William IV, though not celebrated as a patron of the arts, was nonetheless of great importance to English porcelain manufacturers. A dessert service was commissioned from Benjamin Flight's factory at Worcester to mark his creation as Duke of Clarence and St Andrews in 1789, and this was followed by several other orders. In celebration of his coronation in 1831, services were ordered from the Worcester factory, from H & R Daniel at Stoke, and from the Brameld brothers' factory on the South Yorkshire estate of Earl Fitzwilliam, known as the Rockingham Works.

William IV's Rockingham service is one of the great masterpieces of English porcelain manufacture. The inventiveness of the designs, and the quality of the modelling, firing, enamelling and gilding, are of the highest order. Some 600 workers were involved in producing the service, which combined national symbols such as oak leaves with the fruits of empire – sugar cane, pineapples and other exotic fruits – celebrating Britain's status as a world power. Among the 760 separate painted reserves are views of India and the West Indies. Such high standards of production came at a heavy price for the factory: the service was delivered six years late, and contributed in large part to the insolvency of the firm.

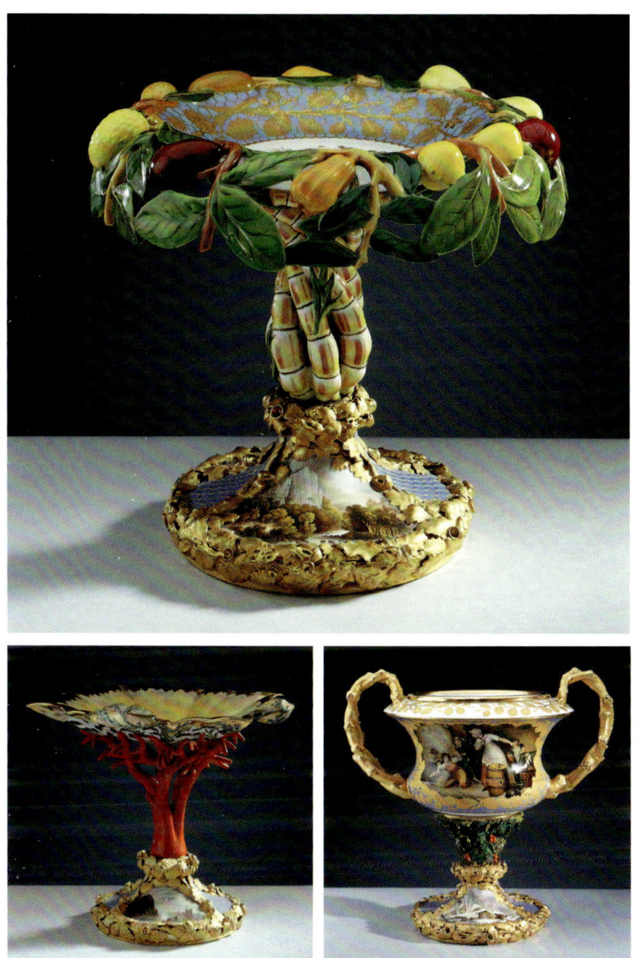

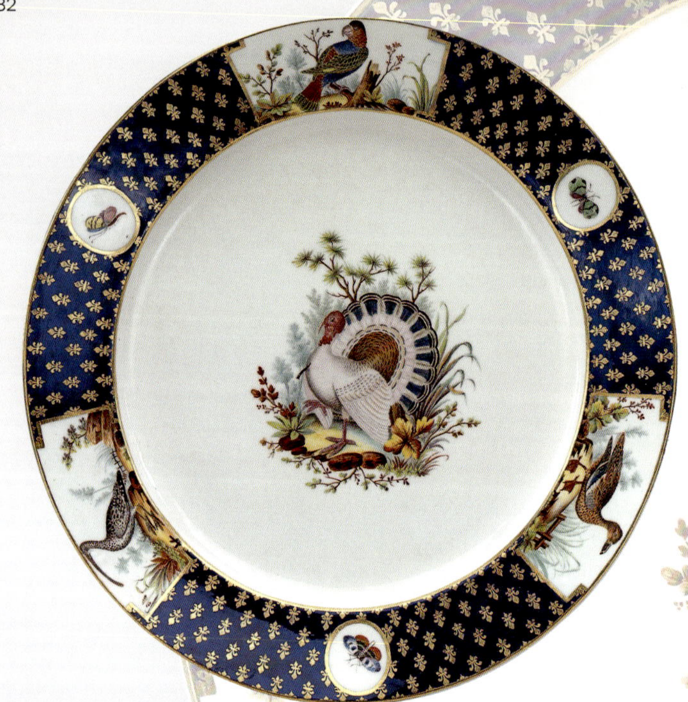

The Tournai Service

c.1787

Often mistaken for the more famous Sèvres porcelain, this service was made at Tournai in modern Belgium, for Philippe, Duke of Orléans (1747–93), possibly as an act of defiance towards his cousin, the French King Louis XVI, proprietor of the Sèvres factory. The service, which includes wares for dinner, dessert, breakfast, tea and coffee, originally comprised 1,603 pieces, each of which was decorated with numerous birds, copied from engravings in the Comte de Buffon's vast encyclopaedia, *Histoire Naturelle* (1770–83). Each bird is named on the back in engagingly unscientific terms, such as 'topaz-throated crested hummingbird from Cayenne' and 'Sea-swallow or scarecrow'.

Many of the designs, such as the bucket-shaped coolers for bottles in descending sizes (the smallest were probably intended for ice cream) and the straight-sided salad dishes, are in an austere neoclassical style and incorporate *trompe l'oeil* paintings of ancient cameos.

The Duke of Orléans was an acquaintance of the future George IV and a frequent visitor to London in the 1780s. Their friendship came to an abrupt end in 1793, when Orléans, who became known during the French Revolution as *Philippe Egalité*, was a signatory to Louis XVI's execution warrant. Later that year, Orléans suffered the same fate and his collections were dispersed. More than 600 pieces of the Tournai service were purchased by George IV through a London dealer, in two batches, in 1803 and 1806.

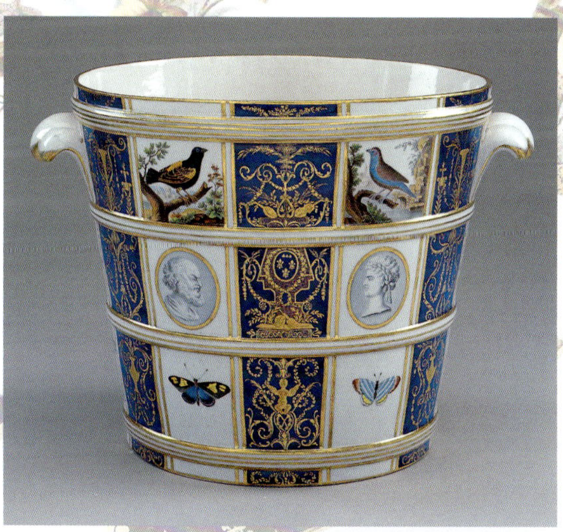

George IV

Sir Francis Chantrey (1781–1841)

1835–6

'Chantrey, I have reason to be obliged to you, for you have immortalised me.' So declared George IV (1762–1830) on first seeing the full-size plaster model for this colossal portrait when it was brought from London to Windsor in 1827. The model had been made for the purpose of casting bronze statues for Brighton and Edinburgh, but the King now asked Chantrey for a version carved in marble. It was not until 1836, six years after the King's death, that the statue was ready to be installed at Windsor.

At around 3.5 metres (11 feet) in height – somewhat taller than the figure of George Washington which Chantrey carved for the State House in Boston at the same time – the statue is nonetheless significantly smaller than Canova's gigantic bronze and marble images of Napoleon. The King is shown as Sovereign of the Order of the Garter, and the pose resembles that of Sir Thomas Lawrence's state portrait. Both derive from the French Baroque tradition exemplified in portraits of Louis XIV.

At the time the statue was first installed, the lowest flight of the Grand Stairs rose directly towards it, so that no visitor was left in doubt as to who had been responsible for the recent restoration of the Castle.

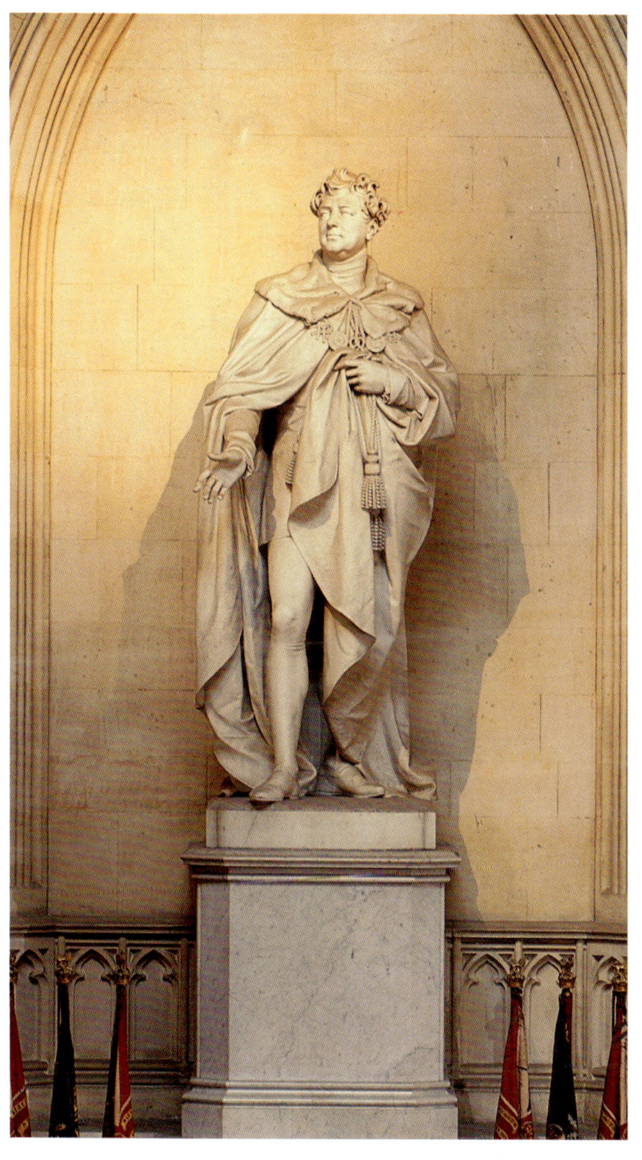

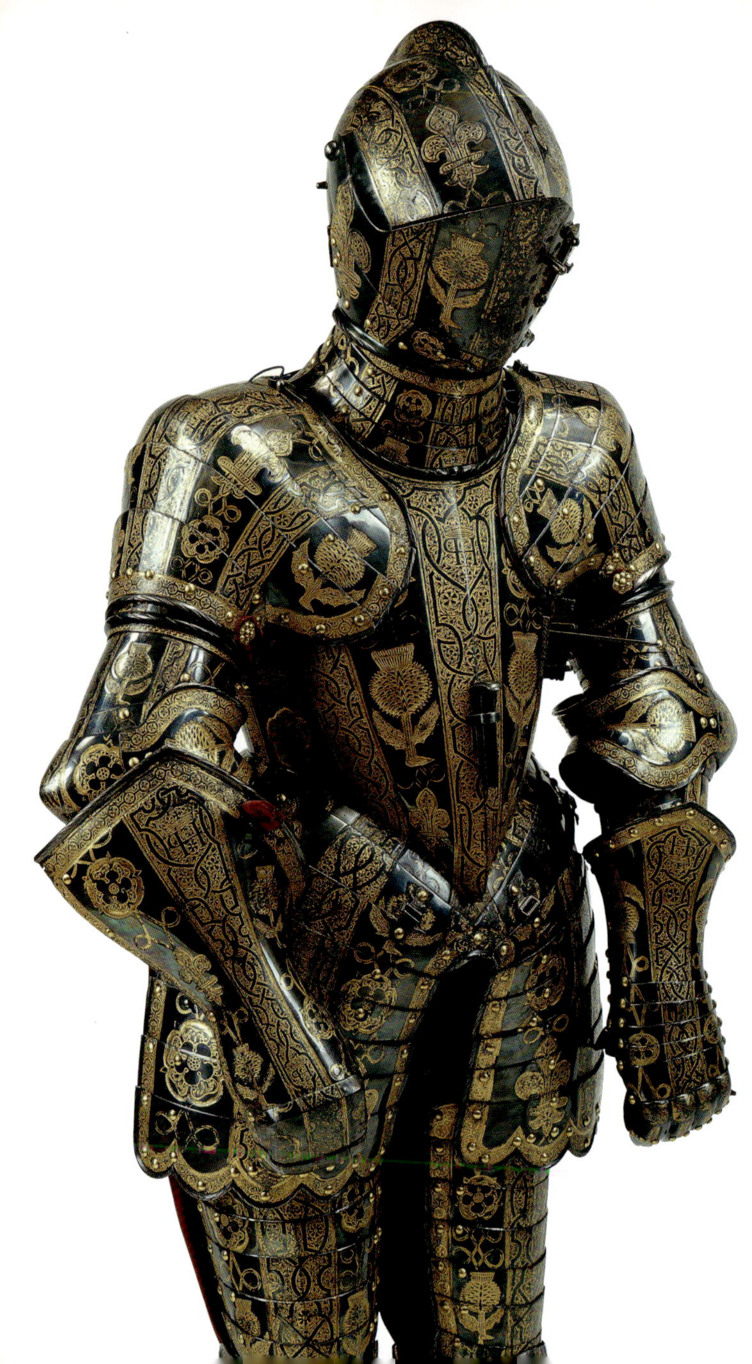

The Armour of Henry, Prince of Wales

Greenwich workshop

c.1608

The eldest son of James VI of Scotland and Anne of Denmark, Prince Henry Frederick (1594–1612) was born at Stirling Castle. Following his father's succession to the English throne (as James I) in 1603, he became Heir Apparent. He was brought up as a Renaissance prince, inheriting a great library at the age of 15, and employing architects and garden designers, including Inigo Jones, who collaborated with the dramatist Ben Jonson on the Prince's court entertainments.

This magnificent armour was made at Greenwich for the 14-year-old Prince's use in the exercises of chivalry, at which he excelled. Of blued steel, with etched and gilded decoration, incorporating Tudor roses, thistles and fleurs-de-lys with the Prince's device 'HP', it can be adapted by means of various 'exchange' pieces for the tilt, barriers or other exercise.
A contemporary said of Prince Henry that he 'performed with so much dexterity and skill that he became second to no Prince in Christendom'.

Henry was created Prince of Wales in 1610, but died suddenly of typhoid two years later, leaving his brother, the future Charles I, to succeed James I in 1625.

Queen Victoria

Joseph Edgar Boehm (1834–90)

c.1869–72

This imposing statue was commissioned by Queen Victoria (1819–1901) herself to stand in the Grand Vestibule. It was the first royal portrait by the Viennese sculptor Joseph Edgar Boehm, and on the strength of it he became Queen Victoria's preferred sculptor, executing numerous commissions for portraits and small bronzes. After his death the Queen paid for a brass tablet in St George's Chapel, 'in heartfelt gratitude for the Memorials his art has left of many who were dear to her'.

When first completed, the statue was exhibited in the porch of the Royal Albert Hall in South Kensington, which had been opened in 1871. In the following year it was included in the Sculpture section of the International Exhibition, on a site adjacent to the Hall. Here it was described by the *Art-Journal* as 'the most careful statue of the Queen that has yet been executed'.

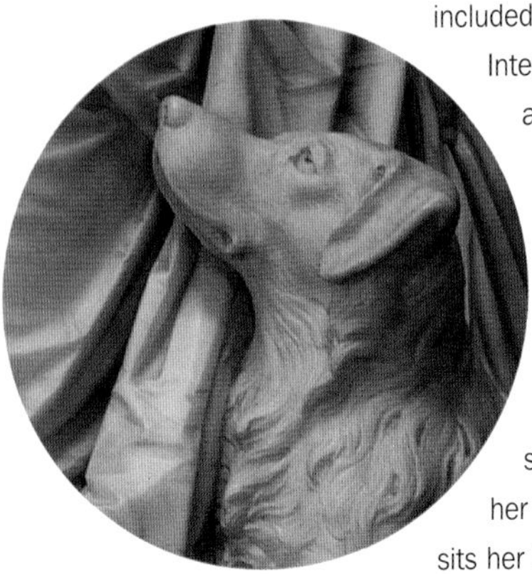

Queen Victoria wears the small diamond crown, made specially in 1870 to be worn over her widow's cap and veil. Beside her sits her faithful collie, Sharp.

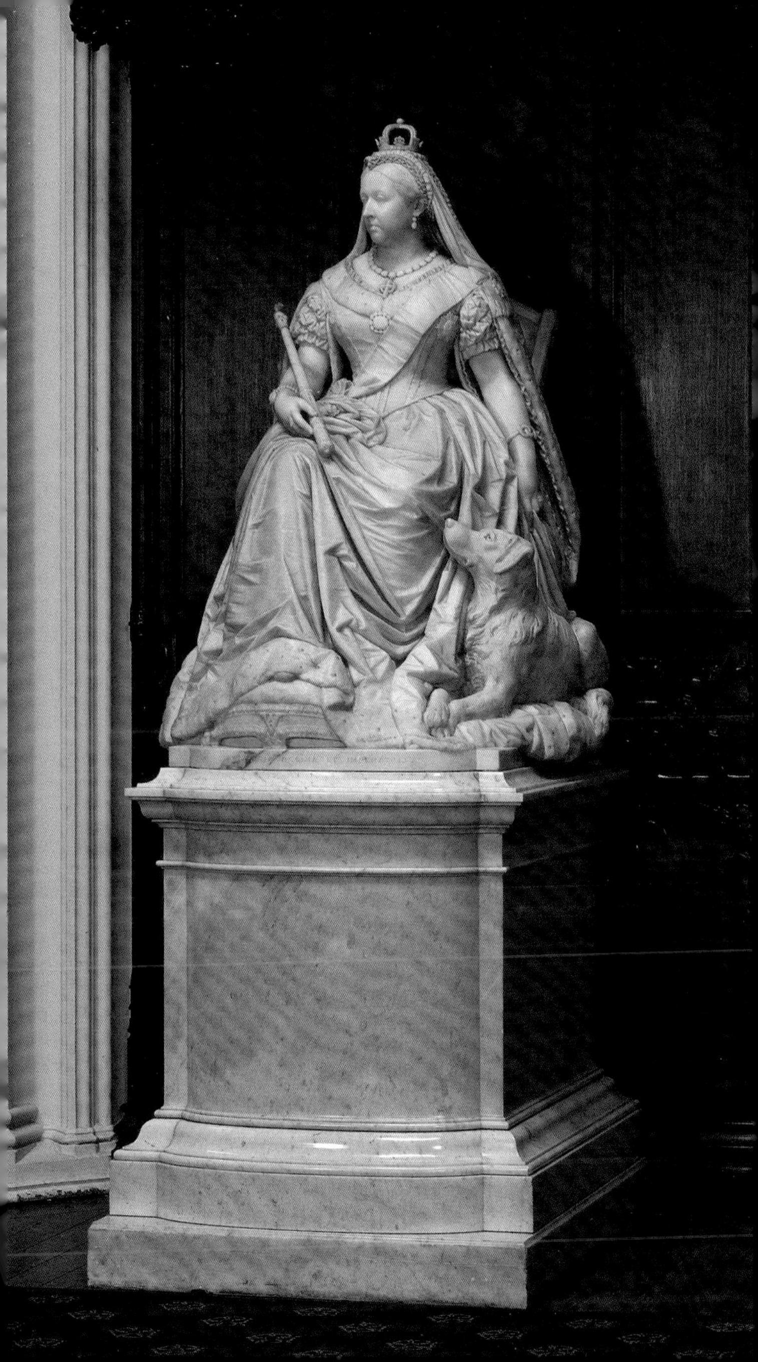

Gold Tiger's Head

Indian

c.1787–91

Tipu Sultan (1750–99) succeeded his father, Haidar Ali, as ruler of the South Indian state of Mysore in 1782, building a sophisticated and modern court around his palace at Seringapatam. For much of his reign he was engaged in hostilities against the British.

The tiger's head was the centrepiece of the octagonal throne which was made for Tipu, but which he may never have used. Every part was covered in sheet gold 2 millimetres thick, and individual parts were set with rubies and diamonds. The tiger's teeth are made from rock crystal and the gold tongue is hinged. Although the tiger was an ancient symbol of kingship in India, Tipu made it his own, declaring that it was 'better to live a single day as a tiger than a thousand years as a sheep'.

The British signed a peace treaty with Tipu in 1792, but the discovery of secret communications with Napoleon brought about a renewed campaign against him, culminating in Tipu's death during the sack of Seringapatam in 1799. The golden throne was broken up and distributed to the troops, but its most important elements were brought back intact as trophies. The tiger's head was presented to William IV by the East India Company in 1831. The silver-gilt inscribed base was made by Paul Storr.

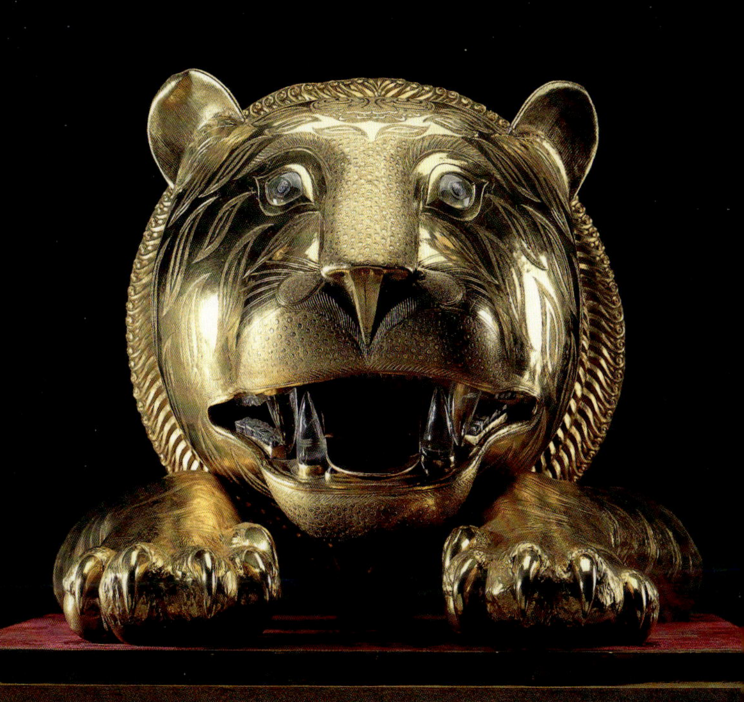
THIS TROPHY WAS TAKEN
AT THE STORMING OF SERINGAPATAM
IV MAY MDCCXCIX
RICHARD EARL OF MORNINGTON
THEN GOVERNOR GENERAL OF INDIA
GENERAL HARRIS COMMANDING THE BRITISH FORCES.

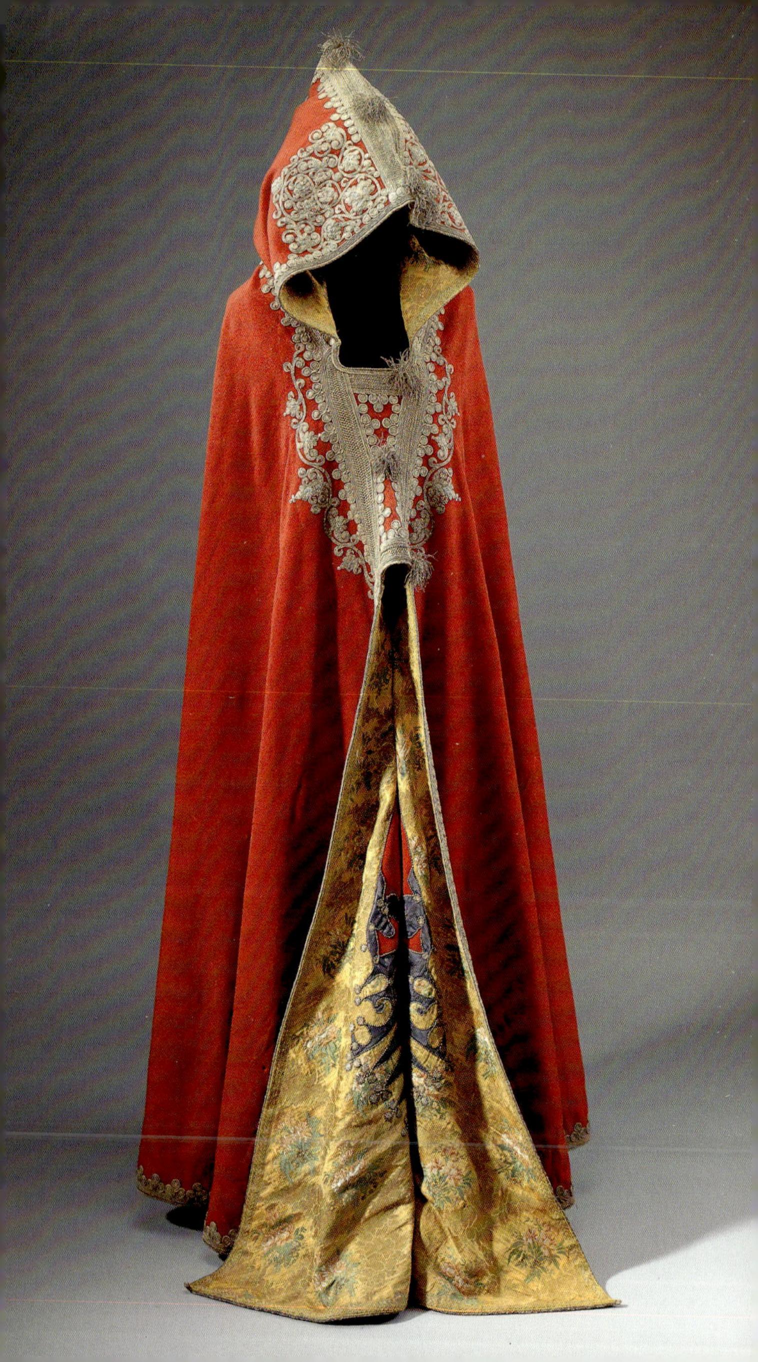

The Cloak of Napoleon Bonaparte

early nineteenth century

Although his position as heir to the throne prevented him from taking the field of battle himself, the Prince Regent (later George IV) took the closest interest in the progress of the allies in the wars against Napoleon, receiving the coalition leaders at Carlton House after the first defeat of the French Emperor in 1814. His fascination with Napoleon became well known, and following the final victory at Waterloo in June 1815 the Prince was presented with a number of 'relics' of his infamous enemy. Among them was this woollen cloak, richly decorated with heavy gold lace and lined with spectacularly patterned brocade, which was said to have been taken from the Emperor's carriage after the Battle of Waterloo. It was presented to the Prince Regent in 1816 by Count von Nostitz, aide-de-camp to the commander of the Prussian cavalry, Marshal Blücher, whose intervention at Waterloo had been decisive. The cloak was first displayed in the Armoury at Carlton House and moved to Windsor in 1837. Prior to Waterloo, it is thought to have been worn by Napoleon during his Egyptian campaign of 1798–1801.

Door Lock

William Walls (*fl.* 1761–5)

1761

The royal arms prominently placed around the keyhole of this mechanical curiosity indicate that it was made for presentation to the King. George III was educated in the mechanical sciences, and from an early age showed a fascination with clocks, scientific instruments and machinery. William Walls, a Birmingham manufacturer of whom almost nothing is known, evidently sought to interest the King in a new and deadly form of security device, for the lock incorporates two flintlock pistols. As originally designed, it was intended that if the lock was tampered with, an alarm would sound and the two pistols would fire at the intruder at close range. A drawback of the device was suggested in the *Gentleman's Magazine* in 1765: 'honest inadvertent people might suffer by it, who not always recollected, might forget the danger, tho' apprized of it and suffer for their want of memory'. The cut and engraved brass work applied to the mahogany cover is of high quality and probably also made in Birmingham. The bit of the key is cut with the King's cipher and the date, 1761.

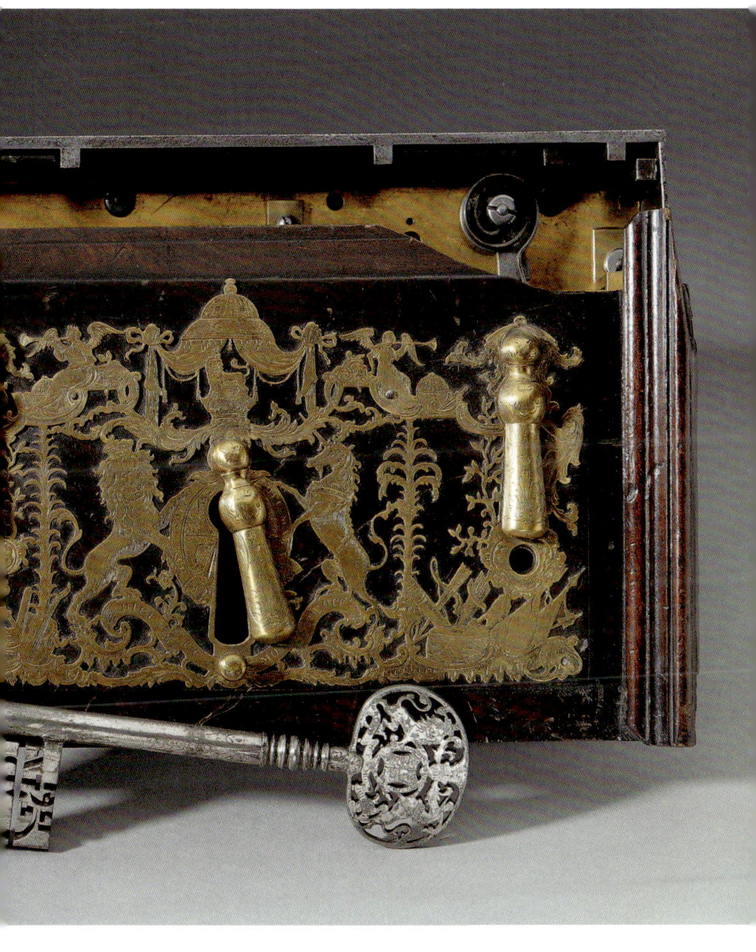

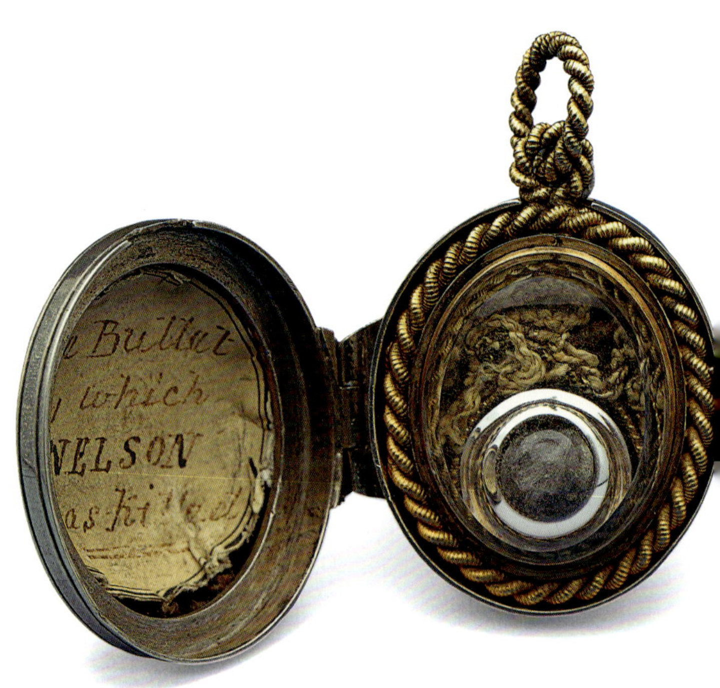
Bullet
which
NELSON

The Musket Ball that Killed Nelson

The death of Admiral Lord Nelson at the height of the Battle of Trafalgar on 21 October 1805 captured the public imagination in England, and numerous artists, poets and composers hastened to satisfy the general hunger for commemorative art. The publisher Josiah Boydell offered a prize for the best painting of the event, but since most of these were made on the basis of scant evidence, they were extremely inaccurate.

This famous and gruesome relic was presented to Queen Victoria around 1842 by the nephew of Sir William Beatty, Nelson's surgeon. The ball was fired at close range from the rigging of the *Redoubtable* alongside Nelson's flagship, *Victory*. It entered the admiral's left shoulder, descending obliquely through the ribcage and spine to lodge in the muscles of the lower back. When Beatty removed it from Nelson's corpse during the return passage to England, traces of gold braid and cloth from the hero's uniform were found embedded in the lead. The relic was mounted in its oval locket by Admiral Sir Thomas Hardy and presented to Beatty, who is said to have worn it suspended from a chain round his neck.

Rudolf II Introducing the Arts into Bohemia

Adriaen de Vries (c.1556–1626)

1609

The Emperor Rudolf II (1552–1612), dressed in Roman armour and seated on a rearing horse, proceeds in triumph through an imaginary city. The scene (overleaf) is framed in the lower foreground by two flanking figures, representing the kingdom of Bohemia (on the left) and Fame with her trumpets (right). To the left of the horse, three female figures representing the arts of Architecture, Painting and Sculpture, each holding an identifying attribute, imitate the poses of the Three Graces, displaying every aspect of female beauty. Further arts, including Music, Poetry, Astronomy and Philosophy, follow in their wake. The Emperor reaches out to give a prize to the figure of Painting, a gesture which may refer to Rudolf's edict of 1595, by which painting was deemed to be a Liberal Art and all court painters were ennobled.

In composing his metallic picture, the Dutch-born sculptor Adriaen de Vries was mounting a challenge on behalf of the art of sculpture. The design, placement and interaction of the figures are calculated with a degree of subtlety normally expected only of painters, exploiting the full range of the sculptor's techniques to create an illusionistic masterpiece.

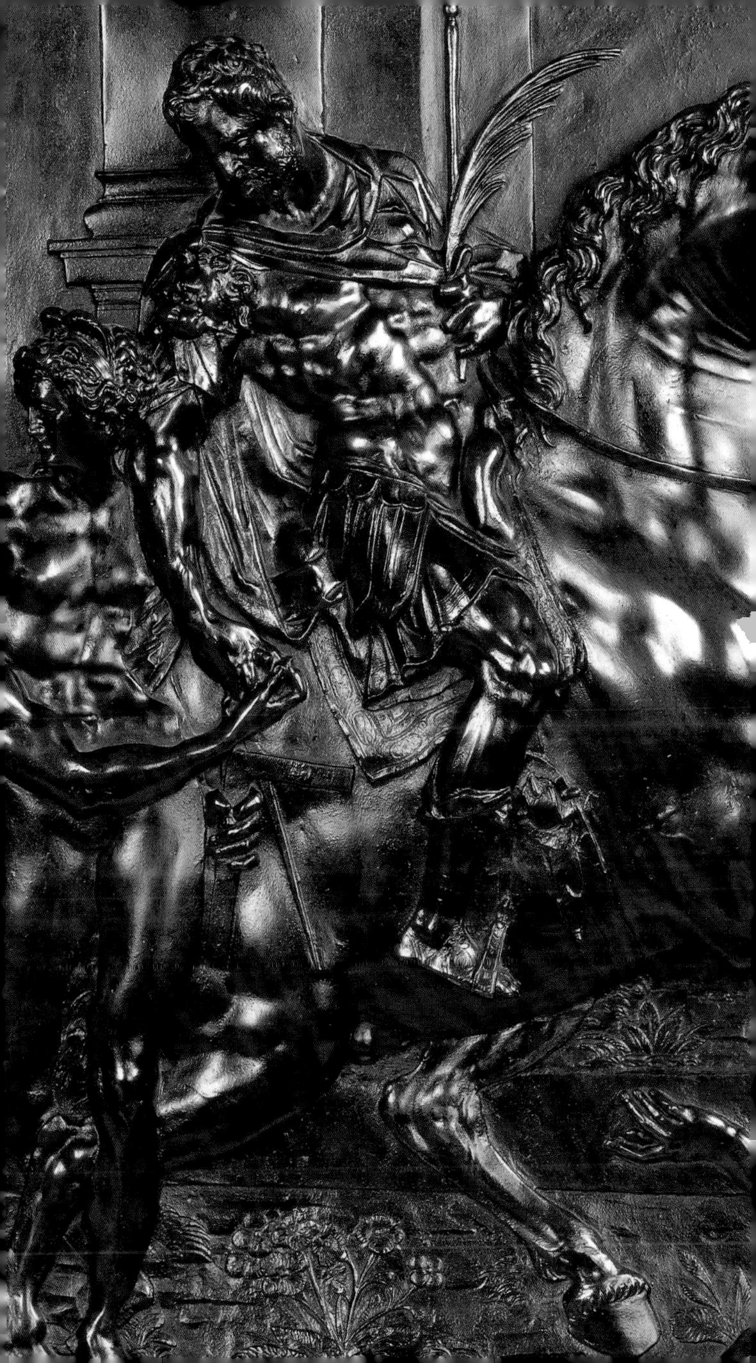

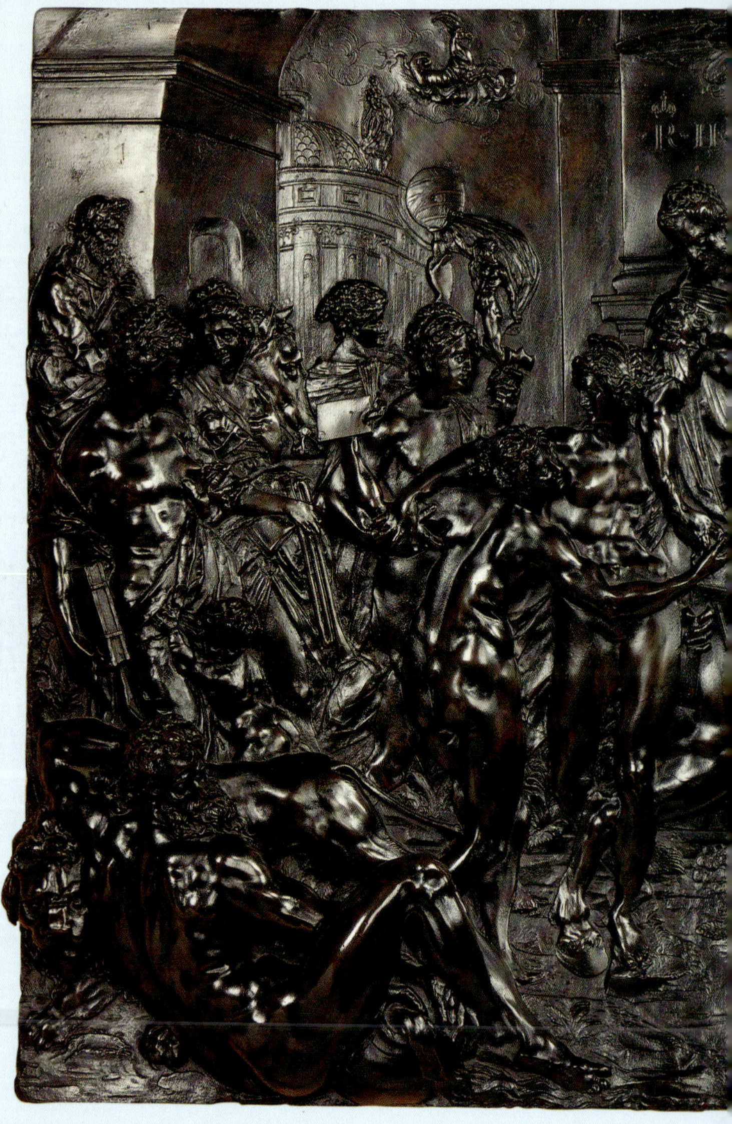

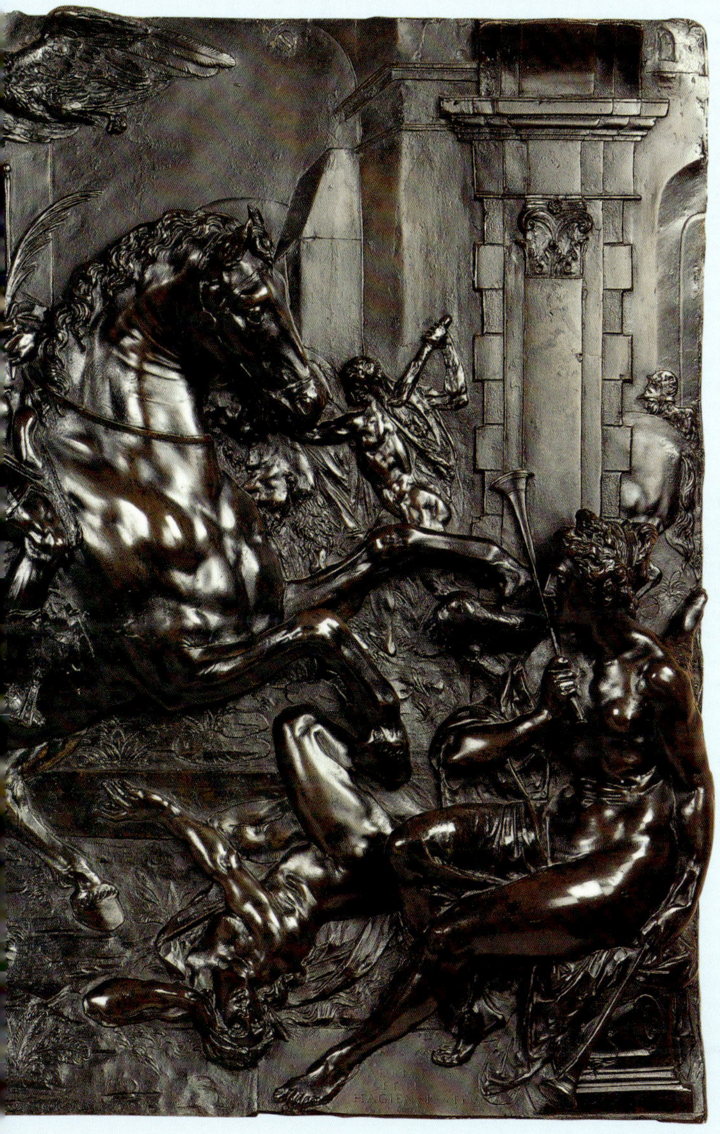

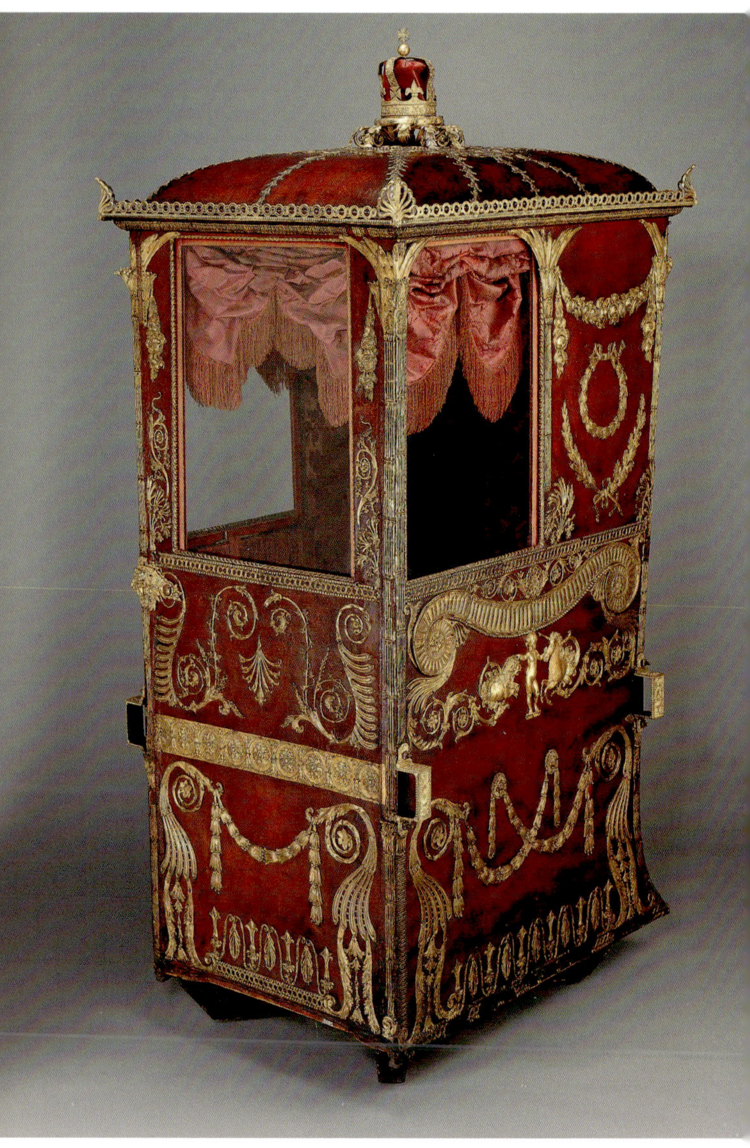

Queen Charlotte's Sedan Chair

Samuel Vaughan (*fl.* 1751–75) and D.N. Anderson

1763

From the seventeenth century until the end of the Georgian era, the sedan chair was the principal means of individual personal transport for the well-to-do. Mainly used for short journeys, sedan chairs were carried by two servants (or 'chairmen'), on long poles fixed at either side. The fact that this chair belonged to Queen Charlotte (1744–1818) is signalled by the prominent crown in the centre of the roof, as well as by the richly upholstered interior, fine plate-glass windows and unusually elaborate (but lightweight) gilt-metal decoration, incorporating the British lion and unicorn, roses, laurel wreaths and oak sprays.

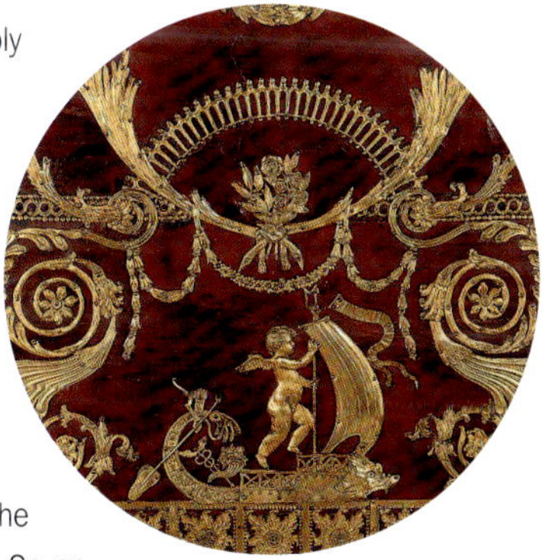

This splendid object was probably supplied by Samuel Vaughan in 1763, at a cost of just over £185 – about three times the cost of a standard chair from this maker. An additional payment of £250 to the metal chaser and gilder D.N. Anderson may have been for the gilt decorations, the theme of which probably refers to the recent successful conclusion of the Seven Years War. Queen Charlotte owned a plainer chair (now also at Windsor), which may have been kept for use in the country; and in 1771 Robert Adam designed a new one for her (which does not survive), with delicate neoclassical decoration, for London use.

Arthur Wellesley, 1st Duke of Wellington

Sir Thomas Lawrence (1769–1830)

1814–15

This triumphant portrait of the Duke of Wellington (1769–1852) dominates the Waterloo Chamber. Lawrence was commissioned by George IV to paint a pantheon of military heroes, diplomats and heads of state responsible for the final defeat of Napoleon at the Battle of Waterloo on 18 June 1815. These portraits were initially proposed for Carlton House, but George IV's plans for Windsor Castle latterly came to include a new room specially created for their display: the Waterloo Chamber.

Lawrence's composition celebrates Wellington as the finest of military commanders and the 'liberator of Europe'. Positioned under a Roman-style triumphal arch, he grasps the Sword of State (symbolising the sovereign's royal authority) in his hand, holding it aloft in a heroic gesture. He wears Field Marshal's uniform and his baton (a symbol of office) rests on a ledge beside a letter addressed to him and signed 'George P.R.', signifying his promotion to Field Marshal and the gratitude of the Crown. In the background we glimpse the procession leading to the special thanksgiving service to celebrate the victory at Waterloo, which took place at St Paul's Cathedral on 7 July 1814.

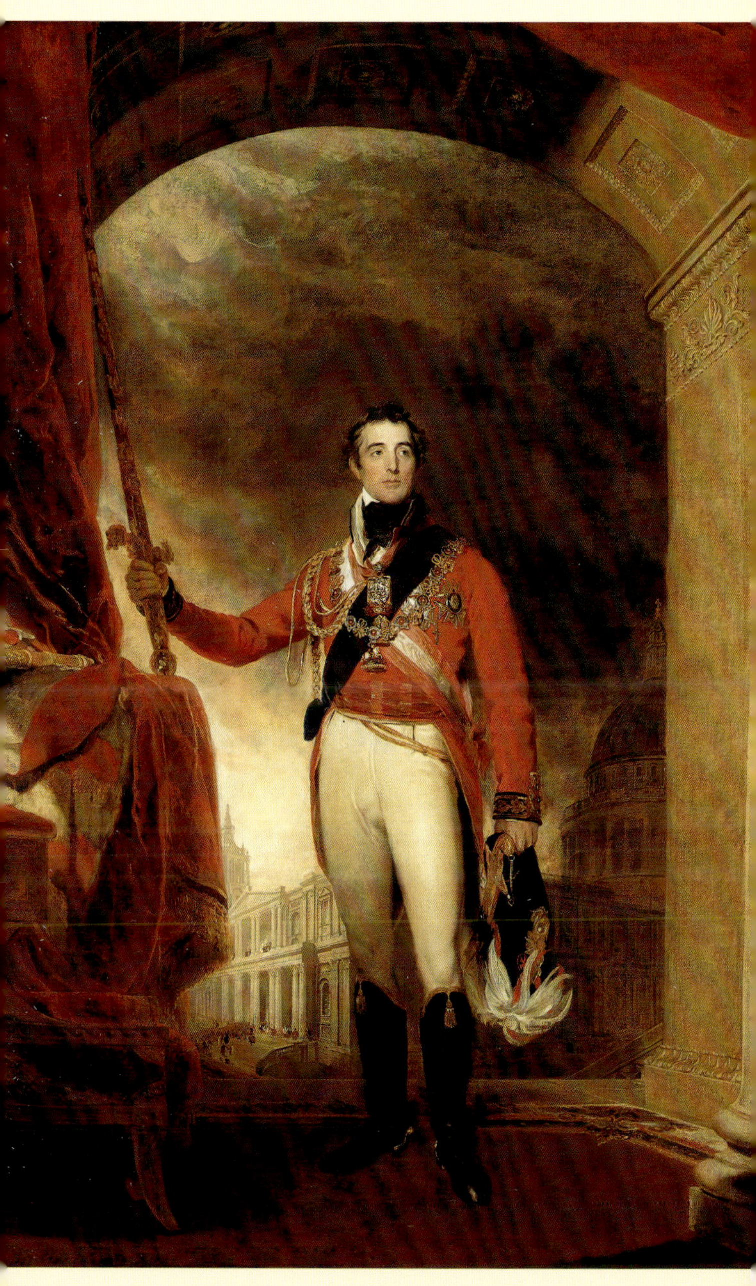

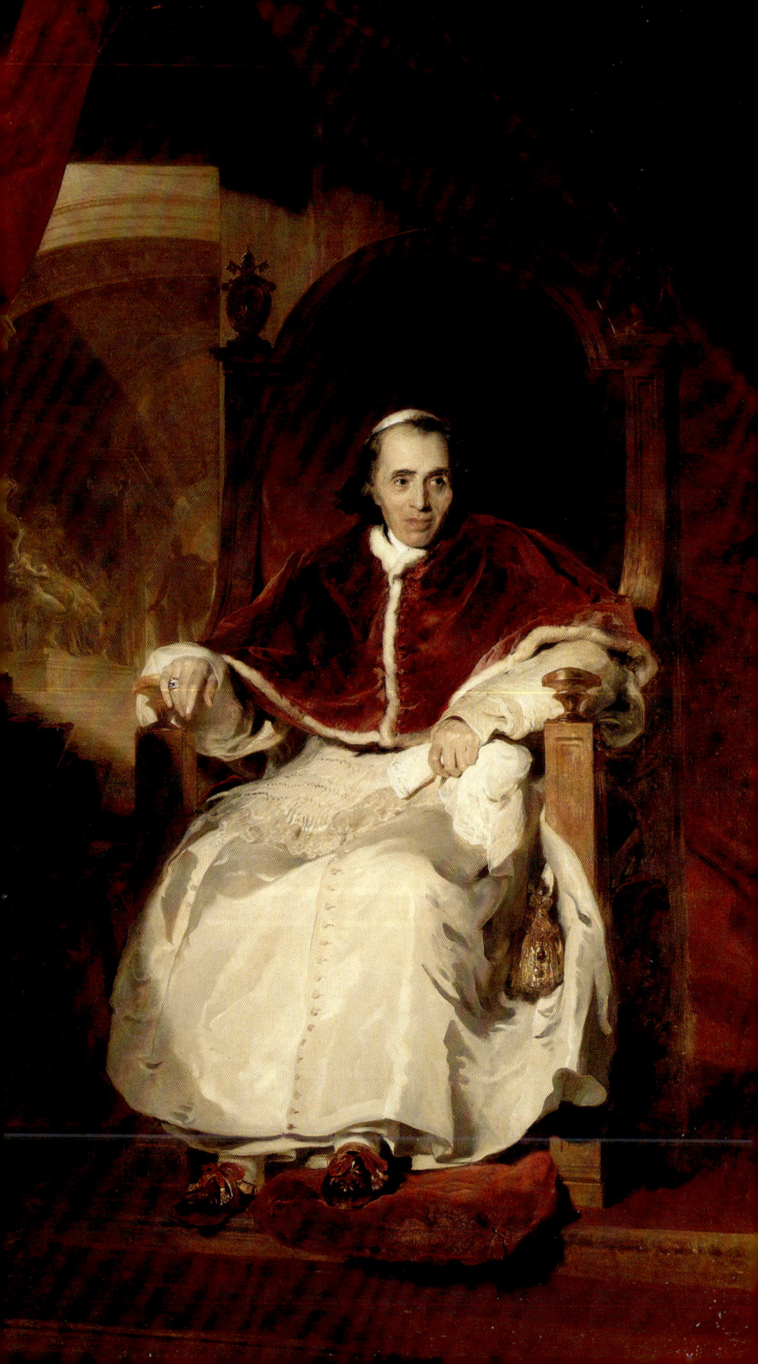

Pope Pius VII

Sir Thomas Lawrence (1769–1830)

1819

Luigi Barnaba Chiaramonti (1742–1823), elected Pope in 1800, was imprisoned by Napoleon in 1809 for opposing his plans for the annexation of the Papal States. After his triumphant return to Rome in 1814, Pius VII became a focus for the political and spiritual regeneration of Europe. Lawrence arrived in Rome in May 1819 and was given nine sittings by the Pope in order to complete the portrait. This work is the most magnificent in the series of portraits commissioned by George IV for the Waterloo Chamber and has long been regarded as Lawrence's crowning achievement.

The Pope, his pale face set off by jet-black hair, is made to appear especially vulnerable by the magnificent papal throne (the *sedia gestatoria*), which almost dwarfs him. With dazzling surface effects, Lawrence portrays the Pope, a symbol in his time for the victory of peace over war, as a spiritual ruler with temporal power and all the trappings of authority.

In the left background, notable pieces of classical sculpture in the papal collections are shown in the *Braccio Nuovo* (New Wing) of the Vatican Palace, created for their display under the supervision of the sculptor Antonio Canova, who had secured the return of the collection from Paris after its removal by Napoleon.

Saint Martin Dividing his Cloak

Anthony Van Dyck (1599–1641)

c.1620

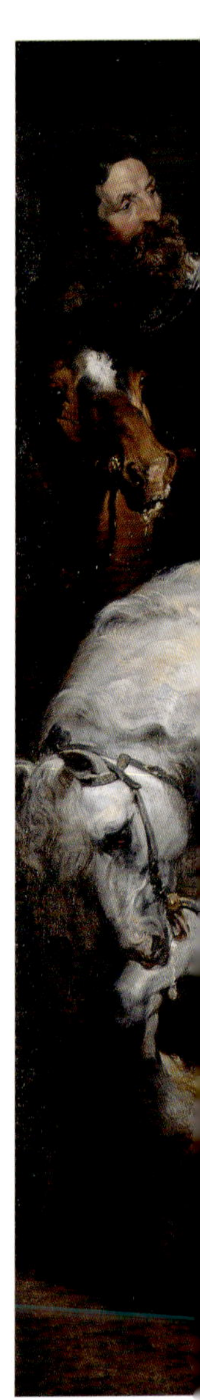

Martin of Tours was one of the most popular and well-known saints in Western Europe. One winter's day Martin encountered a beggar at the gates of Amiens, and cut his cloak in two with his sword, giving half to the beggar as an act of charity.

The painting dates from the early part of Van Dyck's career, when he was still working in Rubens's studio and was much influenced by his master. It is even possible that it was painted as a present to Rubens, at a time when the artist was contemplating leaving Antwerp. Van Dyck based the painting on an earlier composition, painted for the church of St Martin at Zaventem, which he made even more monumental, expanding the right side to incorporate the women and children behind the beggars. The painting was bought by Frederick, Prince of Wales in the mid-eighteenth century.

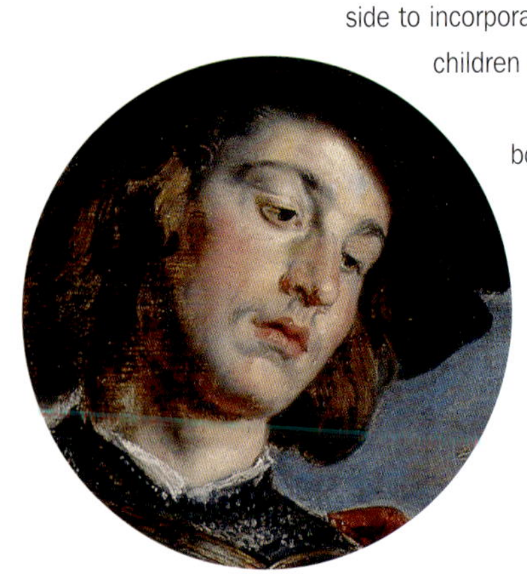

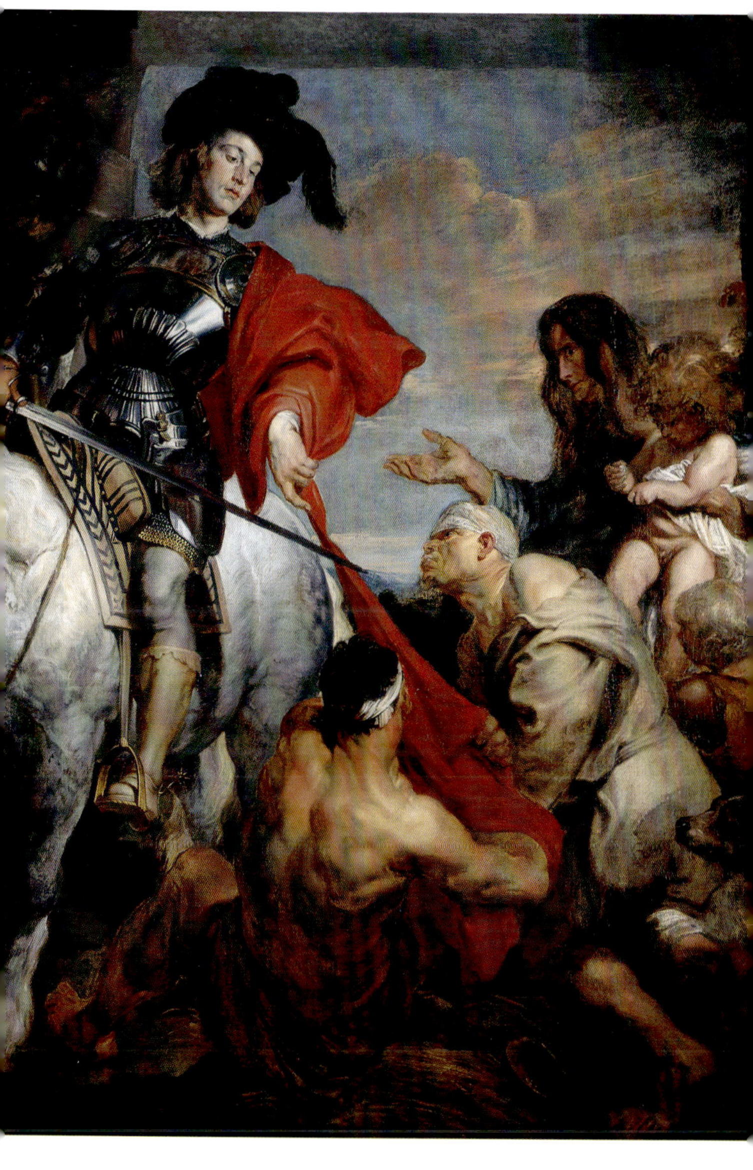

The Holy Family with Saint Francis

Peter Paul Rubens (1577–1640)

1626–8 and *c*.1635

This painting was first referred to in the notebooks of the antiquarian scholar George Vertue, who records that in 1723 George I 'bought 6 Large paintings...[including] two other of Rubens for all of which he paid 4000 pounds'.

As so often with Rubens's paintings, the composition evolved in several stages. The figures were originally only three-quarter length, but were extended to full-length by the addition of an extra piece of canvas along the lower edge when the infant St John the Baptist and the lamb were added.

The mood is formal and solemn; St Francis's pose is matched and balanced by that of Joseph. Recent cleaning of the painting has confirmed the outstanding quality of the figures, particularly the faces of the Virgin, the Holy Child and Saint Anne. There is only a glimpse of landscape, but Rubens has managed to saturate the scene with the quality of a dusky evening light. This effect and the composition as a whole reveal the artist's debt to the great Venetian Renaissance masters, Titian and Veronese.

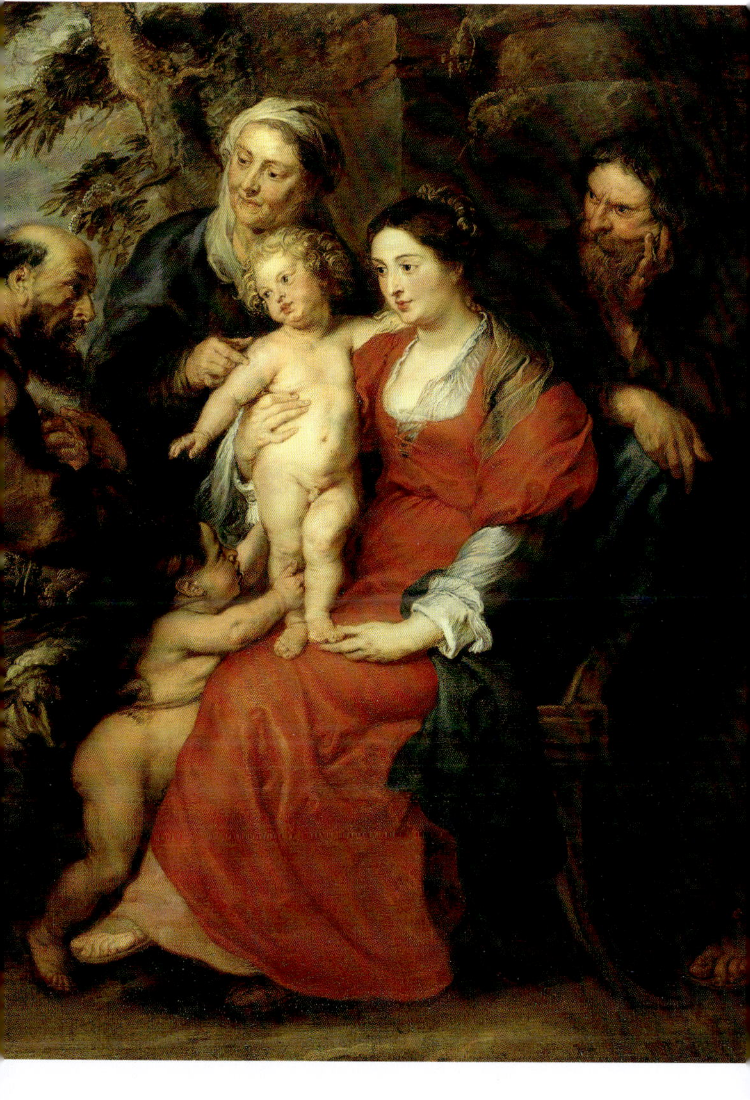

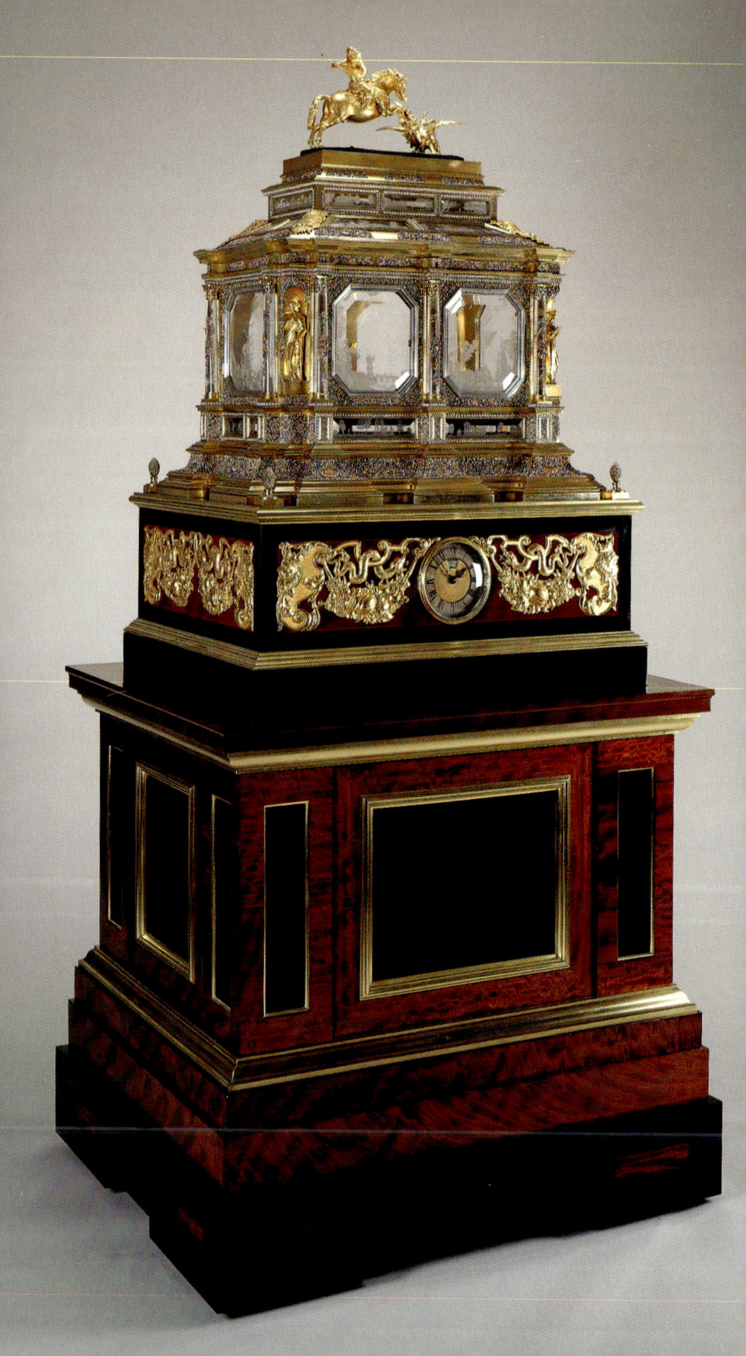

Organ Clock

Charles Clay (d.1740)

c.1740

This most unusual object disguises its real function very effectively. The modest clock face scarcely registers among the gilt-bronze serpents, masks and swags of fruit around the centre; and only a small opening on the dial reveals, one at a time, the names of the ten tunes that the barrel organ can play – five of them specially set by the great composer Handel. The organ mechanism itself is completely concealed within the plain and solid-looking mahogany and ebony plinth. This also serves as a support for the elaborate seventeenth-century German casket that Clay, who specialised in the manufacture of mechanical organ clocks, decided to place on the plinth.

The casket, which is made of silver gilt, enamel, gilt bronze and finely engraved rock crystal, is signed by the Augsburg cabinet-maker Melchior Baumgartner (1621–86) and dated 1664. The complete object was probably sold by Clay's widow to Frederick, Prince of Wales, or possibly to his wife Augusta, some time after 1743. In George IV's time, the seventeenth-century gilt-bronze group of St George and the Dragon by Francesco Fanelli was added to the top of the casket; and later in the nineteenth century Queen Victoria placed inside it the Bible of the great imperial hero and adventurer General Gordon, murdered at Khartoum in 1885.

The Grand Canal with Santa Maria della Salute

Canaletto (1697–1768)

1744

This view (overleaf) is of the south end of the Grand Canal, close to where it emerges into the Bacino di San Marco, the hub of Venice. To the right (shown in the detail opposite) appears the church of Santa Maria della Salute, built by Baldassare Longhena to celebrate the end of the terrible plague of 1630 and one of the finest Baroque buildings in Venice. On the left are numerous palaces once inhabited by noble families, with glimpses of the great monuments of the Piazza San Marco beyond: the Palazzo Ducale (Doge's Palace), and the Campanile and column of San Marco, topped by the winged lion, the symbol of St Mark and thus of Venice.

Canaletto painted this particular view of the Grand Canal on several occasions. The version depicted here was conceived from a viewpoint on the first floor of the nearby abbey buildings of San Gregorio. His paintings often appear to be topographically accurate, but here he has skilfully manipulated the view to suit the composition by widening the left-hand side of the vista in order to include more detail of the buildings.

This is one of around fifty paintings by Canaletto in the Royal Collection, purchased by George III from Consul Joseph Smith in 1762. Smith was an English merchant banker and collector, who resided in Venice from c.1700 and was Canaletto's main patron.

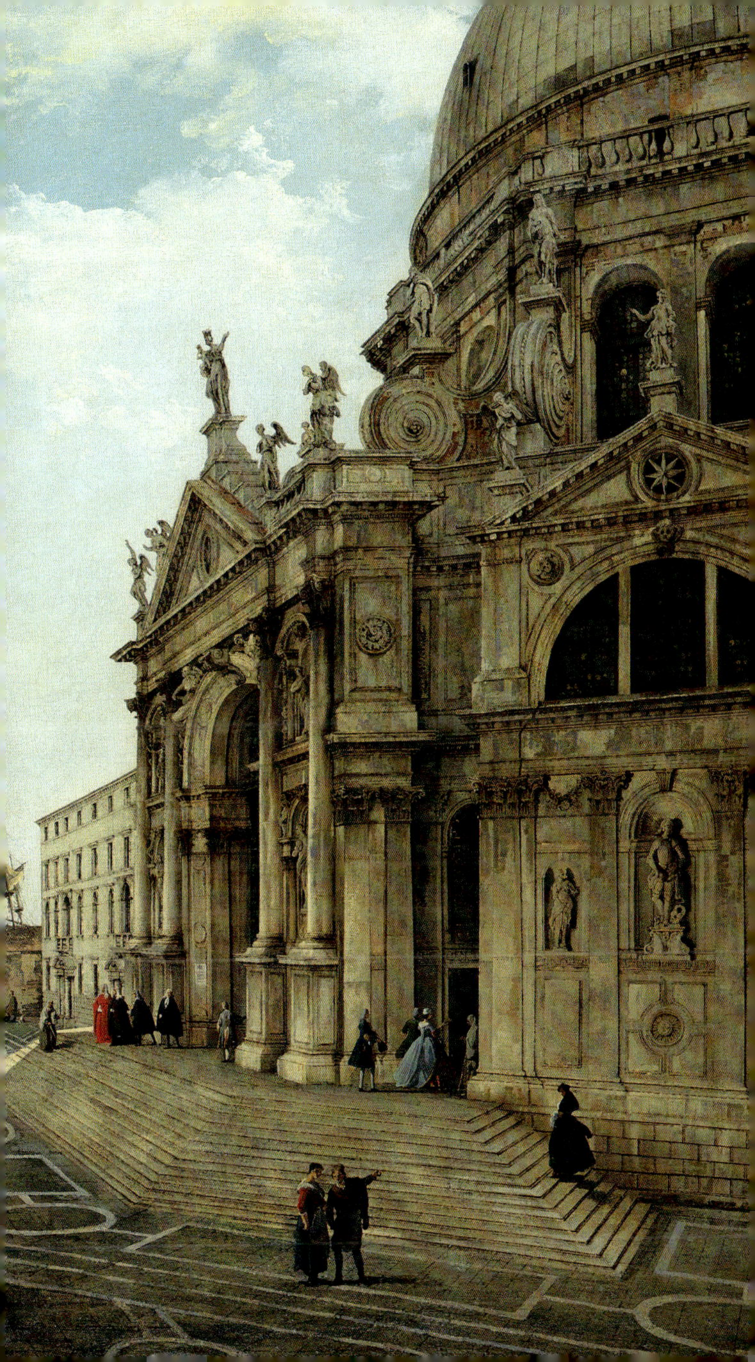

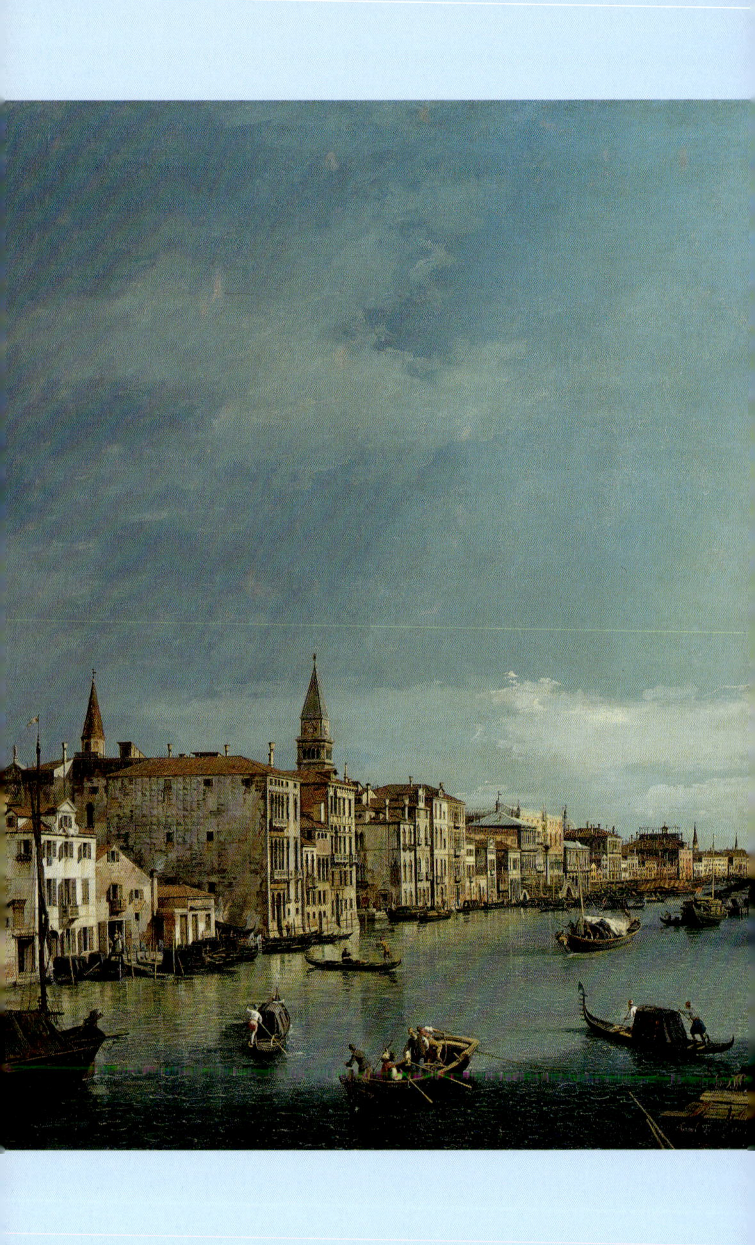

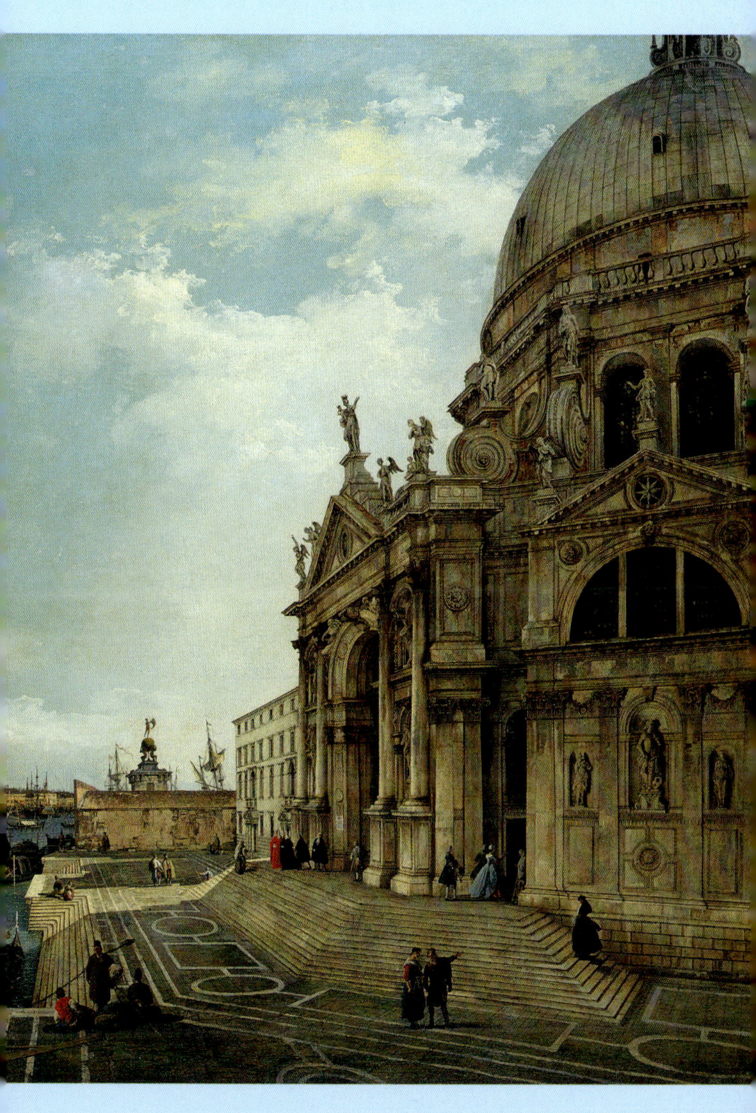

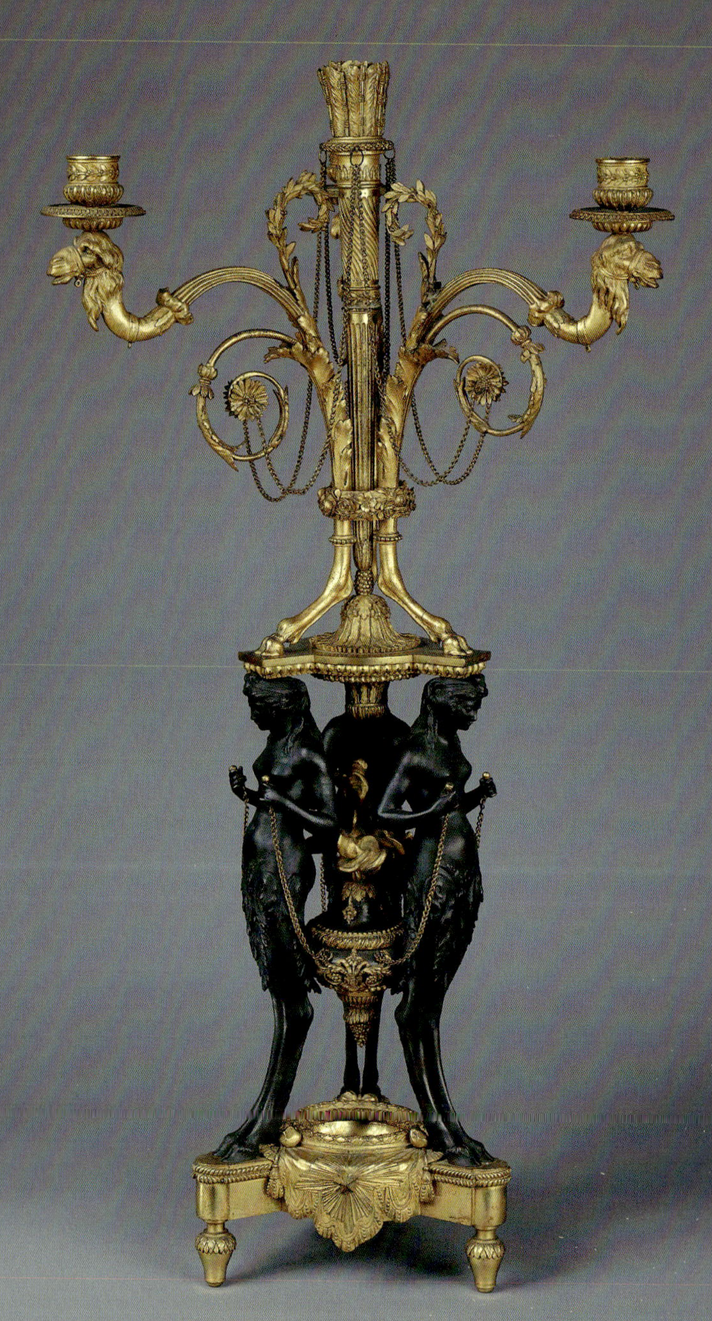

Pair of Camel Candelabra

attributed to François Rémond (1745/7–1812)

c.1790

The fashion for all things Turkish, which swept Paris in the late 1770s, claimed as one of its earliest enthusiasts King Louis XVI's brother, the Comte d'Artois. He created a Turkish room at his residence in the Temple in 1776–7, and a second more lavish example in 1781 in his apartment at Versailles. For the latter, the bronze-maker François Rémond supplied, at very considerable cost, a clock and five pairs of gilt-bronze candelabra, including a pair of this distinctive model, with their elegant tripod supports and candle-branches terminating in camel heads.

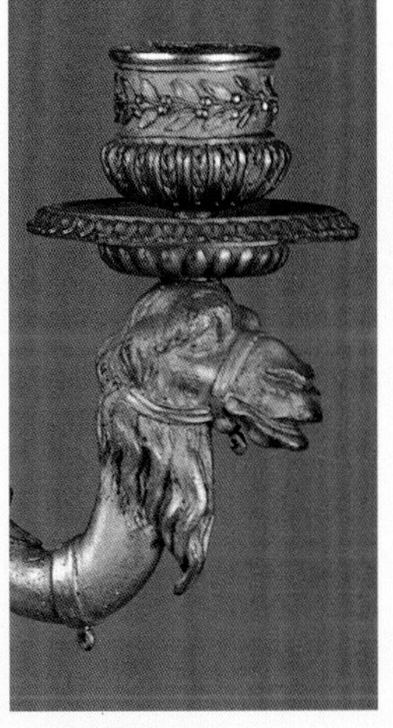

The design, which may have come from the ornamental draughtsman J.-D. Dugourc, evidently proved popular and Rémond supplied several more examples with slight variations, such as this pair with its partly patinated satyresses, which was first recorded at Carlton House, the London residence of the Prince of Wales, in 1792. As Rémond worked extensively for the fashionable dealer-decorator Dominique Daguerre, and as Daguerre had been invited by the Prince, in about 1786, to help decorate and furnish Carlton House, it was almost certainly via this route that these candelabra came into the Prince's collection. In 1828 they were transferred by George IV to his new apartments at Windsor.

'Polonaise' Bed

attributed to Georges Jacob (1739–1814)

*c.*1790

Domed beds, known as *à la polonaise* in the eighteenth century, provided an elegant way of displaying to advantage the luxurious and richly ornamented hangings which generally constituted the most expensive part of a bed of this kind. The bed was probably supplied by the Parisian dealer-decorator Dominique Daguerre for the Prince of Wales's new residence, Carlton House, which he was furnishing and decorating in the late 1780s and early 1790s. Daguerre had access to highly sophisticated makers, including the carver and gilder Georges Jacob, and provided the Prince with substantial quantities of expensive furniture in the most up-to-date Parisian taste: the bed, upholstered in blue silk brocade, was made for the Prince's London bedroom.

In the 1820s, George IV had the bed modified – adding the ostrich plume finial, among other things – and placed it in the principal visitors' suite at Windsor. Queen Victoria selected the bed for the use of the Empress Eugénie, when on a State Visit to Windsor with Emperor Napoleon III in 1855. Under the direction of the firm of J.G. Crace, the blue hangings were replaced with new ones in the imperial colours of green and purple, ornamented with finely worked flower borders, made originally by the girls of Mrs Pawsey's embroidery school to decorate George III's throne canopy at Windsor. At the same time, Crace provided an embroidered panel for the footboard, worked with the monograms of the imperial couple.

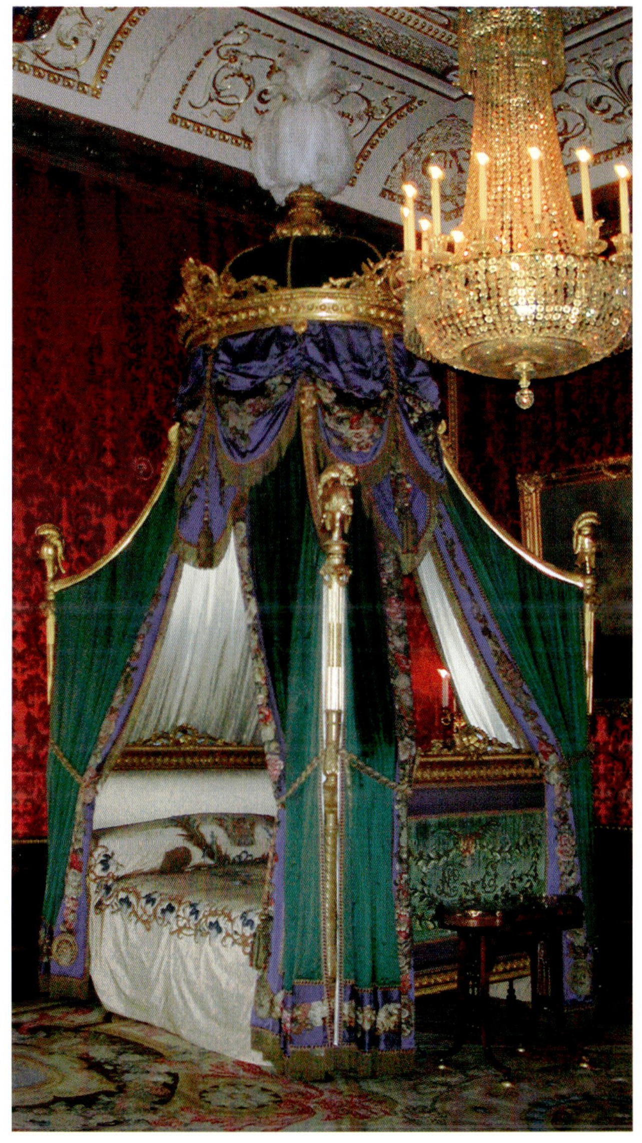

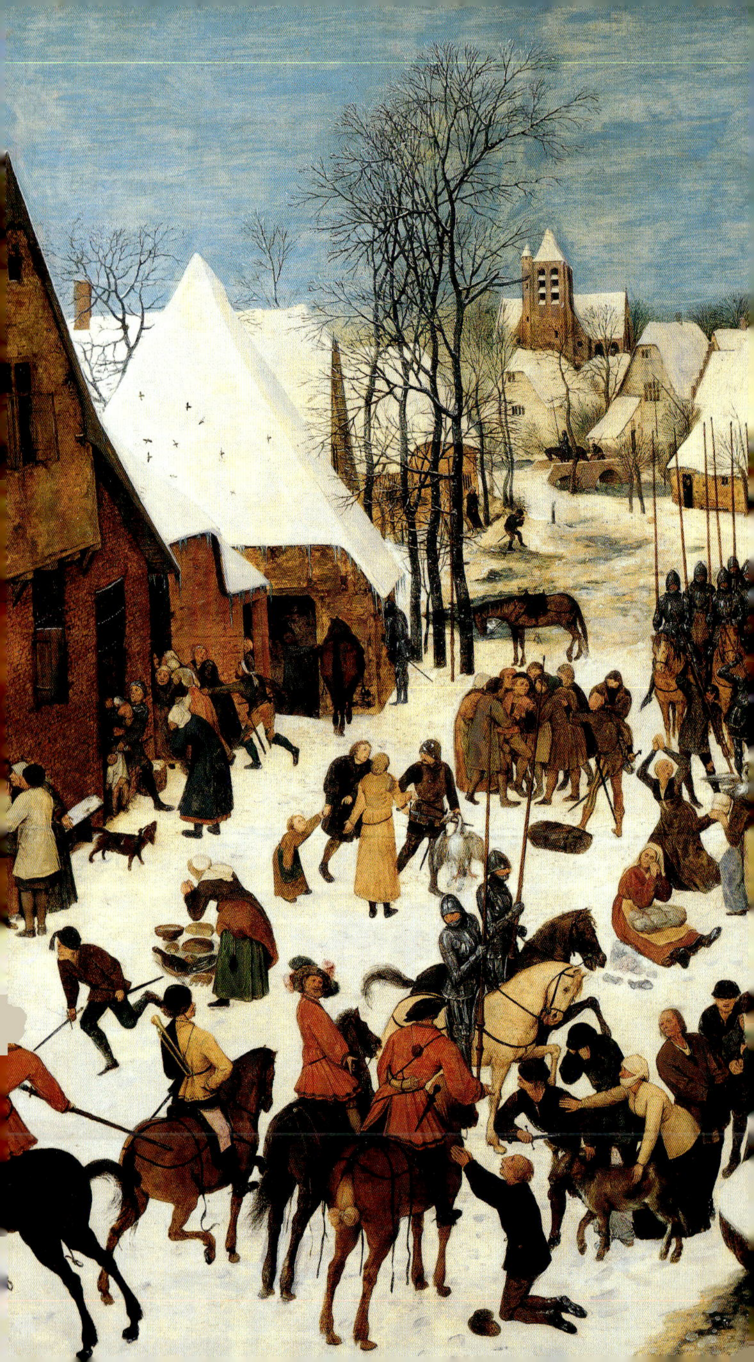

The Massacre of the Innocents

Pieter Bruegel the Elder (1525–69)

1565–7

King Herod is troubled to learn from the Wise Men of a child born in Bethlehem who is to be King of the Jews, and orders the slaughter of all children below the age of two (Matthew 2:16). Bruegel retells the story in modern times: the troops of the Spanish King (the supreme ruler of the Netherlands) descend upon a remote Flemish country town in the depths of winter; they beat down the doors and climb in at the windows; they drag out every child and, ignoring pleas, make a pile of their corpses.

The painting belonged to the Emperor Rudolf II, the King of Spain's cousin, who found it so brutal that he had it altered into a scene of looting, with stolen animals and other booty painted over the top of the children. The painting itself was looted from Prague by Swedish troops and subsequently bought from Queen Christina of Sweden by Charles II in 1660.

A number of other versions of this composition exist, but this one is clearly executed by Bruegel himself, as can be seen in the expressive, almost cartoon-like drawing of the figures, in the brilliant details, and in the beautifully observed depiction of the colours and patterns of a fresh snowfall and a winter's sky.

Derich Born

Hans Holbein the Younger (1497/8–1543)

1533

Soon after Holbein returned to England from his native Basel in 1532, he painted a group of portraits of members of the community of German merchants in London. Each portrait is inscribed with the sitter's name and age, as well as the year it was made. This is the 23-year-old Derich Born from Cologne, the youngest of the merchants to be portrayed. This information appears to be carved into the stone balustrade, along with the following words: 'Once you add the voice, it would be Derich himself here, such that you wonder whether it was the painter or his father who made him'. The painter tells us in so many words that he is trying to deceive us with a wholly lifelike image. We almost believe that the inscription is really carved in stone; we almost believe that Derich Born can talk. The artist plays further tricks on us: are the leaves 'real' or part of the wallpaper? The answer, of course, is that they are painted, like everything else.

This is a typical man of the Renaissance: his posture is self-confident and stylish, but his gaze is direct and open, as if greeting the viewer as an equal with whom he can do business. The idea of the arm resting on a balustrade derives from Titian, the greatest portrait painter of the Italian Renaissance.

The wood on the back of the panel is branded with the letters 'CR', indicating that the painting once belonged to King Charles I.

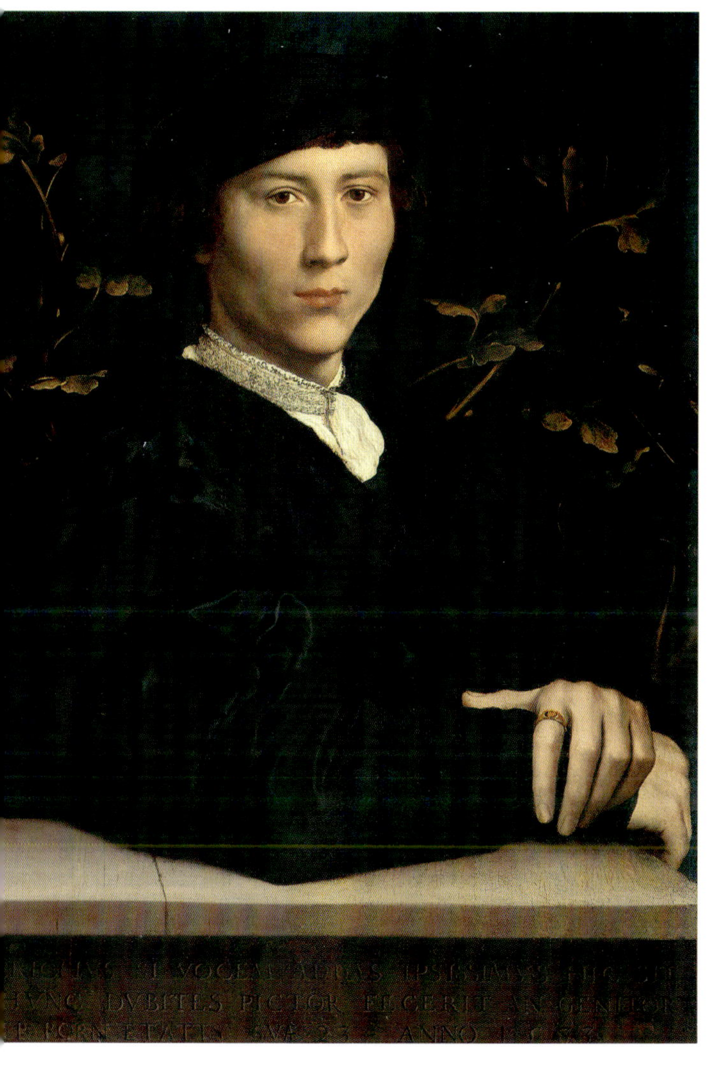

KING'S DRESSING ROOM

The Children of Christian II of Denmark

Jan Gossaert, called Mabuse (1478–1532)

c.1526

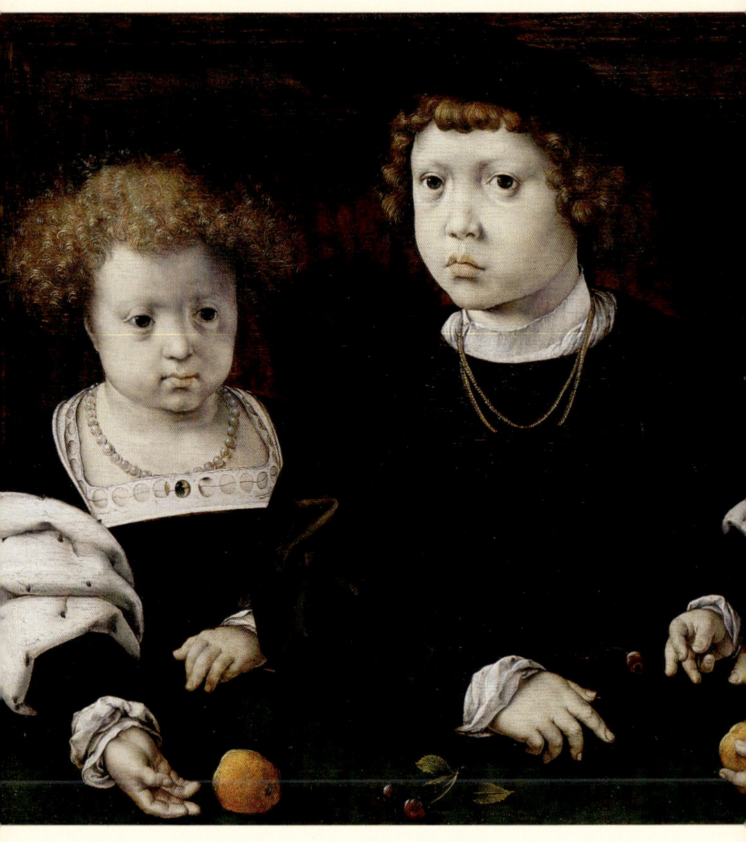

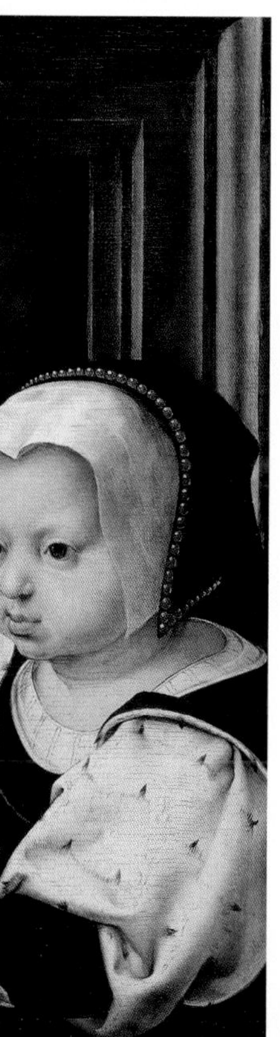

The children in this portrait wear mourning clothes and were probably painted by Gossaert soon after the death of their mother, Isabella of Austria, in January 1526. Dorothea, John and Christina are depicted at around the ages of 5, 8 and 4 respectively. Following their mother's death, the children were left in the care of their great-aunt, Margaret of Austria, when their father, Christian II, left the Netherlands later that year. Little Christina, later Duchess of Milan, is better known in her celebrated portrait by Holbein (National Gallery, London), painted for Henry VIII in 1538 as a possible bridal candidate.

Like his northern European counterparts, Dürer and Van der Goes, Gossaert delights in detail. The children's hair and clothes and the fruits are all minutely observed. However, following a visit to Italy in 1508 his work shows the influence of artists of the Renaissance. The mood of the painting is solemn and there is little direct eye contact between the children or with the spectator. The children are enclosed within their own painted frame, in their own world. Children are often depicted in art with fruit, to suggest that they are 'ripening' with the years.

This portrait is recorded in the collection of Henry VIII at Whitehall in 1542.

The Judgement of Paris

Lucas Cranach the Elder (1472–1553)

c.1537–40

Cranach has based his painting on medieval interpretations of this Greek myth, such as the *Story of the Destruction of Troy* (*Historia destructionis Troiae*) by the thirteenth-century writer Guido delle Colonne. In these accounts the story is brought up to date (and somewhat parodied): Paris is a medieval knight who has lost his way in a thicket; he tethers his horse to a tree before falling asleep. Mercury appears to him in a dream and introduces three goddesses – Venus, Minerva and Juno – asking him to choose the fairest. Paris agrees to do this on condition that the goddesses undress, which they duly do. The theme presents the artist with the opportunity to depict his trademark nudes – lithe, elongated and erotic – while at the same time providing a tongue-in-cheek retelling of a familiar story.

Twelve different versions of this theme are known, all of which include the same compositional elements, but there are differences in the arrangements and poses of the figures. This picture differs from the others only in the fact that it lacks a distant landscape: here the hedge closes off the composition and Cranach accordingly arranges his figures as in a frieze.

The painting was possibly first recorded in the collection of James II.

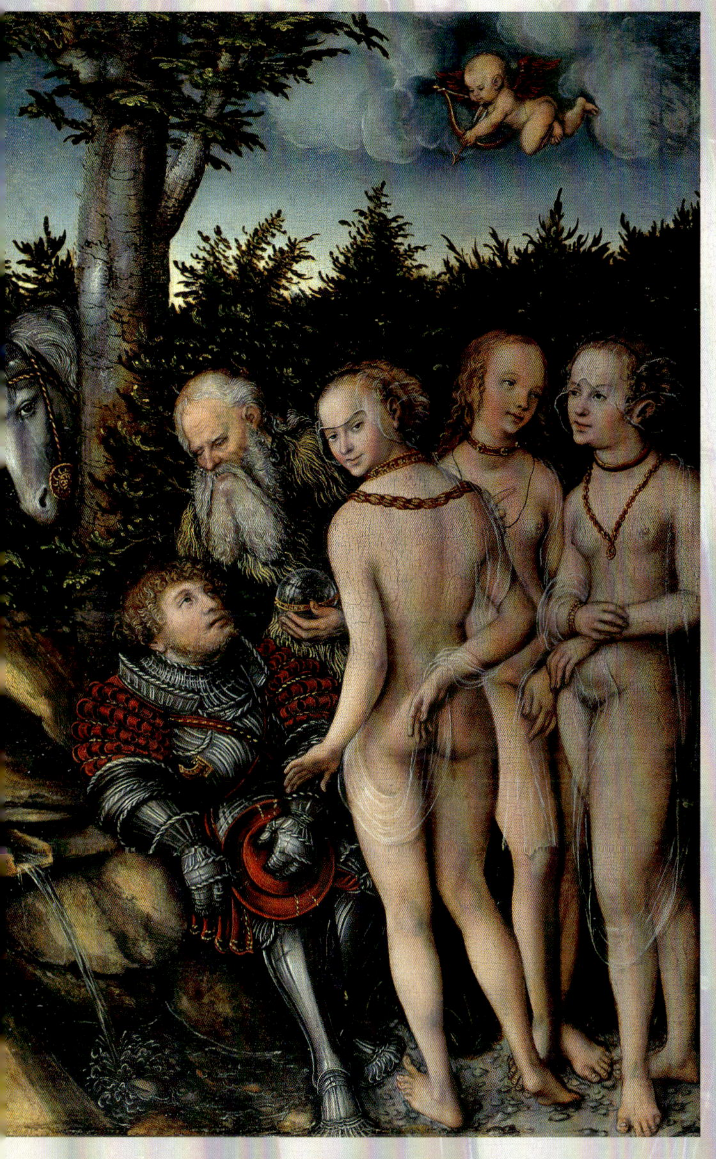

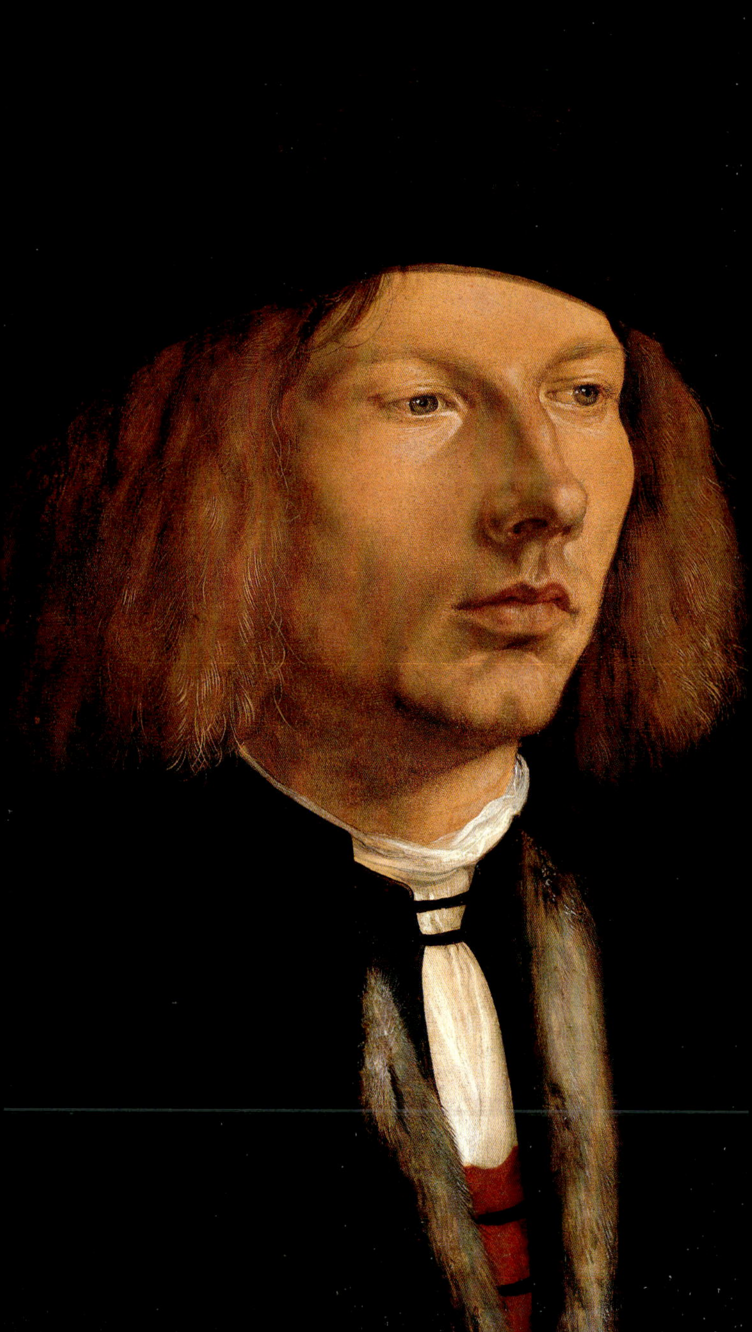

Burkhard von Speyer

Albrecht Dürer (1471–1528)

1506

This portrait was painted during Dürer's second visit to Venice, in 1506–7, and has been identified as Burkhard von Speyer (of whom little is known). In September 1506 Dürer wrote that he would be ready to leave Venice in about a month's time, 'but first I must take the portraits of some people I have promised'. This portrait may have been among them. Von Speyer was portrayed with other members of the German community in Venice in Dürer's famous altarpiece *The Feast of the Rose Garlands*, painted for the church of San Bartolommeo.

Dürer's mastery of fine detail is exemplified in the hair and the fur trim. The portrait also reveals the artist's admiration of Bellini, of whom he wrote while in Venice: 'I am really friendly with him. He is very old, but is still the best painter of them all.' Dürer was instrumental in introducing Italian Renaissance forms and ideas to Northern Europe.

The painting was acquired by Charles I and bears his brand on the back. It is recorded hanging in the Chair Room at Whitehall, in which the King had placed some of his most precious and finely wrought small pictures.

A Lady in Green

Agnolo Bronzino (1503–72)

*c.*1528–32

The celebrated nineteenth-century critic William Hazlitt thought that the green and white sleeves in this portrait looked like 'the leaves and flowers of the water-lily, and as clear!' This glamorous outfit is either Florentine or north Italian, and includes slashed sleeves, green velvet overdress with puffed shoulders, an embroidered chemise and a headdress into which the hair is gathered, called a *balza*. These colours are set off by an unusually deep red background. However splendid the costume, this remains an informal and intimate portrait.

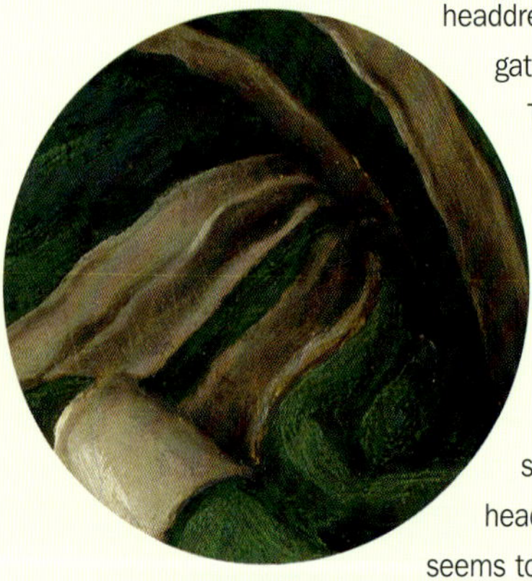

The sitter has a slight smile, a beguiling tilt of the head and a direct gaze that seems to beckon through the frame and engage the viewer. The artist here is almost certainly Bronzino, whose portraits always have this polished and refined surface, though they usually convey a demeanour of glacial hauteur. The sitter may be the daughter of Bronzino's friend Matteo Sofferoni, which might explain its unusual warmth and directness.

This portrait was almost certainly in the Gonzaga collection at Mantua, which was acquired by Charles I in 1628–32.

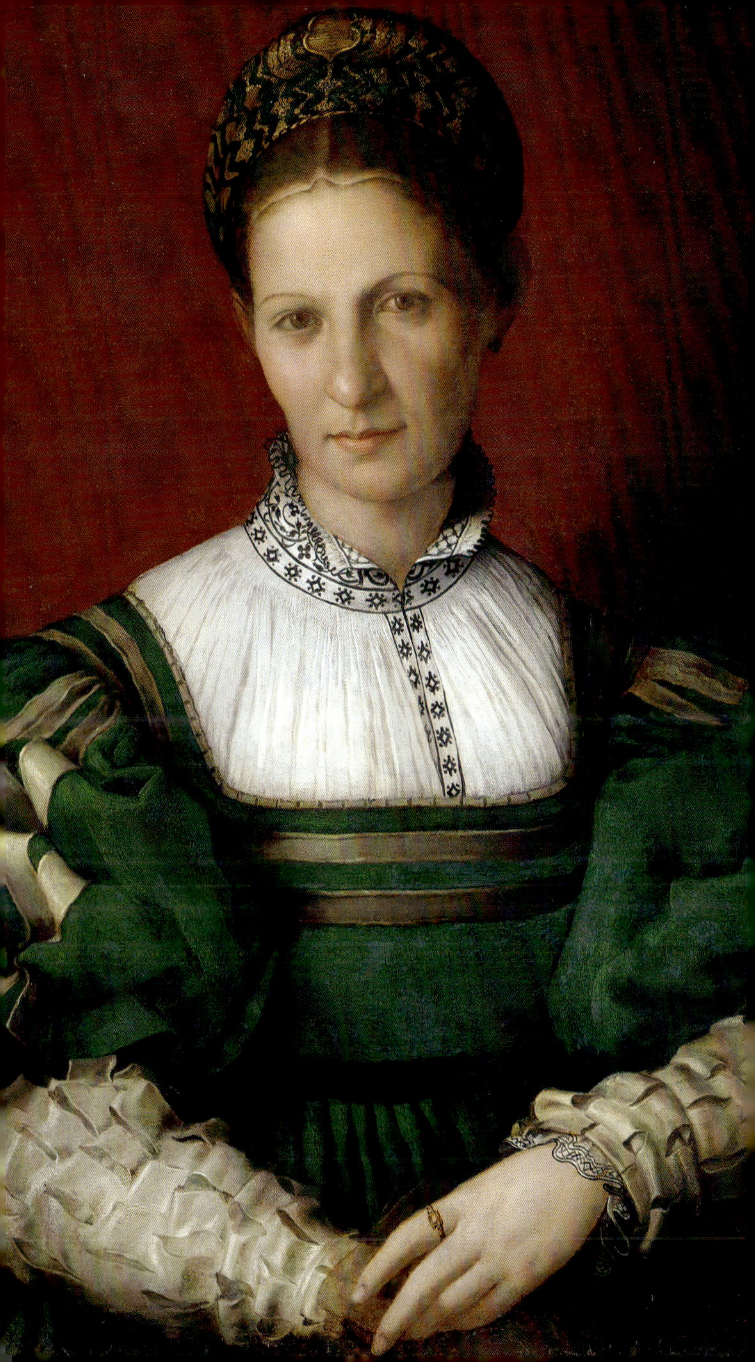

French Lacquer Commode

Bernard van Risamburgh (after 1696–c.1766)

*c.*1750

The elegant and graceful furniture produced by the Parisian cabinet-maker Bernard van Risamburgh, invariably known by the initials BVRB, is very distinctive: gently undulating surfaces, embellished with finely chased and richly gilt bronze mounts, are decorated with veneers of lacquer (as in this commode, or chest of drawers), floral marquetry in exotic woods or plaques of Sèvres porcelain.

BVRB worked principally for the leading Parisian dealer-decorators and this piece was undoubtedly supplied to a highly fashionable – possibly even royal – client. As was frequently

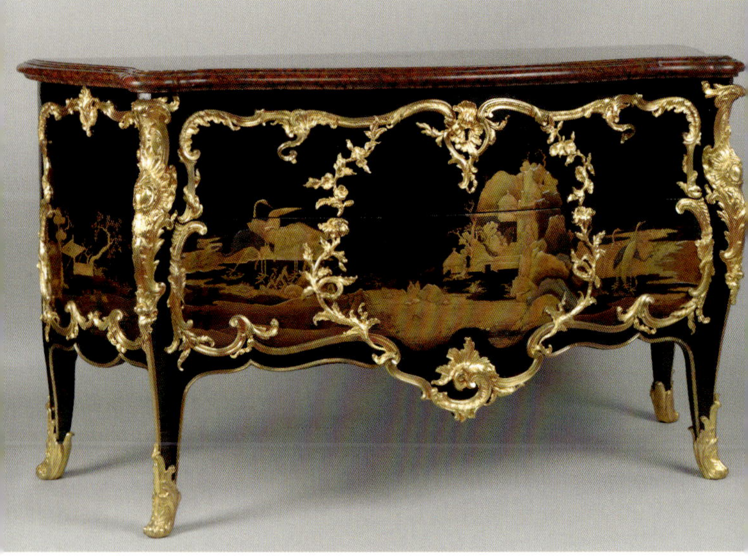

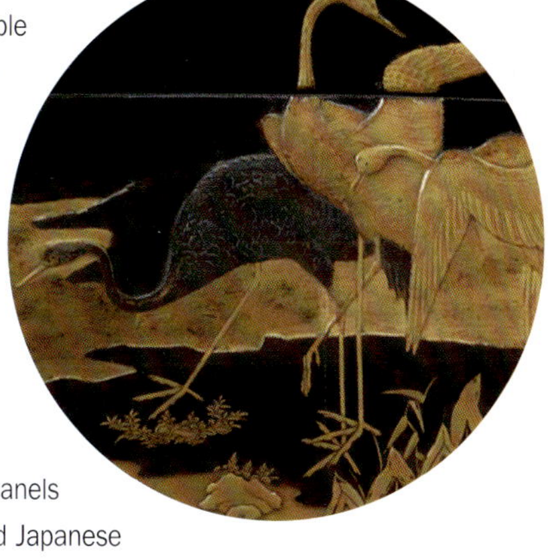

the case with the grandest French furniture, the marble top – in this case a deep red *griotte*, with elaborately moulded edge – may have been selected to match the chimneypiece of the room for which the commode was originally intended. The front and sides are veneered with panels of very fine black and gold Japanese lacquer, probably taken from a seventeenth-century coffer or screen. These panels have been carefully pared down from behind, reapplied to the newly made oak carcase of the commode, and then framed by beautifully modelled scrolls and a central wreath of flowers in sparkling gilt bronze. In places, joins or damage to the lacquer have been disguised by French lacquer additions.

This commode is one of six lacquer pieces by or attributed to BVRB in the Royal Collection, all of which were acquired by George IV in the early nineteenth century.

The Fall of Simon Magus

Benozzo Gozzoli (c.1421–97)

1461–2

This is one of five predella panels surviving from a *Madonna and Six Saints* (now National Gallery, London), which Gozzoli was contracted to paint on 23 October 1461 for the oratory of the Compagnia di San Marco, Florence. The high altarpiece of the church had already been painted by Fra Angelico in about 1440. It is hardly surprising, therefore, that his assistant and pupil, Gozzoli, should have been commissioned to paint the altarpiece for the Compagnia. Gozzoli was an able narrative painter, aware of the latest advances in Renaissance art. His colouring is always fresh and the predella panels to this particular altarpiece are among his finest work on a small scale.

The Fall of Simon Magus is a subject taken from *The Golden Legend* of Jacobus de Voragine, and it involves a contest between Saint Peter and a sorcerer at the court of Emperor Nero. Nero is seen enthroned on the left, while Saint Peter and Saint Paul are on the right. Simon Magus endeavours to prove his magical powers by launching himself from a wooden tower towards heaven. Despite being supported by demons, his stunt fails and he falls to the ground.

This panel was owned by William Ottley, an important authority on early Italian art, and was bought by Prince Albert in 1846.

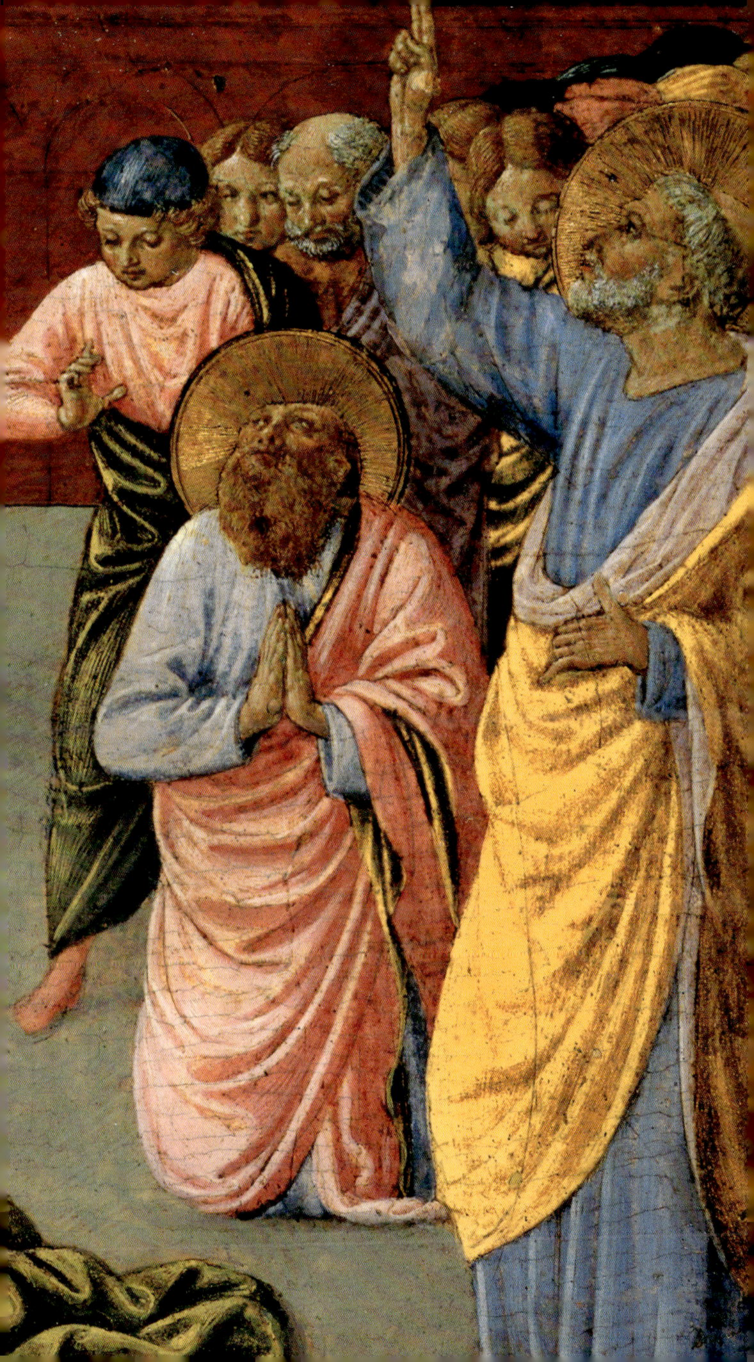

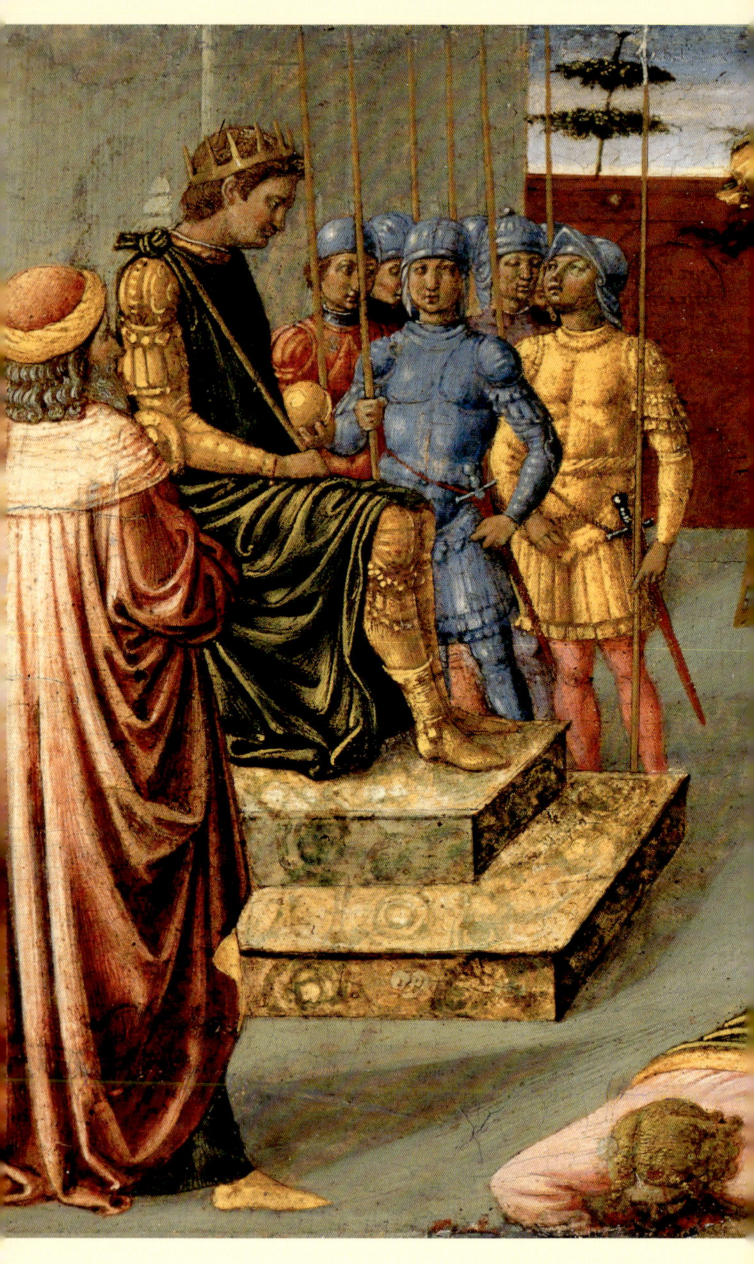

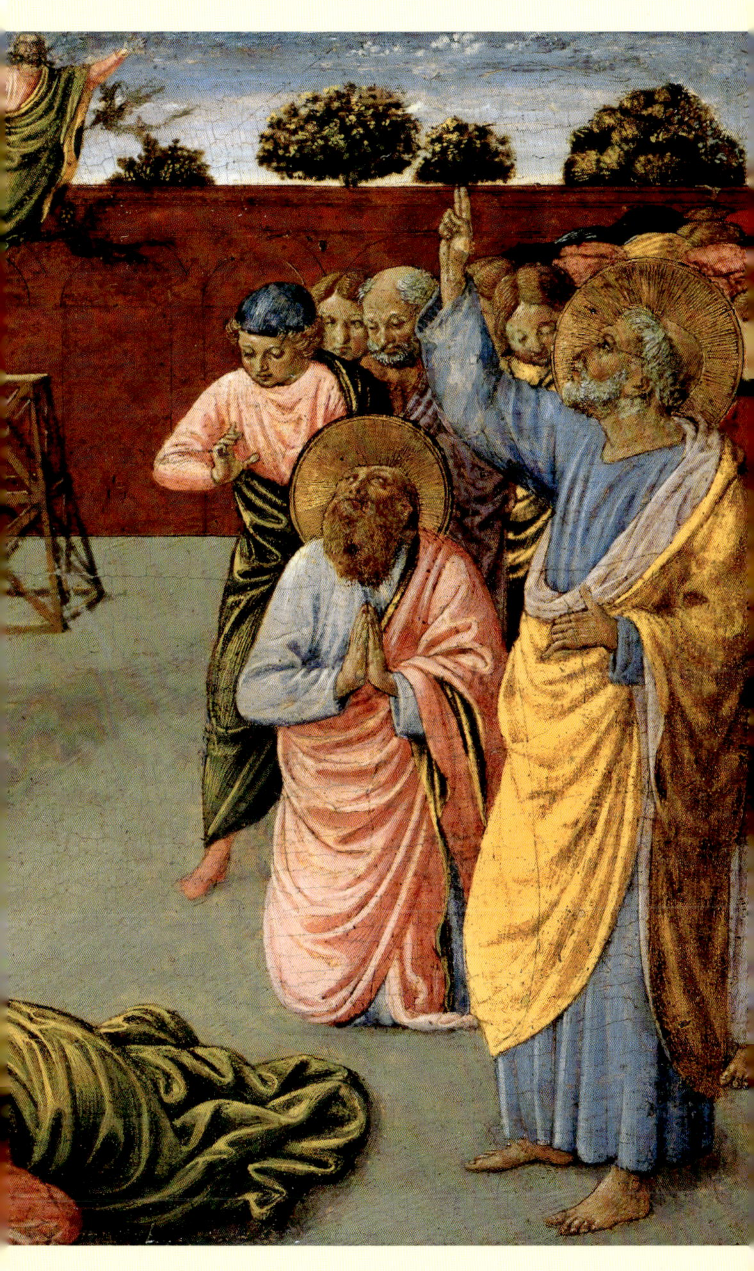

A Lady with a Lapdog

Lorenzo Costa (c.1460–1535)

c.1500–1505

This lady probably belongs to one of the ruling northern Italian families. The high degree of finish in this painting, most apparent in the careful delineation of the strands of hair and the use of gold highlights on the dress, suggests that the portrait was an important commission. Her dress is typical of the fashion of the north Italian courts: it has detachable sleeves, decorated with stripes and tied to the dress, worn over a white shift, decorated with a gold border. The band round the crown of her head is called a *lenza* and sometimes held a jewel.

It has been suggested that this painting originally formed part of a diptych (a hinged double-panel that opens and closes like a book). If this were so, it may have been commissioned to celebrate a marriage or betrothal. In the context of a marriage, the presence of the lapdog would symbolise fidelity.

It is not known how this painting entered the Royal Collection, but it is first recorded in the collection of Charles II, hanging at Whitehall.

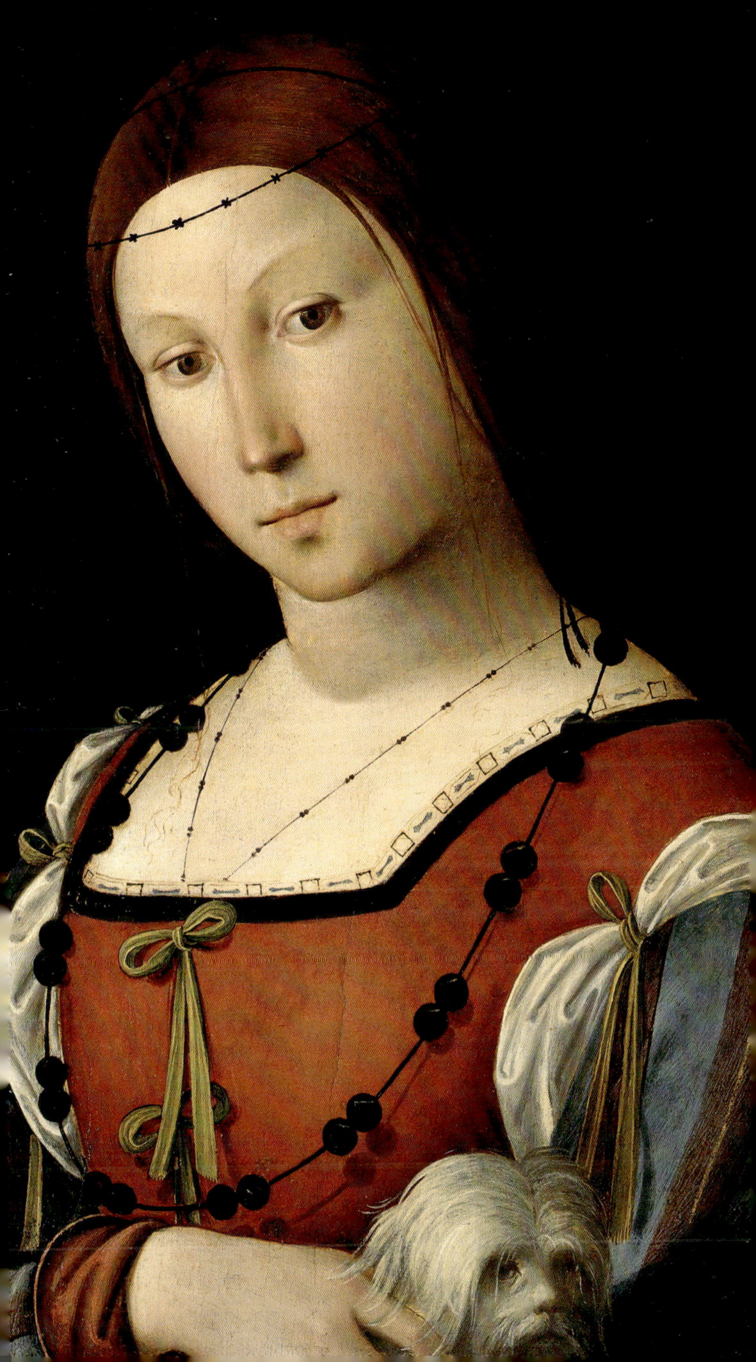

Elizabeth I when Princess

attributed to William Scrots (*fl.* 1537–53)

*c.*1546

This painting is the finest and most compelling portrait of the great Queen (1533–1603) before her accession. It conveys something of her beauty, dignity, gentleness and learning. Although it was probably painted for her father, Henry VIII, it is first recorded (in 1547) in the collection of her half-brother, Edward VI, where it is described as 'the picture of the Ladye Elizabeth her grace with a booke in her hande her gowne like crymsen clothe'.

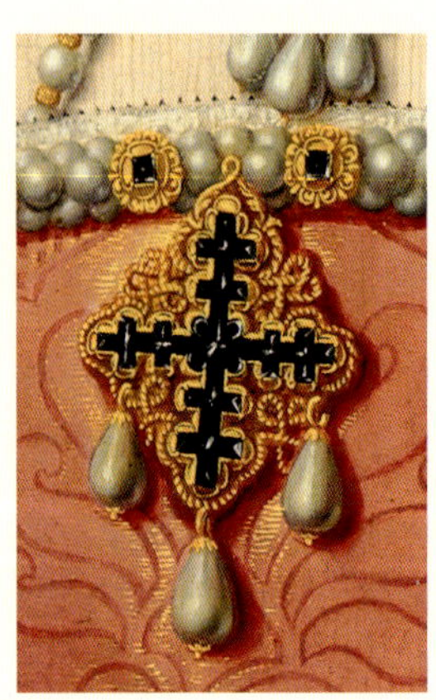

Elizabeth's costume is meticulously painted, drawing attention to the richness of the fabric of her dress and jewellery. However, there is evidence of a number of changes to the portrait by the artist before its completion. Alterations have been made to the fingers of her right hand and to the position of the small book that she holds, as well as to the large book, possibly a Bible, beside the Princess. The background curtain was painted over an earlier wall with architectural features.

This portrait seems to form a pair with one of Edward VI, which also hangs in the Queen's Drawing Room at Windsor: the style is similar and the panels are constructed in the same way, from the wood of the same tree. It has been suggested that the painter of these two works was William Scrots, who was employed by Henry VIII from 1545.

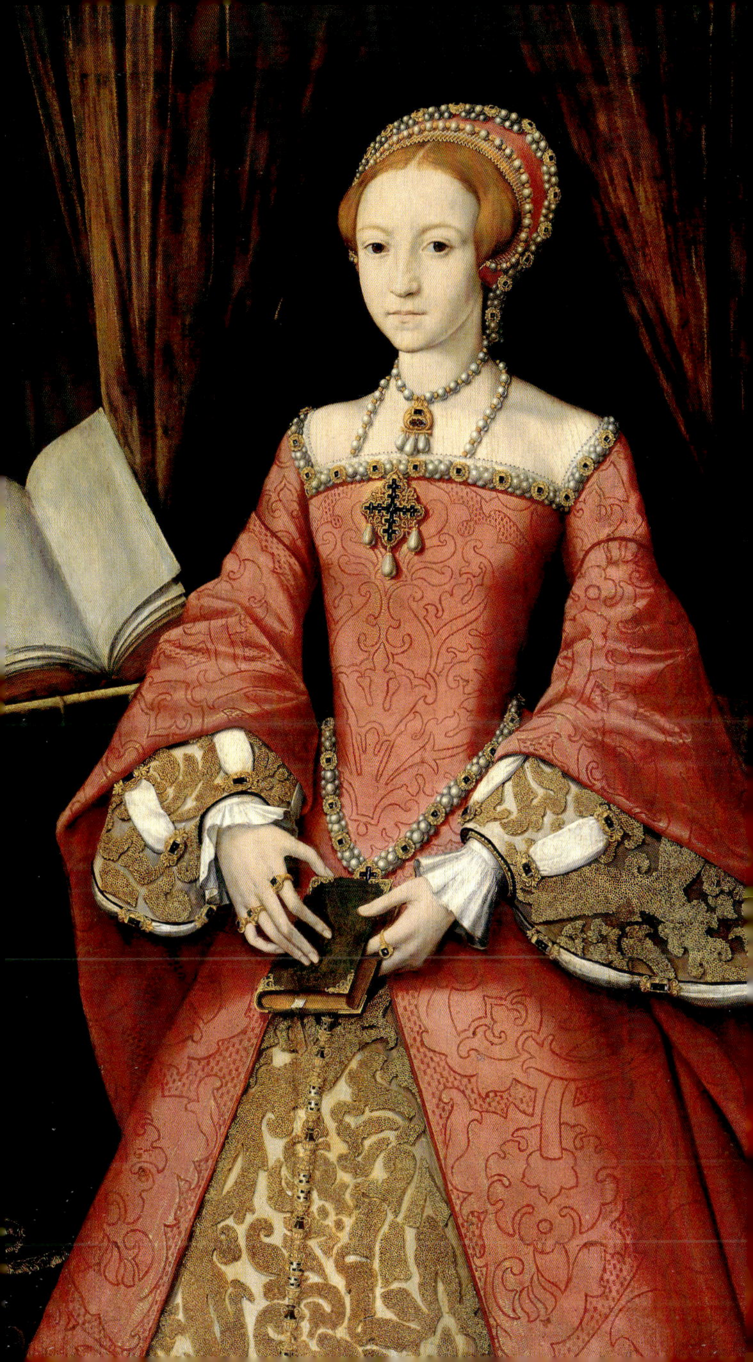

Charles I in Three Positions

Anthony Van Dyck (1599–1641)

1635

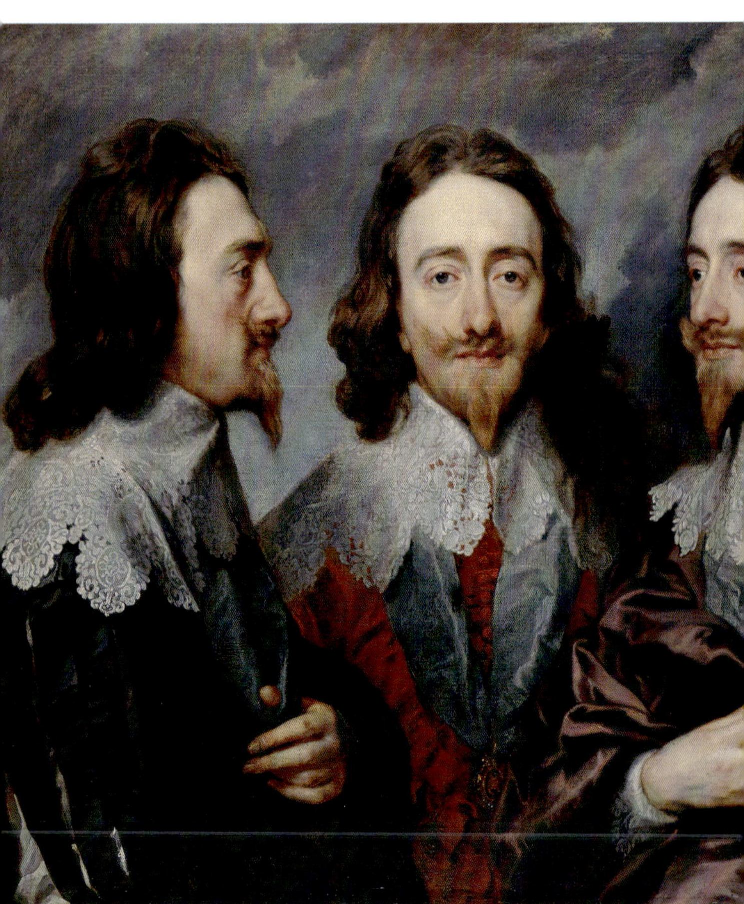

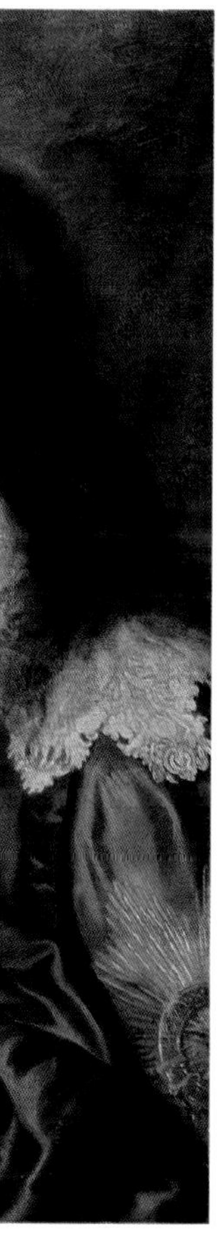

This painting was probably begun in the second half of 1635. In a letter to Gianlorenzo Bernini in March 1636, Charles I (1600–1649) expressed the hope that Bernini would execute 'our portrait in marble after the painted portrait which we shall send to you immediately'. The bust was to be a papal present to the Catholic Queen Henrietta Maria, and Pope Urban VIII had arranged its creation specially, at a time when hopes were entertained in Rome that Charles might lead England back into the Roman Catholic fold.

The heads in the painting are drawn and modelled with a care and restraint unusual in Van Dyck. The contrast between the blue Garter ribbon and the three different colours of the King's costume, which includes three differently patterned lace collars, against the richly worked sky, contributes to the transformation of a utilitarian commission into a transcendent work of art.

Van Dyck had presumably been influenced by Lotto's *Portrait of a Man in Three Positions* (Vienna, Kunsthistorisches Museum), which was in Charles I's collection at this time. The King's portrait, in turn, probably influenced Philippe de Champaigne, who in 1642 painted a *Triple Portrait of Cardinal Richelieu* (London, National Gallery) to assist Bernini (or another sculptor) with a bust of the Cardinal.

Although the portrait was painted for Charles I, it was kept by Bernini after he had completed his bust, and was only acquired for the Royal Collection in 1822 by George IV.

Windsor Castle

Leonard Knyff (1650–1722)

c.1703

This is one of the most accurate early views of Windsor Castle (reproduced in full on pages 2–3). Painted during the reign of Queen Anne, it shows a prospect of the north front of the Castle and part of the area of land acquired by William III in 1699, stretching from the Castle to Datchet in the east. The area was known as the Maestricht Garden and takes its name from the mock-military display performed in 1674, when James, Duke of Monmouth (illegitimate son of Charles II), re-enacted the successful attack of the Anglo-French forces on the fortified town of Maestricht in the Netherlands in June 1673.

William III had great plans for landscaping this site, inspired by French garden design. Work was interrupted by William's death in March 1702, but the garden area was enclosed within a high wall following the line of the river, leaving a roadway by the river's edge for travellers to and from Windsor and Datchet.

The garden shown in this painting probably dates to about 1703, when, under the instruction of Queen Anne, the terraces on the north slopes were constructed and lines of trees planted. However, it does not include the proposed canal that ran north to south, from the Castle to the river. Queen Anne's garden was abandoned on her death and although nothing of it survives, traces of the layout can still be seen from the air.

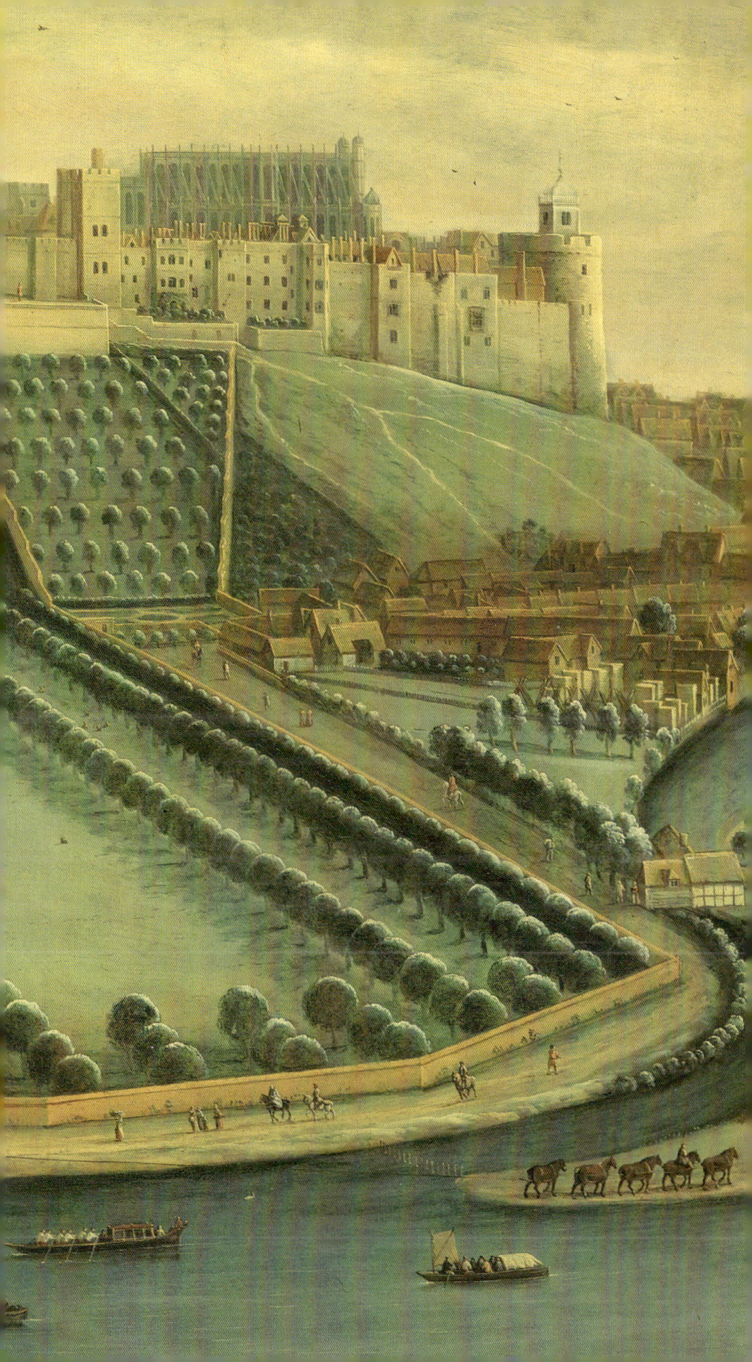

Ebony Cabinet
Paris
c.1650

Cabinets of this type – veneered all over with ebony and elaborately carved in low relief – were among the grandest pieces of furniture made in Paris in the first half of the seventeenth century. The French word to describe cabinet-making – *ébénisterie* (ebony work) – derives from precisely this use of costly ebony veneers, and on the best examples, such as this one, perhaps by Pierre Gole (c.1620–85), enormous care and attention were lavished. Even the insides of the drawers are veneered and inlaid with elaborate geometric designs, and among the interior fittings are chess and backgammon boards and a number of concealed drawers.

The carved decoration is partly based on the engraved illustrations of two popular early seventeenth-century French novels, *L'Ariane* and *L'Endymion*. Among the additional scenes

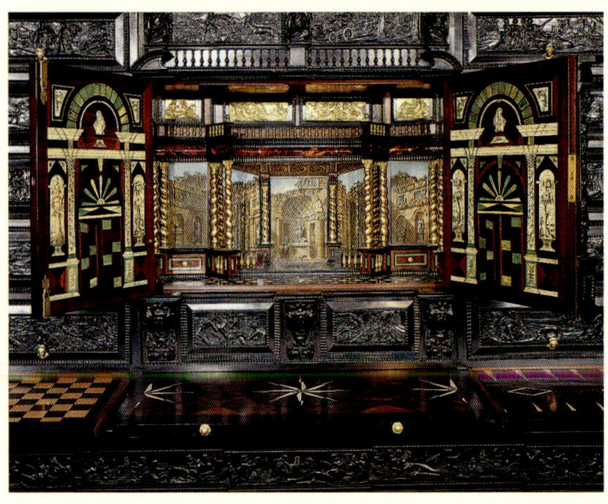

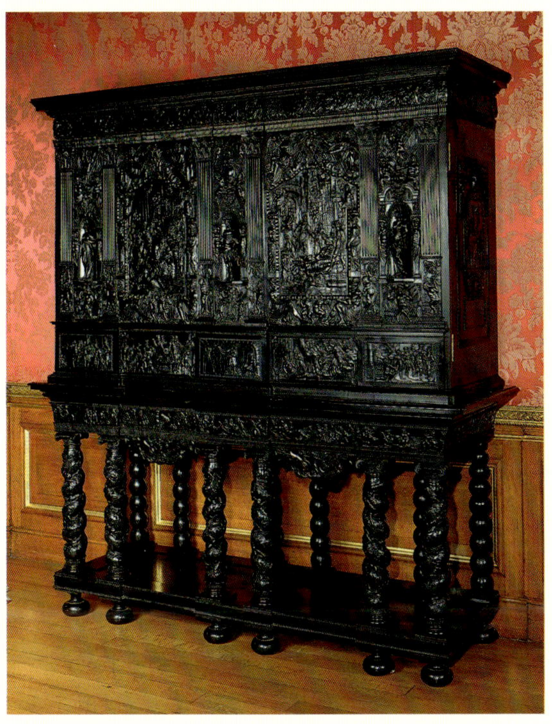

portrayed are two which include the infant Louis XIV, his parents Louis XIII and Anne of Austria, and Cardinal Richelieu. How and when this seemingly royal cabinet came to England is not known: perhaps it was a gift from Louis XIV to his first cousin Charles II; alternatively, it might have come via Louis XIV's childless sister-in-law, Liselotte, Duchess of Orléans, to her Hanoverian cousins. It was certainly in George III's collection – the feet were replaced in 1765 by the cabinet-maker John Bradburn. A set of gouaches of classical ruins by C.-L. Clérisseau was added to the interior at a later date, either for George III or George IV.

Augsburg Clock

Jacob Mayr (c.1648–1714)

c.1710

Clocks of this kind, with cases as elaborate as their movements, were a speciality of southern Germany in the late seventeenth and early eighteenth centuries. The unusually complicated spring-driven movement of this one, signed by the Augsburg maker Jacob Mayr, is fitted with numerous intricately worked dials. These, in addition to showing the time, indicate the day of the week, hours of daylight and darkness, position of the sun in the Zodiac, and other astronomical and lunar information, as well as an annual calendar with the Saints' Days.

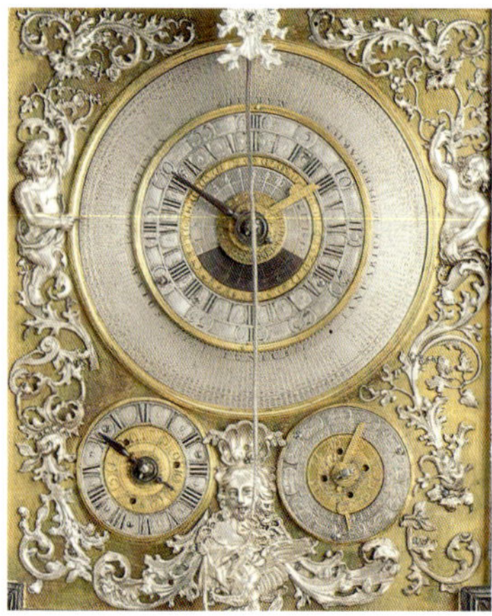

The architectural case, which is decorated with red-stained turtle-shell, ebony, chased silver plaques and pink glass columns, and contains a pin-barrel mechanism in the base, was once surmounted by a silver group of Atlas supporting the globe. This and other silver ornamental features were lost when the clock case was damaged during a bombing raid on Buckingham Palace (where the clock then was) during the Second World War. The lengthy restoration of the case was undertaken in the Royal Collection workshops.

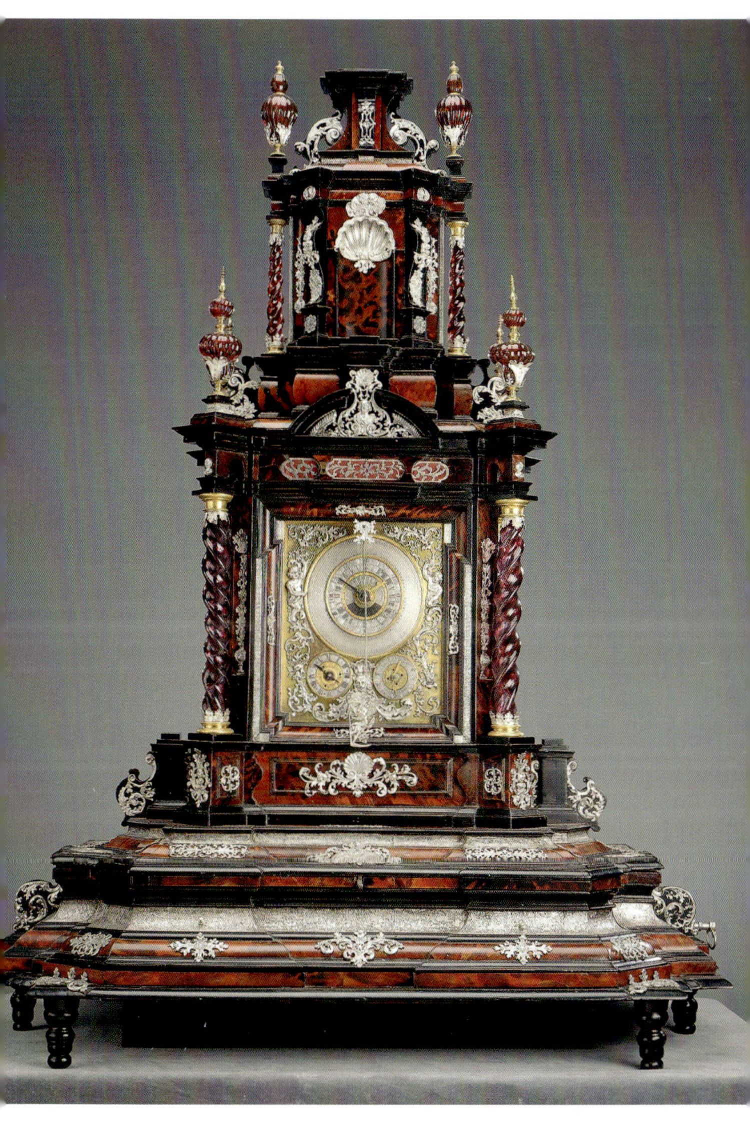

Marquetry Cabinet

attributed to Gerrit Jensen (*fl.*1680–1715)

*c.*1695

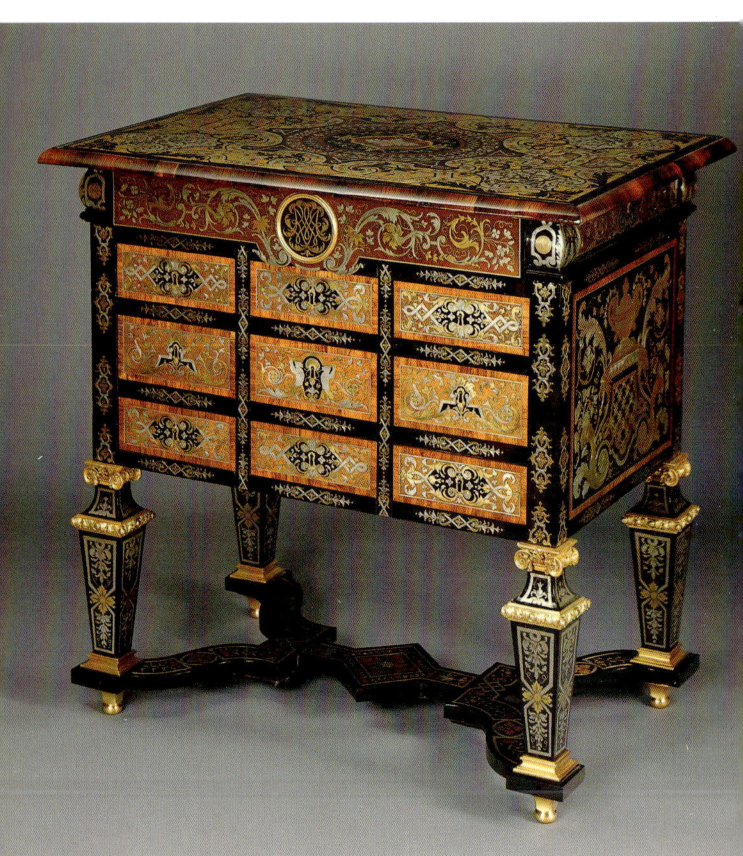

The practice of inlaying metal (usually brass and pewter), tortoiseshell and exotic woods in intricate formal patterns was first popularised by the French royal cabinet-maker André-Charles Boulle, from around 1670. This technique, to which Boulle gave his name, was widely imitated in northern Europe, but in England the only known practitioner was Gerrit Jensen, cabinet-maker to William III and Mary II. Jensen, who may have come to England from the Low Countries, would certainly have known the King and Queen's architect and designer, the Huguenot Daniel Marot, one of whose designs (for a tablecloth) was adapted by Jensen for the top of this table.

The table itself has often been identified with a payment of 1694/5 in the Royal Archives to Jensen for £70, for a 'fine writeing desk Table Inlaid wth metall'. While the table is undoubtedly a royal piece – the frieze drawer is inlaid with the double cipher of William and Mary – the description is too vague to allow much certainty. What we do know is that the cipher would not have been used after Queen Mary's death in December 1694, and that the table itself was adapted to incorporate the cabinet section with a nest of drawers at a slightly later date. In order to achieve this change, which was certainly carried out by the same cabinet-maker, the original legs would have been changed and the medallion containing the cipher shaved down to allow the new drawers to fit below it.

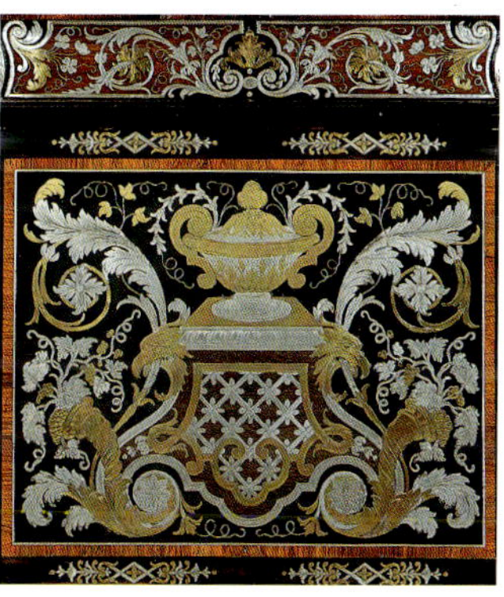

Stump-work Casket

c.1670

Stump-work embroidery, invariably executed by young girls as part of their preparation for adulthood, developed from the Elizabethan tradition of raised needlework. The use of relief, achieved by means of wadding and wire, enabled the embroideress to create livelier scenes than were possible using other techniques. The provenance of this particularly large and spectacular stump-work casket, made during the reign of Charles II, is unknown, but in the twentieth century it formed part of a notable collection of early English furniture and decorative arts assembled by the financier Lord Plender (1861–1946), who presented it to Queen Mary in 1932.

The scenes chosen for stump-work embroidery were often taken from the Old Testament, and were selected for their morally uplifting qualities. The front and back of the casket tell the story of David and Bathsheba, warning of the terrible consequences of unrestrained desire and upholding the importance of virtue and chastity. On one of the sides is the story of Jephthah, whose daughter gave up her life to fulfil her father's vow to God. Perhaps the most extraordinary decoration is reserved for the lid, where a three-dimensional rural scene has been created using silk wrapped around pieces of wire, complete with trees, sheep and a shepherdess.

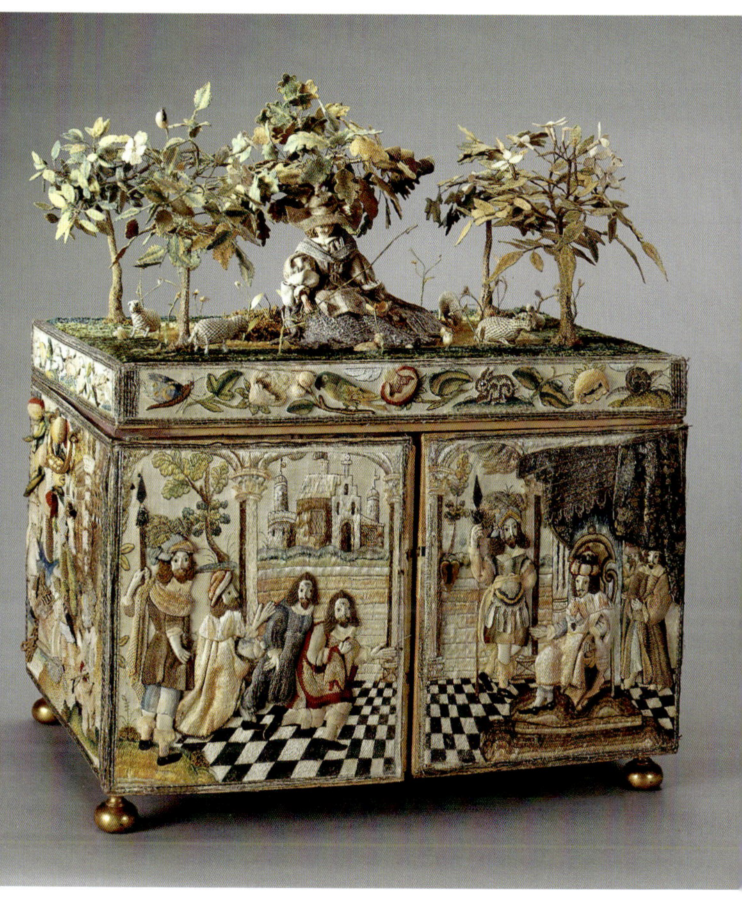

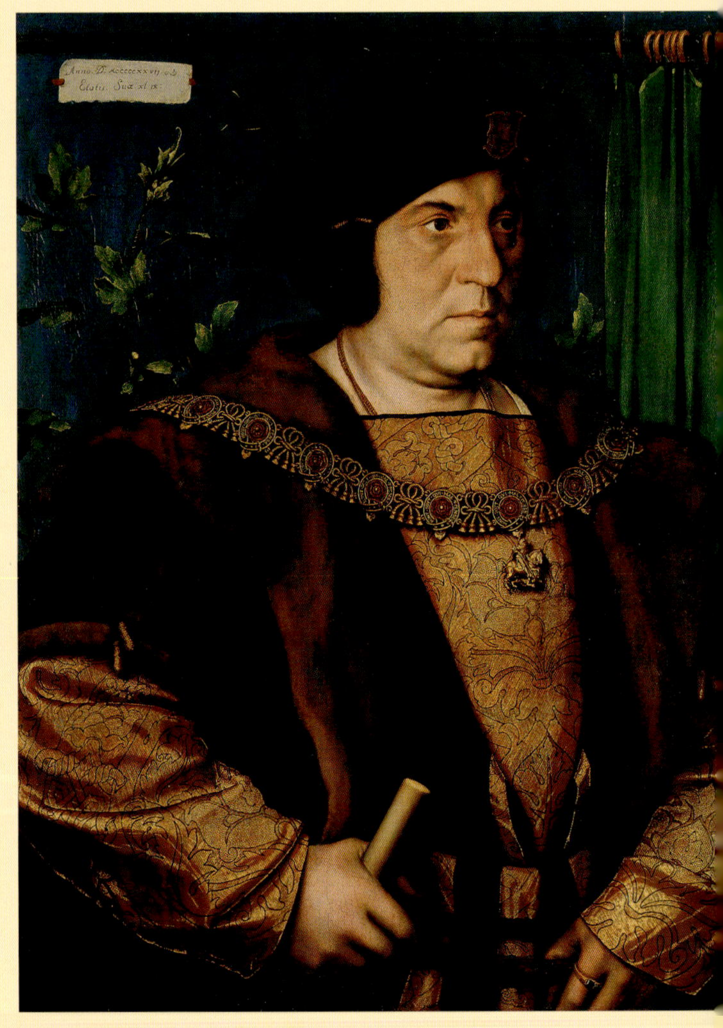

Sir Henry Guildford

Hans Holbein the Younger (1497/8–1543)

1527

Sir Henry Guildford (1489–1532) was an eminent courtier and held several high offices in Henry VIII's household, including that of Comptroller, as indicated by the white staff of office he carries in this picture. He became a Knight of the Garter in 1526, and is depicted wearing the gold collar of the Order. As Comptroller, Guildford was responsible for authorising payments to a 'Master Hans', who is assumed to be Holbein.

Holbein and Guildford were also linked through their friendship with the philosopher Erasmus. Guildford's interest in learning, unusual for a courtier at this time, is suggested by his hat badge. This is decorated with a design composed of a clock and surveying instruments, to demonstrate the importance of geometry in understanding the universe.

This portrait was painted during Holbein's first visit to England, in 1526–8. During this time he made a great impact on the artistic sensibilities of those at court, most of whom had never sat for a painter before. His portraits combine truth and subtlety to a degree that was extremely rare in European painting at this date. The painting is lavish in its use of gold and rich contrasting colours, such as the brilliant green leaves against the blue background and the rich fur collar.

The painting was bought by George II, in about 1735.

Japanese Porcelain Vase and Cover

late seventeenth century

The fashion for arranging oriental porcelain jars, bowls and cups on cabinets, over doors and fireplaces, and on wall brackets was introduced to England by Queen Mary II (1662–94), who ruled jointly with her Dutch husband William III. To satisfy demand, porcelain was imported in vast quantities, chiefly through the Dutch East India Company and mainly from Japan, as civil wars had disrupted the trade with China. Queen Mary owned several thousand pieces. Nearly 800 were included in an inventory of her apartments at Kensington Palace in 1694, including several 'coloured jars of six squares', which probably refers to this form of vase.

Made of milk-white soft-paste porcelain with a colourless glaze, the vase is painted in the *Kakiemon* style and palette, used in the Arita province of Japan from the mid-seventeenth century. The decoration of the main panels includes cranes among flowering plants, with more stylised fantailed birds and geometric patterns on the shoulders and lid. These colours and motifs were devised for the Western market and such wares were not available within Japan.

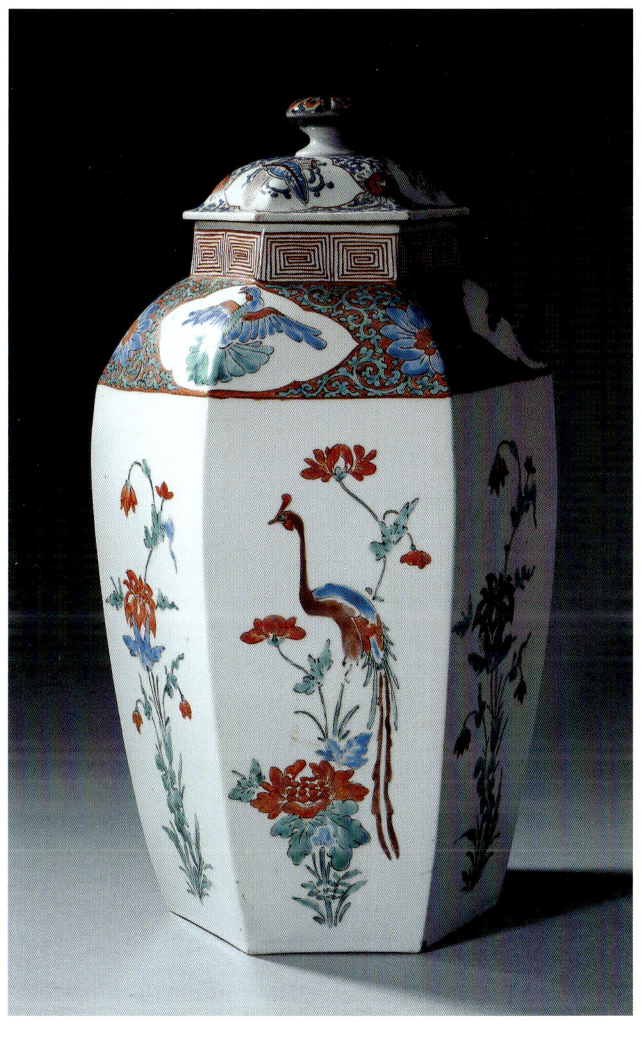

'Nell Gwyn's Bellows'

c.1680–85

Following the Restoration of the Monarchy in 1660, furniture made of, or embellished with, silver first made its appearance in England. This fashion, adopted enthusiastically by Charles II and his successors, James II and William III, soon extended to such relatively minor areas as chimney-furniture – particularly grates, andirons and fire-irons. This pair of bellows is among the most luxurious of these minor articles to have survived: its spout, vent and handles are mounted in silver gilt (the gilding adding an extra dash of quality). The royal origin of the bellows is proclaimed by the prominent crowned cipher of linked 'C's inlaid in the marquetry of the front, and by the raised crown and crossed sceptres on the silver handle – set just above an infant's head blowing a gust of wind from which a phoenix emerges. The silver is marked by the leading London goldsmith Benjamin Pyne (c.1650–1732), with the stamp that he used from shortly after 1680, thus narrowing the date of manufacture to the five years before the King's death in 1685.

If the traditional but undocumented connection with Charles II's mistress Nell Gwyn (?1651–87) has any substance, it may not be too fanciful to imagine that the bellows were given to her for use at Burford House, the substantial mansion that the King built for her a few hundred metres to the south of the Castle in the late 1670s.

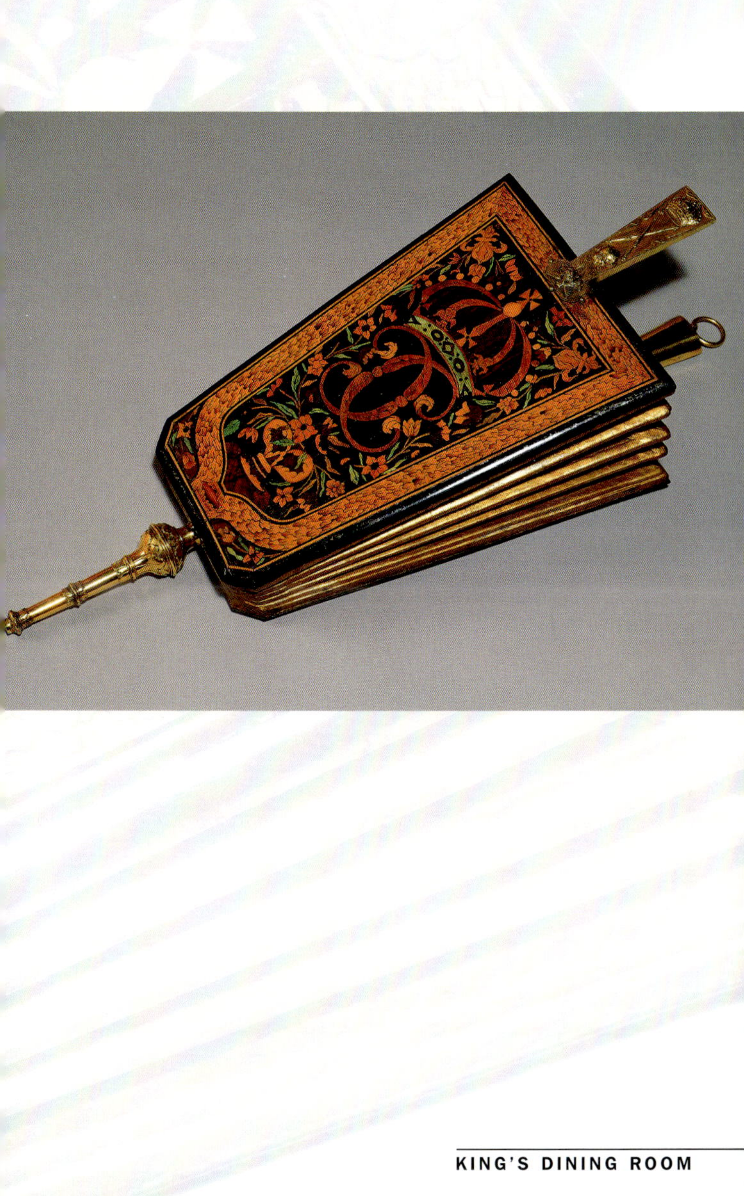

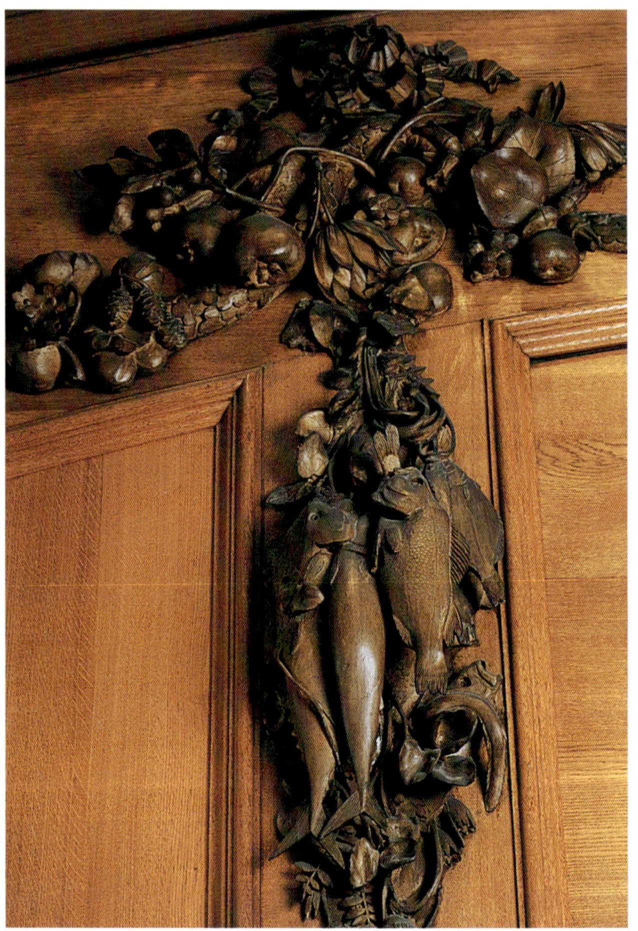

Limewood Carving

Grinling Gibbons (1648–1721)

1676–8

Much of the magnificence of the new State Apartments built at Windsor for Charles II in the 1670s was due to the painted ceilings and murals of Antonio Verrio and the illusionistic limewood carvings of Grinling Gibbons. In many parts of the Castle their work was destroyed by the transformations of George IV and Sir Jeffry Wyatville in the 1820s. Many of the carvings were re-employed in that process, but in the King's Dining Room the whole scheme has survived, no doubt owing to the harmony of subject matter between Verrio's ceiling of the *Banquet of the Gods*, his cove of fish, fowl and game, and Gibbons's astonishing carved equivalents.

Gibbons had first been brought to Charles II's attention in 1671, but it was Hugh May, the Surveyor of the Works at Windsor, who secured the first royal employment for him, at the age of only 28, initially working alongside the much older Master Carver to the King, Henry Phillips. The success of the Windsor work secured Gibbons and his workshop a further 20 years of royal work at Kensington Palace and Hampton Court. In this example, each of the intricate carved groups is made up of several thicknesses of wood, which are gradually built up in layers so that the resulting carvings are sometimes as much as 30 centimetres (1 foot) in depth.

Bridget Holmes

John Riley (1646–91)

1686

Bridget Holmes is shown here at the age of 96, playfully wielding her mop at the fashionably dressed Page of the Backstairs, who peeps out from behind a curtain. She was a 'Necessary Woman' (one of the lower servants in the Royal Household), whose task it was to dispose of the contents of chamber pots. Her period of royal service began during the time of Charles I and continued into the reign of William III and Mary II, but this painting was probably commissioned during the reign of James II.

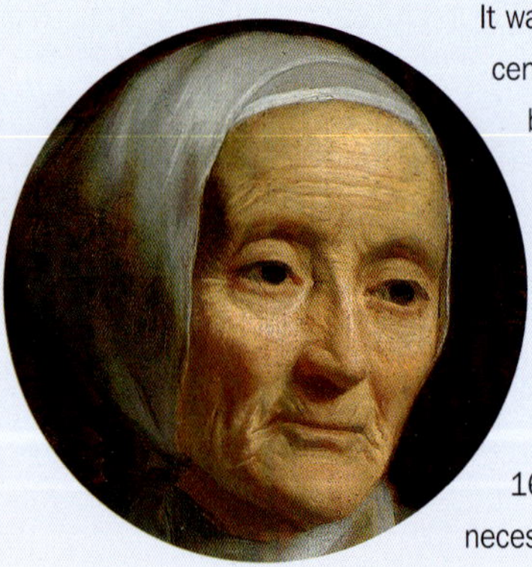

It was rare in the seventeenth century for a domestic servant to be the subject of a portrait, but Bridget Holmes's age and dutiful service presumably earned her this accolade. Riley, who was appointed Principal Painter to William III and Mary II (jointly with Sir Godfrey Kneller) in 1688, has included all the props necessary in fashionable portraiture. The cascading curtain, and the column and vase with classical frieze, would be a more fitting background in a portrait of someone with a higher social status. This is an affectionate, mock-heroic portrait: the faithful servant is portrayed as an inspiration to her fellow servants and countrymen, who had not all been as faithful in their royal service during the same period.

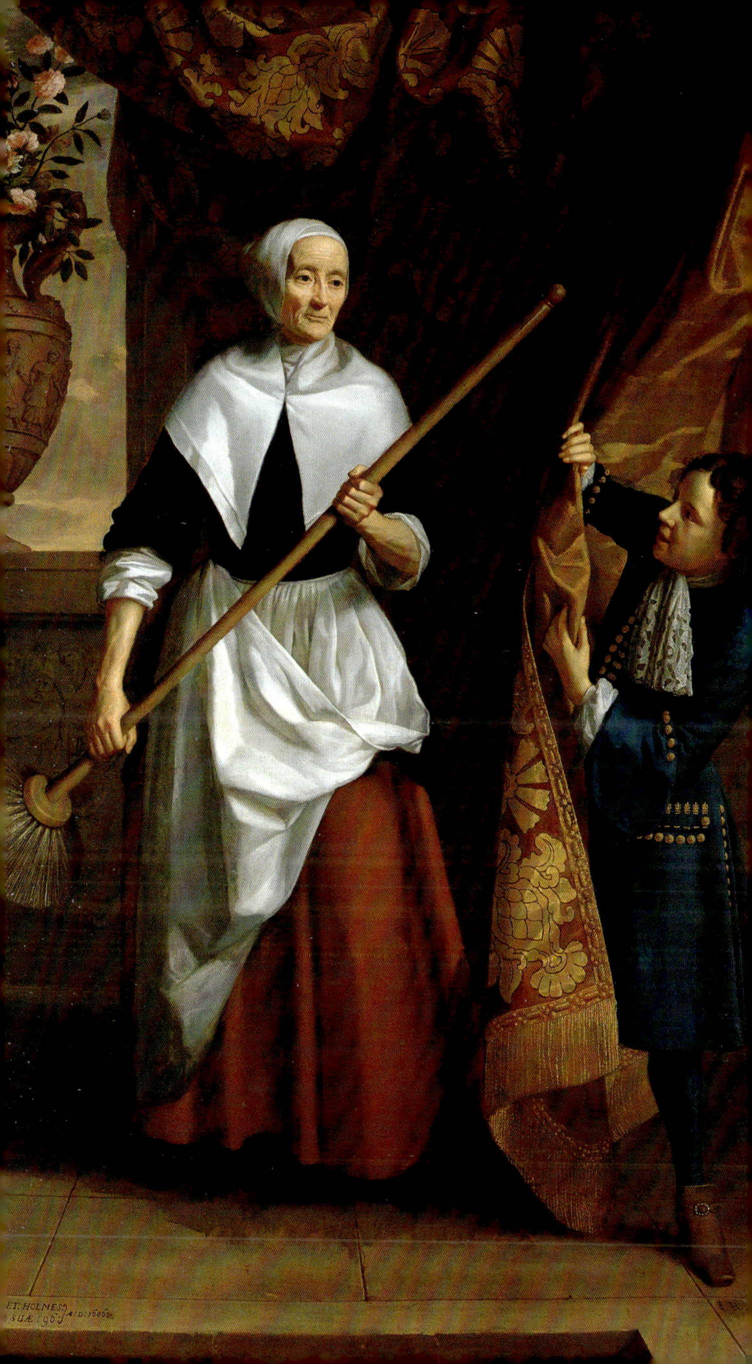
ET. HOLMES
SUÆ : 96

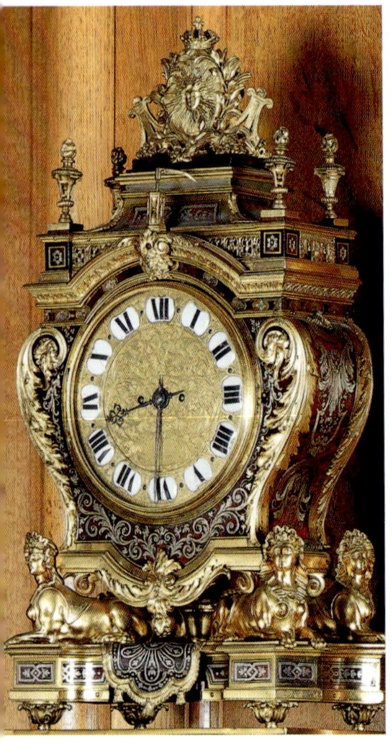

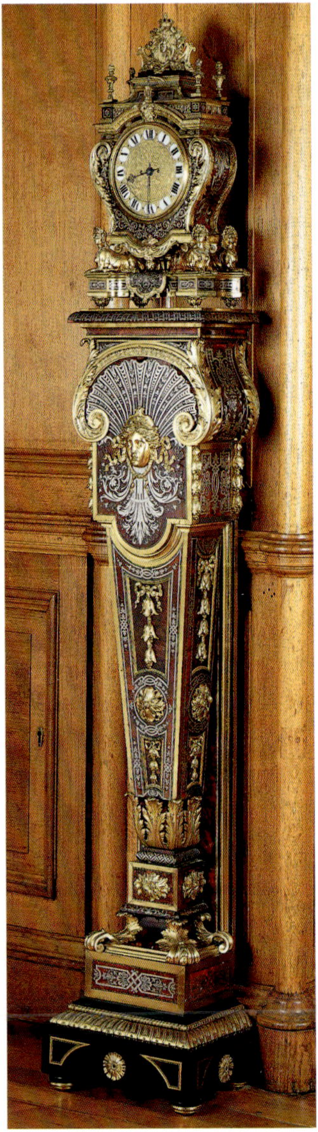

Long-case Clock

attributed to André-Charles Boulle

(1642–1732)

*c.*1695

This richly decorated, small-scale clock, intricately veneered with pewter and tortoiseshell marquetry and lavishly mounted with fine gilt-bronze ornaments, is characteristic of the style of Louis XIV's principal and most celebrated cabinet-maker, André-Charles Boulle. In terms of design, the case for the clock movement and the pedestal on which it rests still retain their separate identities. This feature, which gives the clock its slightly transitional character, disappeared over the following 20 years, as Boulle developed fully integrated designs for his clock cases.

The striking imagery of the double-sided Apollo mask surmounted by a crown on the cresting of the clock strongly suggests a royal origin. Not surprisingly therefore, when the clock was purchased by George IV in 1820, it was claimed that it had come from Versailles. Three other clocks of the same model are known, all supposedly made for Louis XIV. The bronzes of the Windsor version are extensively struck with the crowned C tax mark, which was applied to all bronzes on the market between 1745 and 1749. This indicates that if it had once been a royal piece, it was no longer so by this time. The original movement, by Gaudron of Paris (probably Antoine, c.1640–1714), was replaced by Vulliamy in 1835, and the following year the clock was brought to Windsor by order of William IV, having remained in store since its purchase 16 years before.

Silver Table and Mirror

1699

Silver furniture is extremely rare. The fashion for it – always seen as the pinnacle of extravagance and never widely followed – began with Louis XIV at Versailles in the 1660s. Ironically, William III's order for this mirror and table, and for a pair of matching candle-stands which do not survive, was given just at the time the French King's silver furniture was being melted down to replenish his war chest (his armies defeated by the Protestant coalition led by King William). They formed the major part of a commission amounting to over £3,600 for new silver furniture to embellish the King's rooms at Kensington Palace.

The table-top, which is elaborately engraved with the King's arms and the emblems of the four kingdoms (including France, to which Britain still laid claim), is signed 'R.H.', perhaps for the Netherlandish engraver Romeyn de Hooghe, while the table frame and the mirror bear the stamp of Andrew Moore, a silver chaser working in the Bridewell district of London. Among the notable decorative features is the realistically modelled pineapple – then a great novelty – resting at the junction of the waved stretchers of the table. In the early nineteenth century George III had the surviving pieces of silver furniture in the Collection refurbished and placed in the Queen's Ballroom, where they remain to this day.

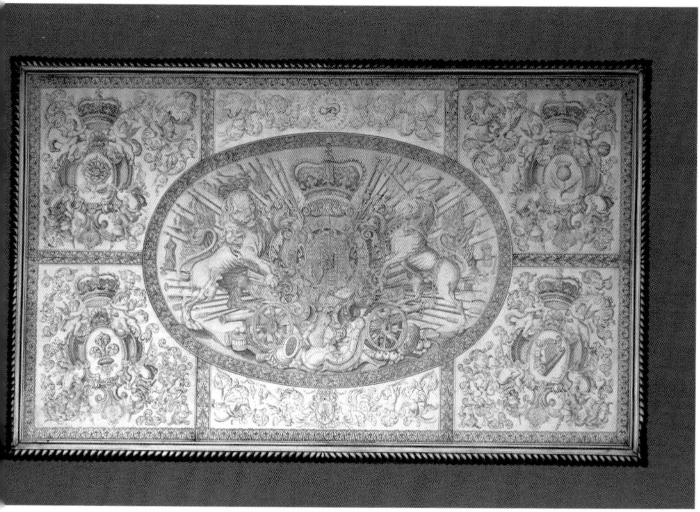

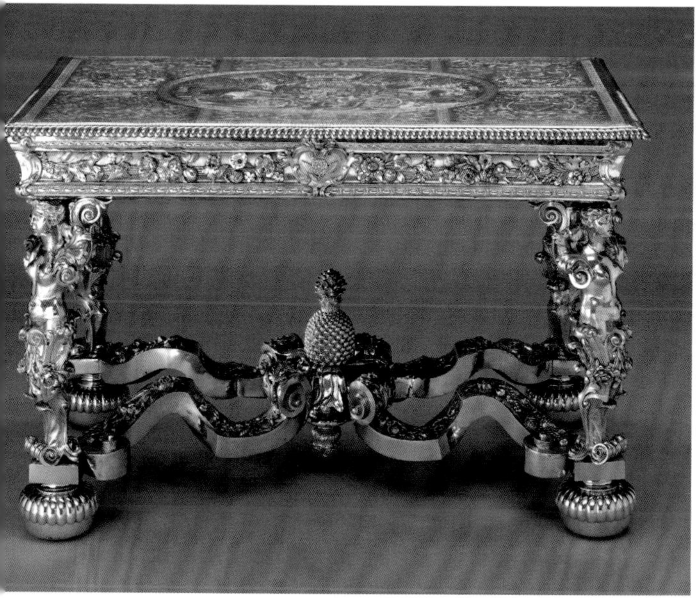

Negress Head Clock

J.-A. Lépine (1720–1814)

1790

At first glance, this unusual object does not immediately reveal itself as a clock, nor is there any indication that the base contains a small pin-barrel organ. However, at ten minutes before the hour, and for two minutes after, the pupils of the eyes of the Negress open to show the hour (with Roman numerals) in her left eye and the minutes (with Arabic numerals) in her right eye. At any other period, her eyes open to reveal the time only when her right earring is pulled. On the hour, or when her left earring is pulled, the organ will play one of eight tunes, all well known in the eighteenth century. These include the popular ditty celebrating Marlborough's victories, *'Malbroogh s'en va-t-en guerre'*.

The Negress herself – representing the eighteenth century's fascination with the exotic, and perhaps intended to personify Africa as one of the Four Parts of the World – wears an elaborate turban and carries on her shoulders a bow and quiver of arrows. Echoing this theme of the huntress, the gilt-bronze relief on the base shows infants returning from the chase, from a design attributed to the sculptor Augustin Pajou. The clock was purchased from Lépine by the Prince of Wales, later George IV, probably in 1790, the year of its manufacture.

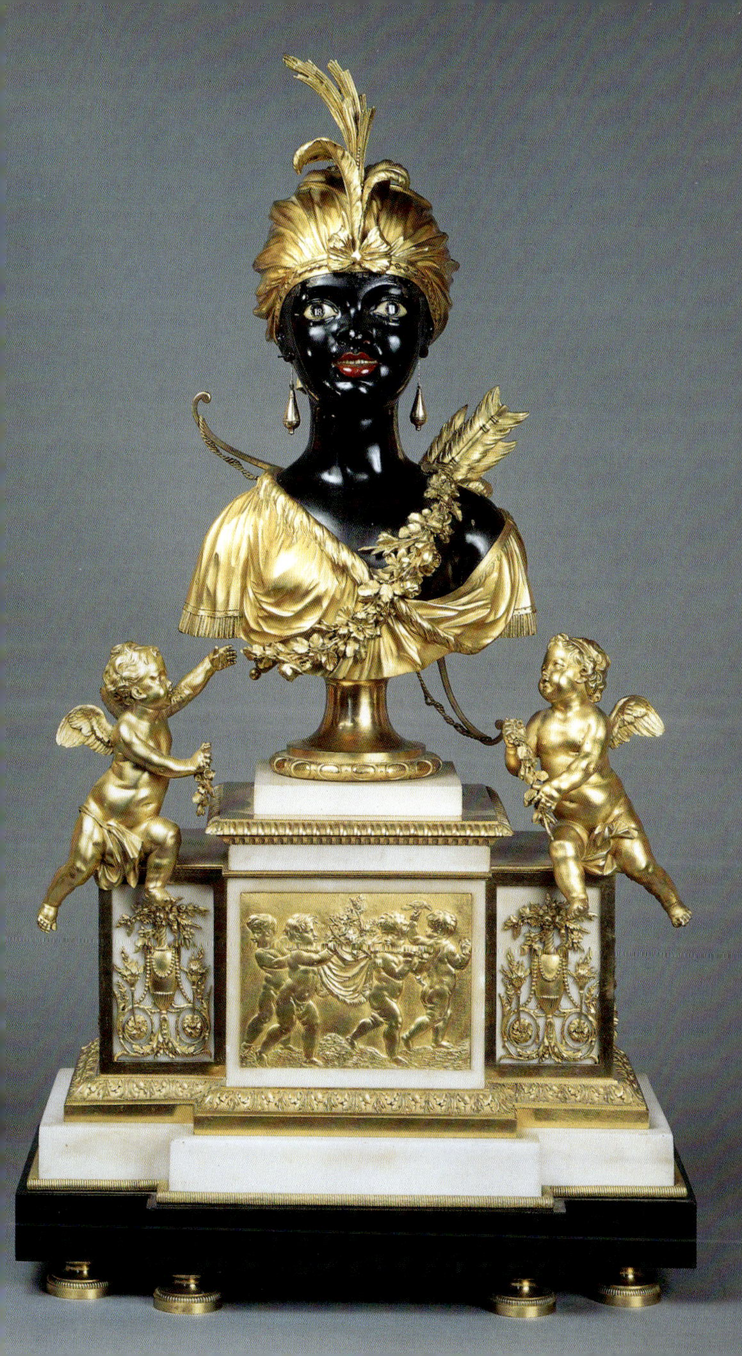

Thomas Killigrew and (?)William, Lord Crofts

Anthony Van Dyck (1599–1641)

1638

In this striking double portrait the man facing us is Thomas Killigrew, the dramatist and leading figure in Restoration theatre. A courtier of Charles I, he was appointed Master of the Revels by Charles II and became known as 'the King's jester'. In stark contrast to the humorous side of his nature, Killigrew is depicted here wearing black and sitting in a melancholic pose, alluding to the recent death of his wife Cecilia, only 18 months after their marriage. Further allusions to her death are provided by the small gold and silver cross attached to his sleeve, bearing her intertwined initials, and a wedding ring bound to his wrist by a black band.

Speculation surrounds the identity of Killigrew's companion, who holds a blank piece of paper, but it seems to be widely accepted that this is Killigrew's brother-in-law, William Crofts. He also wears black, perhaps in mourning for the death of his recently lost sister. The broken column in the background can be read as a symbol of fortitude, implying that both men are bearing their sorrows stoically.

The majority of works by Van Dyck in the Royal Collection were commissioned by Charles I. However, this portrait only entered the Collection in 1748, when it was bought by Frederick, Prince of Wales.

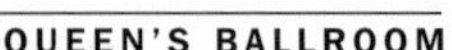

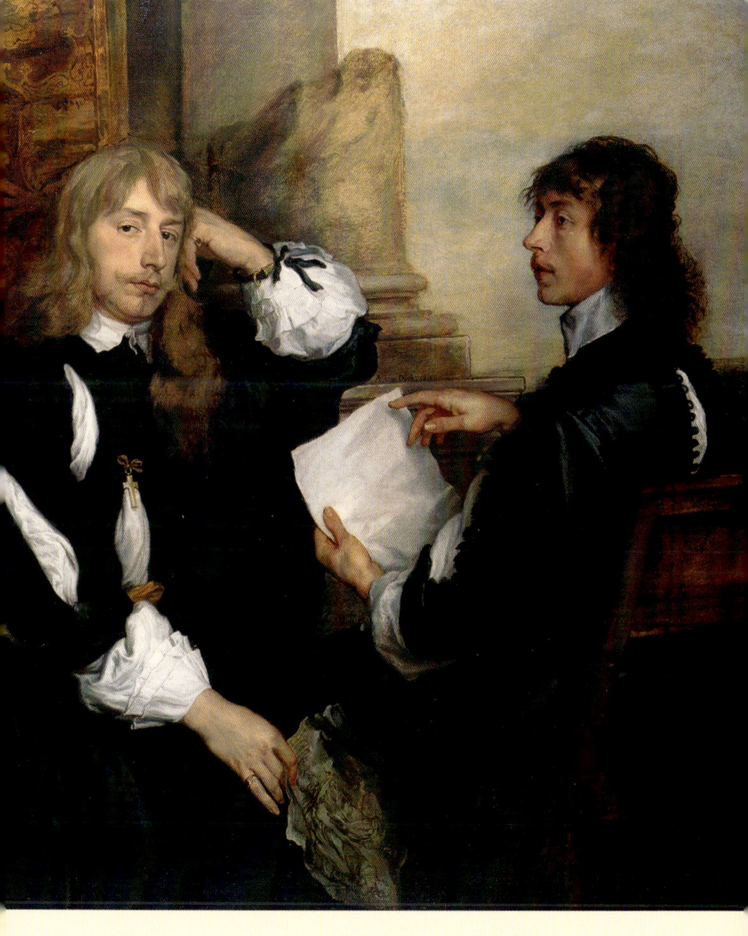

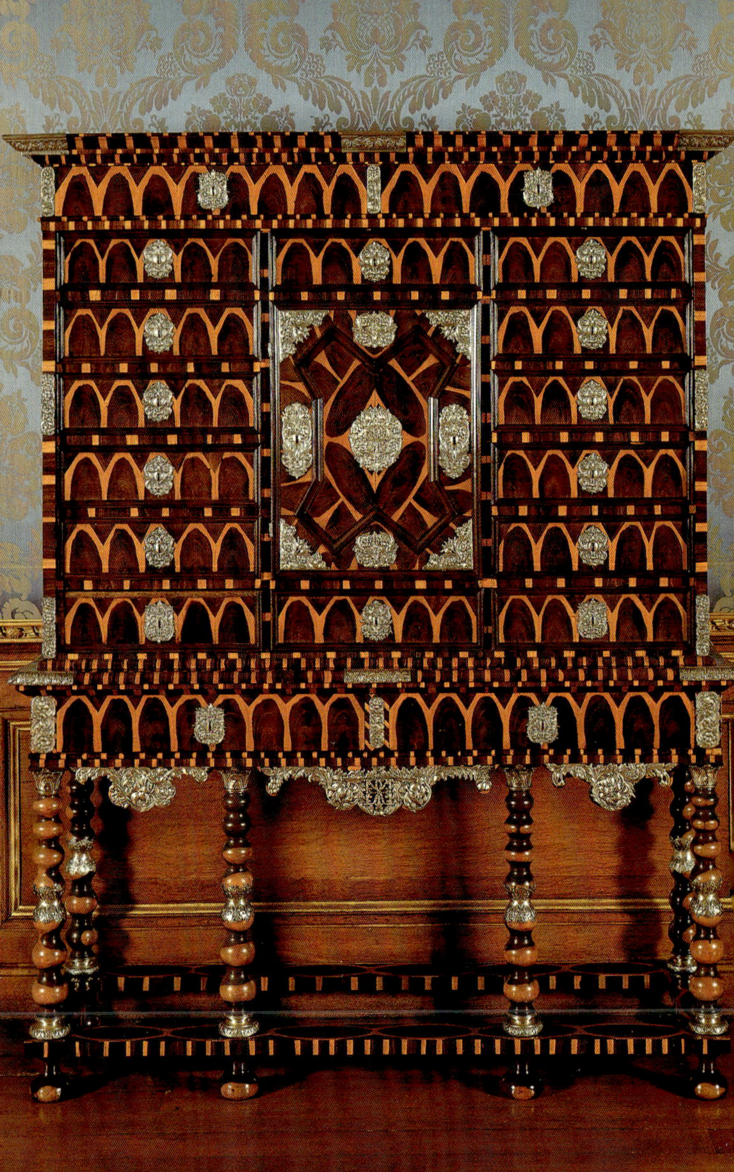

Pair of Silver-mounted Cabinets

c.1660

Cabinets with ranks of lockable drawers were intended for the safekeeping of precious or fragile objects, and were often to be found in libraries or rooms containing collections of curiosities and rarities. They were fashionable in France from the mid-seventeenth century onwards, and the French-born Queen Henrietta Maria, for whom these outstanding examples were almost certainly made, would no doubt have been familiar with the type from the time of her exile in France following the execution of Charles I in 1649. The cabinets were probably made for the Queen's apartments at Somerset House, which she occupied for five years after the Restoration of the Monarchy in 1660. They are strikingly decorated with oyster-shaped veneers of West Indian cocus-wood, sometimes called Jamaica ebony and often mistaken for laburnum or lignum vitae. Cocus is both hard and heavy and is recognisable by the dark brown heartwood and bright white sapwood.

The most unusual feature of the cabinets, again French in inspiration, is the applied decoration with silver plaques – 98 on each cabinet, two with the Queen's monogram 'HMR'. After the Queen's death in 1669, the cabinets were probably given to her Vice Chamberlain and Secretary Henry Jermyn, Earl of St Albans, in whose family they descended at Rushbrooke Hall, Suffolk, until 1910. In that year they were acquired by the Rothschild family and presented to King George V and Queen Mary.

The Five Eldest Children of Charles I

Anthony Van Dyck (1599–1641)

1637

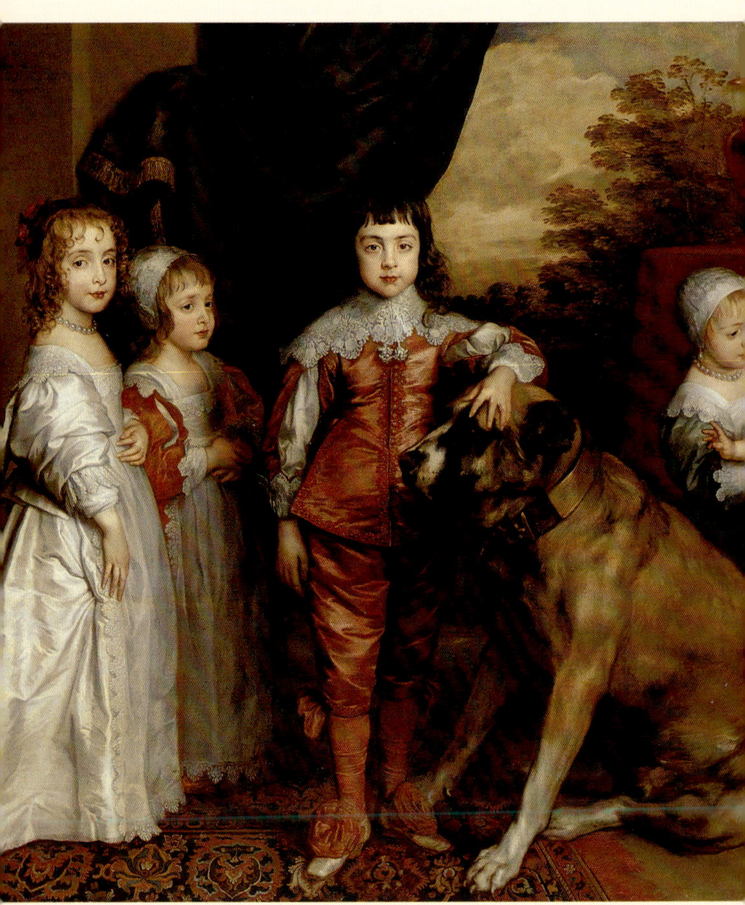

Van Dyck excelled at child portraiture and this masterful painting acknowledges both the youth and the status of its royal subjects, breaking with the earlier tradition of presenting royal children as miniature adults. In this intimate composition the future Charles II is placed in the centre, surrounded by his younger siblings: Mary, Princess Royal stands to the left in a white dress, beside James, Duke of York, who wears an orange petticoat. On the right sits Princess Elizabeth, holding the infant Princess Anne who was born only a few months earlier.

Van Dyck has cleverly indicated the scale of the sitters by the inclusion of the huge Lyme mastiff dog that sits beside the young Charles II, appearing to guard the children and dwarfing the King Charles spaniel sitting at the feet of Princess Anne. Lyme mastiffs were used as guard dogs, as well as for hunting, and were favoured as pets because of their docility with children. The breed died out in the early years of the twentieth century.

The picture was commissioned by Charles I (1600–1649), but it left the Royal Collection twice, once during the Interregnum and again during the reign of James II, before being re-purchased by George III in 1765.

Cabinet

Louis-François Bellangé (1759–1827)

c.1820

This striking piece of furniture, which is fitted with two doors and a drawer in the frieze, incorporates a large group of seventeenth-century Florentine *pietra dura* (literally, hard stone) panels. The technique of inlaying and carving in relief with multicoloured marbles and semi-precious stones was first perfected in the Grand Ducal workshops of the Medici in Florence during the sixteenth century. The fashion spread rapidly to other centres, including Rome, Prague and Paris, and from the late seventeenth to the early nineteenth century, cabinet-makers regularly used both large and small panels such as these to decorate furniture.

The two small rectangular panels below the flower vases, inlaid with dwarf swordsmen and musicians, are based on drawings by Baccio del Bianco (1604–54), Director of the Medici workshops, and may have been inspired by engravings of dwarfs by Jacques Callot, published in 1616. This cabinet, constructed by a member of one of the leading dynasties of early nineteenth-century Parisian furniture-makers, was one of seven decorated with *pietra dura* acquired by King George IV in 1825 at the auction of the celebrated collection of George Watson Taylor.

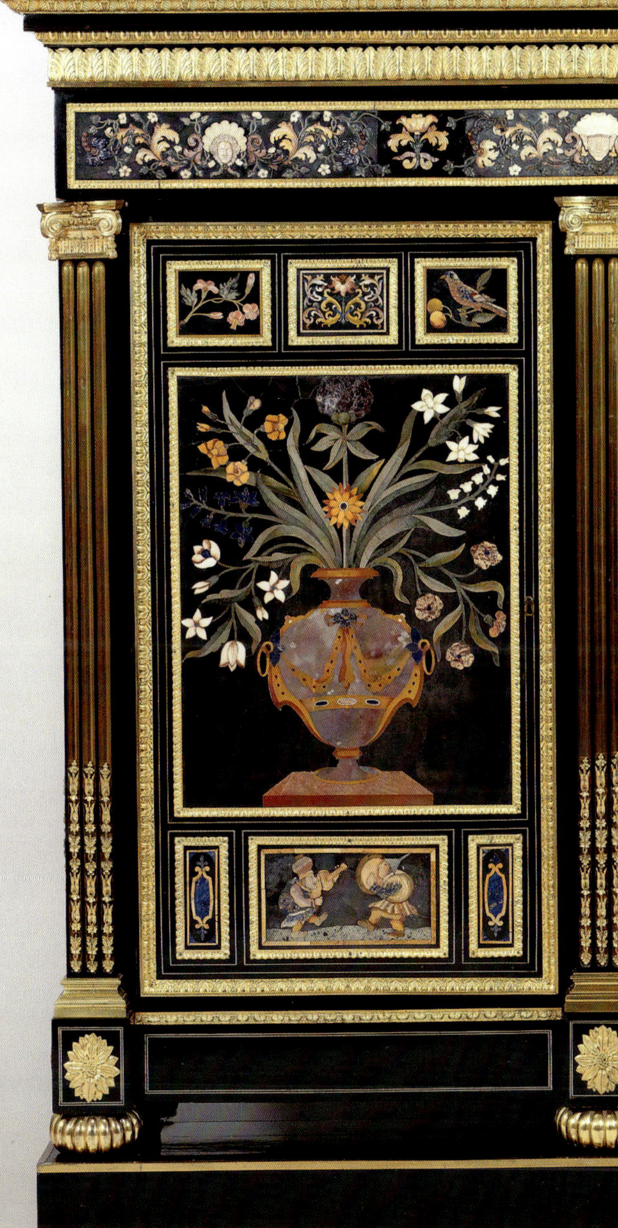

George Frederick Handel

Louis-François Roubiliac (1702–62)

1739

Born at Halle in Saxony, but resident for almost 50 years in England, Handel (1685–1759) was the most celebrated composer in eighteenth-century Britain. His appearance was described as 'somewhat heavy and sour; but when he did smile…there was a sudden flash of intelligence, wit and good humour beaming in his countenance'.

One of five separate likenesses of Handel made by Roubiliac over a period of 20 years, this one belonged to the composer himself. At the time it was made, Handel was at a turning point, having faced ill health and a dwindling demand for his Italian operas, and before his English oratorios (such as *Messiah* of 1741) gained popularity.

The informal style of the portrait captures the great man *en négligé*, in the sort of clothes he would wear about the house. Roubiliac was unsurpassed in his ability to distinguish the relative qualities and weight of material – such as the soft velvet cap and the heavier cloth of the coat – despite the constraints of working in marble. His portraits are often animated by some 'accidental' detail, such as the way the coat appears to be caught askew on the tasselled button. The bust was given to George III by the son of Handel's secretary, together with the composer's harpsichord and his manuscripts, around 1773.

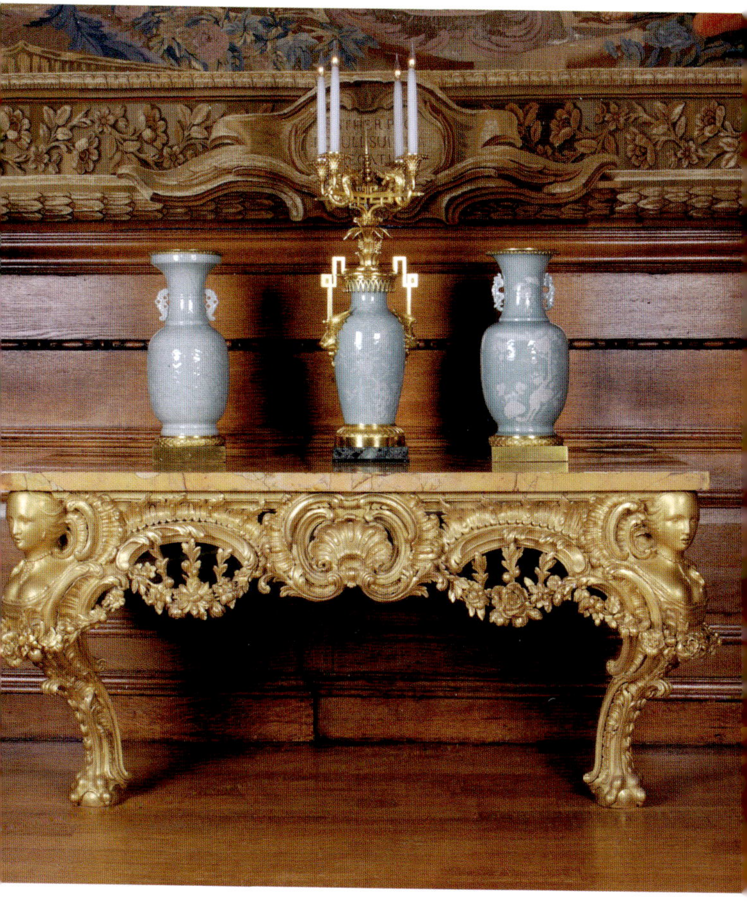

The Story of Esther

Gobelins factory

after Jean-François de Troy (1679–1752)

1779–84

In the late 1730s the leading French painter Jean-François de Troy designed a set of seven scenes from the Old Testament story of Esther for the French royal tapestry factory. The designs proved enduringly popular, and seven sets were woven between 1738 and 1794.

Esther, the beautiful niece of Mordecai, was taken by the Persian King Ahasuerus as his second wife. Mordecai took a stand in refusing to bend his knee before the King's haughty Chief Minister, Haman. On discovering that Mordecai was Jewish, Haman persuaded the King to sign an order for the extermination of all Jews in the Kingdom. Following Esther's supplications, the decree was reversed, Mordecai was exalted and Haman was sentenced to death.

Like Racine's dramatic version of the story, written for the court of Louis XIV, the tapestries illustrated the special power of kings to administer divine justice. For de Troy, the commission offered a rare chance to work on the grand scale of Italian masters such as Veronese, and the subject was rich in scenic and colourful possibilities, from the luxurious apparel of the protagonists to the marbled halls of the palace Shushan, described in detail in Scripture.

These tapestries were purchased, with 23 others, by Sir Charles Long in Paris in 1825, specifically for Windsor Castle. They had earlier been used by the Revolutionary authorities as payment in kind to one of the suppliers of their army, Jacques de Chapeaurouge.

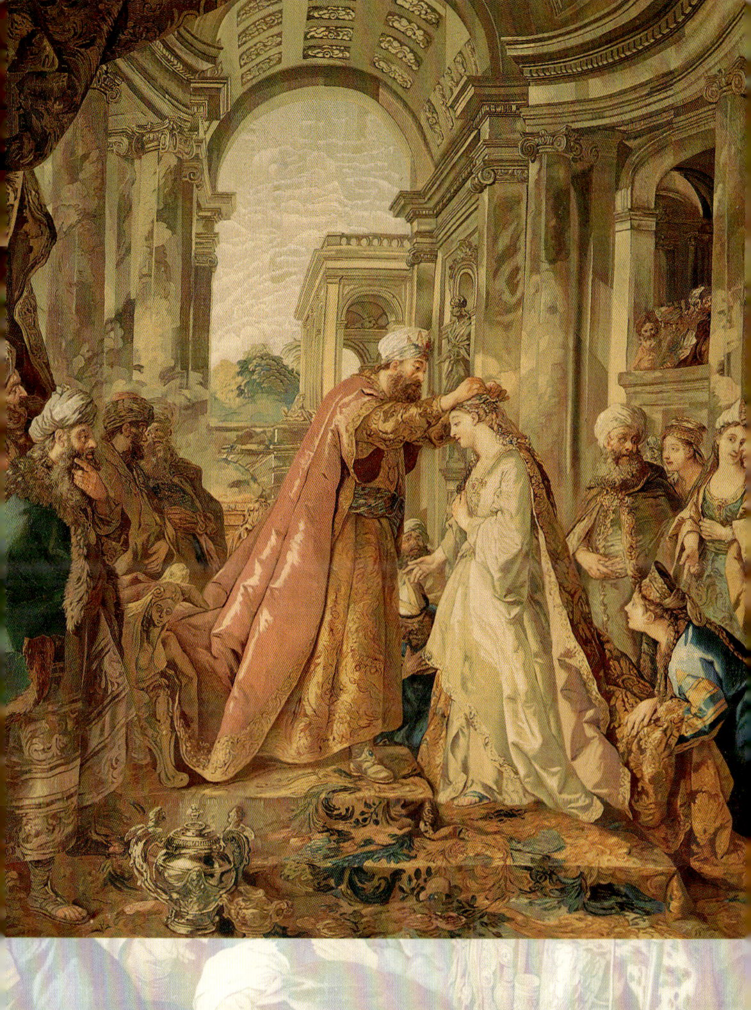

The Apotheosis of Catherine of Braganza

Antonio Verrio (1639–1707)

1675–c.1684

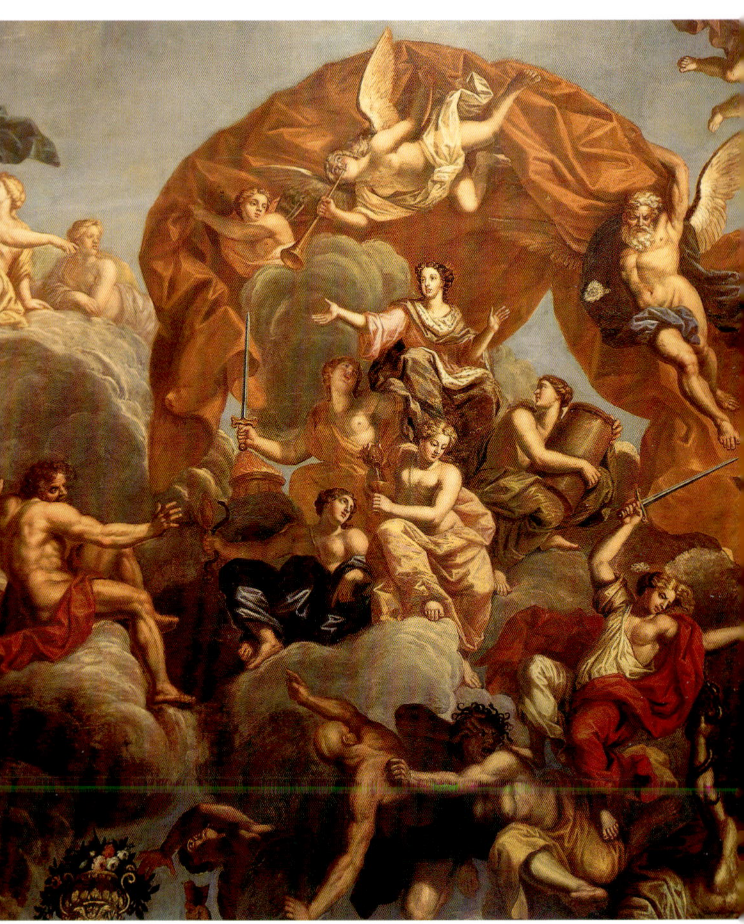

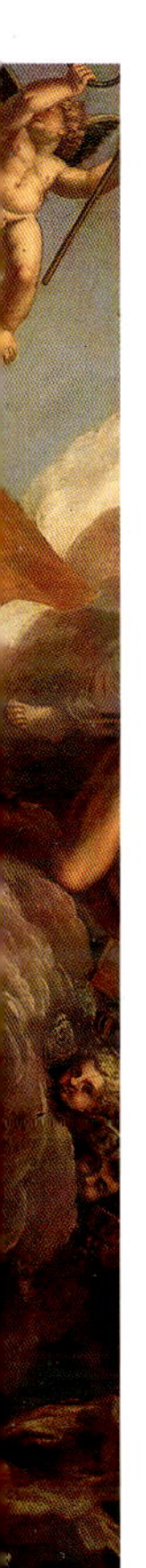

This ceiling painting is one of only three by Verrio at Windsor to survive. Most of the artist's 20 decorative schemes were destroyed during George IV's reconstruction of the Castle in the early nineteenth century. The ceiling depicts Charles II's queen, Catherine of Braganza, seated under a canopy held by zephyrs, while figures of Envy and Sedition retreat before the outstretched Sword of Justice.

Verrio relied on a decorative formula which opens up the room by including mythological or allegorical figures in a 'sky' rising from a painted ledge or balcony, often decorated with putti (representations of naked children, especially cherubs or cupids in Renaissance art), swags of fruit or flowers, or brightly coloured birds. Much of his inspiration derived from decorative schemes created for Louis XIV at Versailles.

Verrio was continuously employed by Charles II from 1678 until 1688, and received about £5,500 for work undertaken at Windsor Castle. His principal task was to decorate the new State Rooms, which were then being rebuilt by the architect Hugh May. The diarist John Evelyn, who saw work being done on 23 July 1679, reported of 'that excellent painter, Verrio, whose works in fresco at the King's Palace at Windsor will celebrate his name as long as those walls last'. In 1684 he was appointed Court Painter, following the death of Peter Lely.

Diamond-hilted Sword

c.1750 and *c*.1820

From the sixteenth century onwards it became fashionable for gentlemen to wear a sword with civilian dress, not merely in self-defence, but as a mark of rank. By the eighteenth century the sword hilt had become a form of costume jewellery at the upper level of society. Designs were prepared by many of the leading decorative artists and reached new levels of elaboration and richness. The gold hilt of this sword, with its pommel in the shape of a helmet with a barred visor, is exquisitely chiselled and set with numerous diamonds, and dates from the mid-eighteenth century. It resembles designs by the French goldsmiths Thomas Germain and Juste-Aurèle Meissonier, and was probably made in Germany by a gold chaser who also made jewelled gold boxes.

The sword was purchased by George IV, who characteristically considered it insufficiently ornate. The royal goldsmiths Rundell, Bridge and Rundell added several hundred further stones in 1820, including the two large diamonds on the scabbard. The blued and gilded steel blade, decorated with the national flowers of Great Britain and other royal devices, was made at the same time.

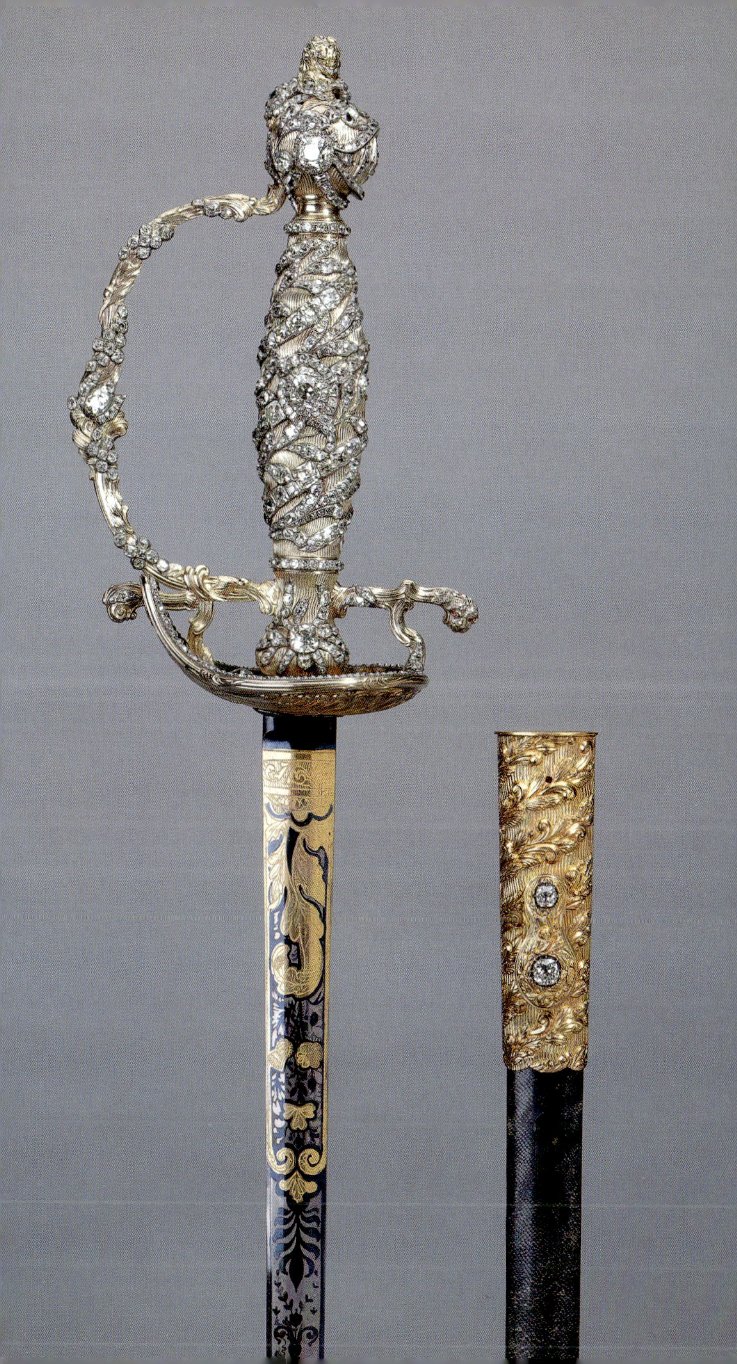

Henry VIII's Hunting Sword and Knife

Diego de Çaias (*fl.* 1535–52)

1544

The outstanding Spanish craftsman Diego de Çaias was sought after by several European rulers for his skill in the decoration of weapons. This is the only known work from the period of his employment by Henry VIII, between 1543 and 1547, the year of the King's death. The sword was intended to be used in hunting and its scabbard also accommodates an auxiliary knife for dealing with dead quarry. The sword blade is decorated with a military scene celebrating Henry VIII's successful siege of Boulogne. The scene is drawn in narrow gold wire, which has been hammered into lines cut into the iron blade. The siege was conducted under the King's direct command between July and September 1544, and the event is celebrated in a lengthy inscription on the reverse of the blade:

> *Rejoice Boulogne in the reign of the eighth Henry. Thy towers are now seen to be adorned with crimson roses, now are the ill-scented lilies uprooted and prostrate, the cock is expelled and the lion reigns in the invincible citadel.*

The sword was acquired for the Royal Collection by Her Majesty The Queen in 1966.

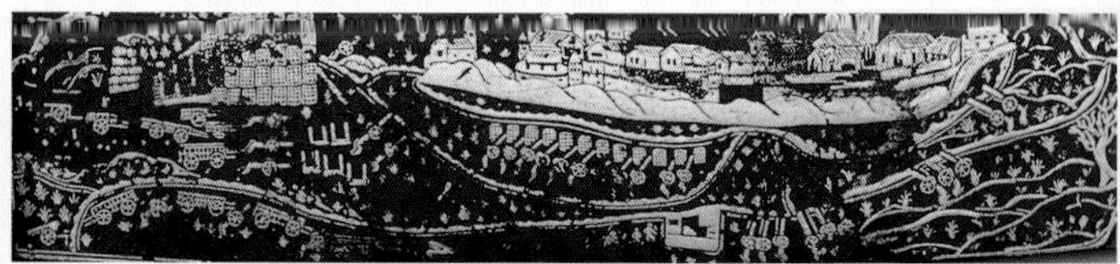

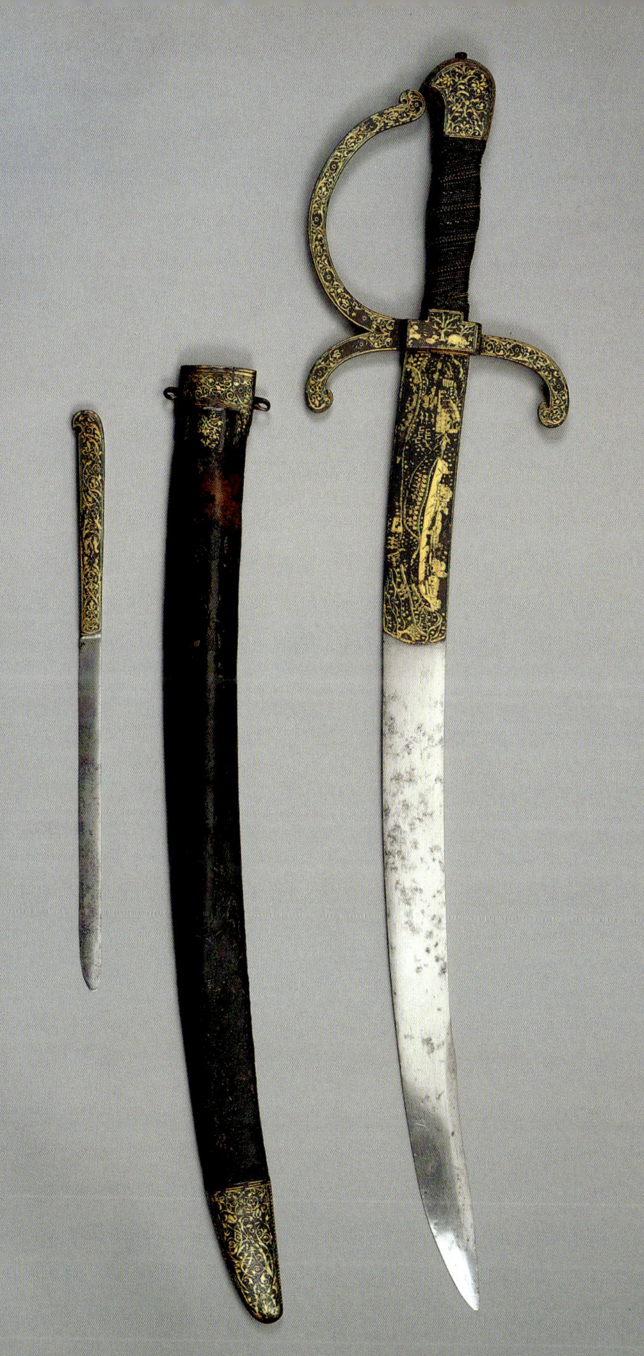

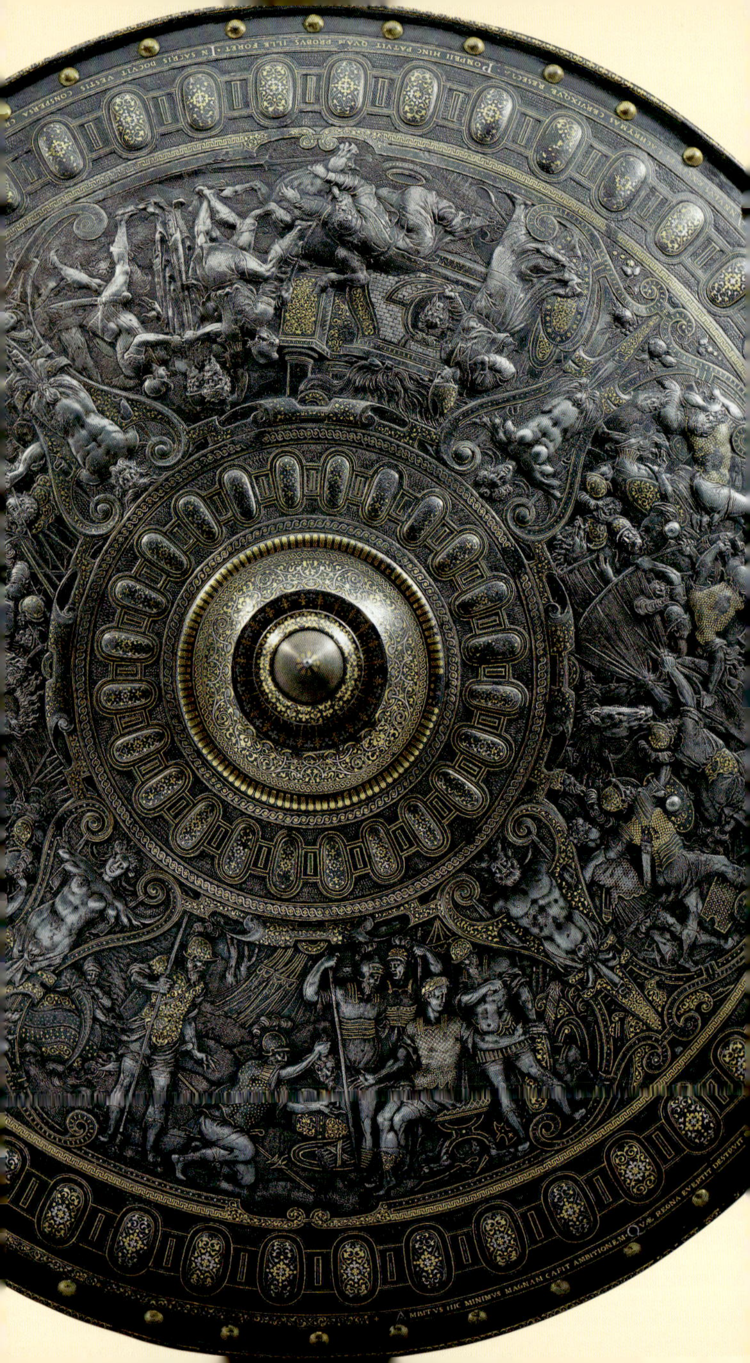
LACHRYMAS CERVIXQVE RESECTA · POMPEII HINC PATVIT QVAM PROBVS ILLE FORET · IN SACRIS DOCVIT VESTIS CONSPERSA
AMBITVS HIC MINIMVS MAGNAM CAPIT AMBITIONEM · QVAE REGNA EVERTIT DESTRVIT

The 'Cellini' Shield
attributed to Eliseus Libaerts
(*fl.* 1557–72)

c.1562–3

The substantial collection of armour and weaponry at Windsor includes just one masterpiece from the European Renaissance, when the work of the armourer, sculptor and goldsmith drew closer together than at any other time. So-called 'parade' armours, made for the Habsburg emperors, for the kings of France and Sweden and the rulers of the German lands, were embossed, etched, inlaid and gilded with symbolic devices and historical scenes which emphasised the military prowess and virtues of their owners.

The shield is decorated with four scenes from the life of Julius Caesar and his adversary Pompey, and the lengthy inscription inlaid around its edge speaks of the evils of ambition. It was almost certainly made for Henri II of France (reigned 1547–59) and designed by his court artist Etienne Delaune (1518/19–83). The decoration was probably the work of Eliseus Libaerts, a Flemish goldsmith who made very similar armour for the King of Sweden.

During the eighteenth and early nineteenth centuries the shield was thought to be the work of the most famous of all Florentine goldsmiths and sculptors, Benvenuto Cellini (1500–1571), but this was later discounted, both on stylistic grounds and because Cellini did not in fact make armour.

The Glaubensschild ('Shield of Faith')

Johann Georg Hossauer (*fl.* 1820–57)

completed 1847

This was the christening present from Frederick William IV, King of Prussia, to his godson, Albert Edward, Prince of Wales, the future King Edward VII. The service took place in St George's Chapel on 25 January 1842, and the King declared his intention to present the Prince with a shield to commemorate the ceremony and to represent the present state of German art. The design, by the painter Peter von Cornelius (1783–1867), in consultation with the King, refers to the Prince's future role as Defender of the Faith. Its manufacture, comprising cast and chased silver and gold, enamels, hardstones and carved cameos, was entrusted to the Prussian court goldsmith Johann Georg Hossauer, head of a large workshop in Berlin. The Queen and Prince Albert were delighted with the 'sense, poetry, taste, art and skill, and above all the idea' of the shield, which was later included in the Great Exhibition in Hyde Park in 1851.

With Christ at its centre, a cross encloses four complementary biblical scenes: the sacraments of Baptism and Communion with their Old Testament equivalents. The outer reliefs include Christ's entry to Jerusalem, His Betrayal, Burial and Resurrection, the foundation of the Church, and an idealised depiction of the sea passage to England of the King of Prussia himself, to be greeted on the shore by Prince Albert and the Duke of Wellington.

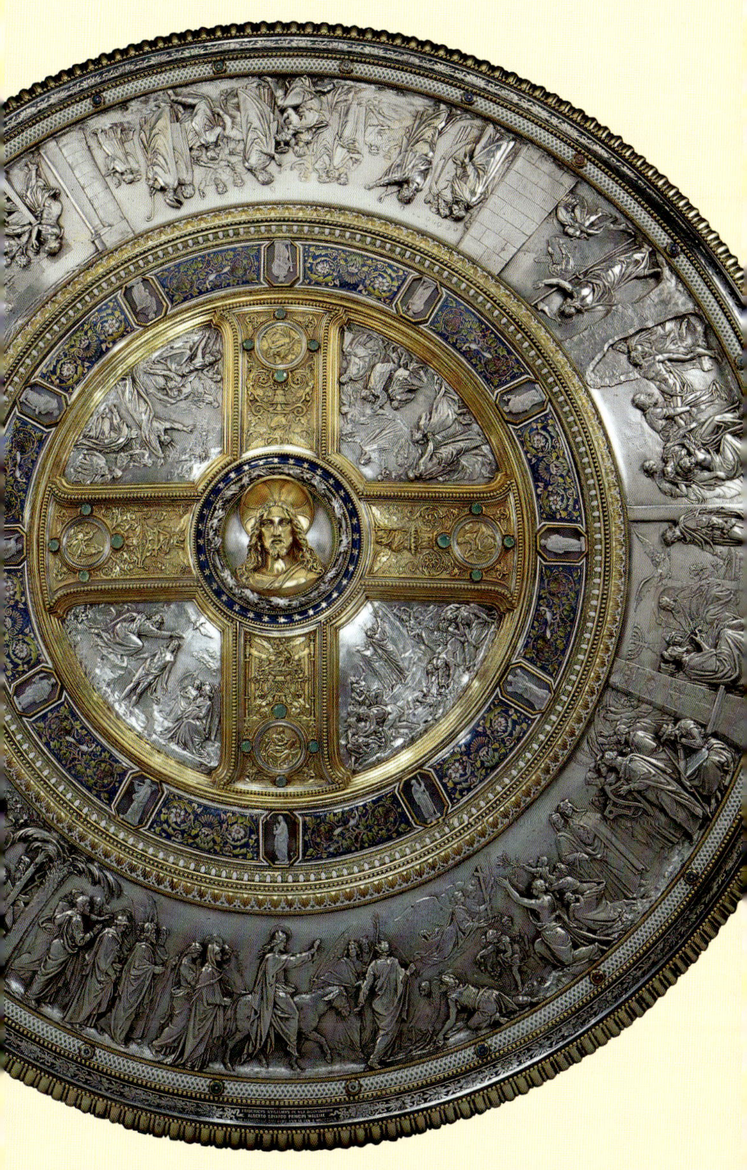

Philip II of Spain

Leone Leoni (1509–90)

c.1555

The Habsburg Emperors Charles V (1500–1558) and his son Philip II (1527–98) are among the most recognisable of European historical rulers thanks to their employment of the Venetian painter, Titian, and the sculptor, medallist and goldsmith from Arezzo, Leone Leoni. This bust is one of three commissioned by the Duke of Alba, chief minister and general in the imperial service, probably during his time as Governor of Milan, where Leoni had his studio. The busts were kept at the Duke's castle near Salamanca in Spain until the Peninsular wars of the early nineteenth century. They were purchased by George IV in 1825, specifically for Windsor Castle.

Milan was a pre-eminent centre for the production of armour, especially 'parade' armour decorated with embossed scenes and figures. Although the King's suit is unidentified, it is highly realistic, and Leoni must have consulted an armourer on details of construction and decoration.

The inscription 'PHI·REX·ANGL·ETC' helps to date the bust between July 1554, when Philip was married to Queen Mary I of England in a magnificent ceremony at Winchester, and January 1556, when he acceded to the throne of Spain and all its dominions. Both Philip and Alba were in England for most of that period, and the bust was probably based on sittings that took place in 1553.

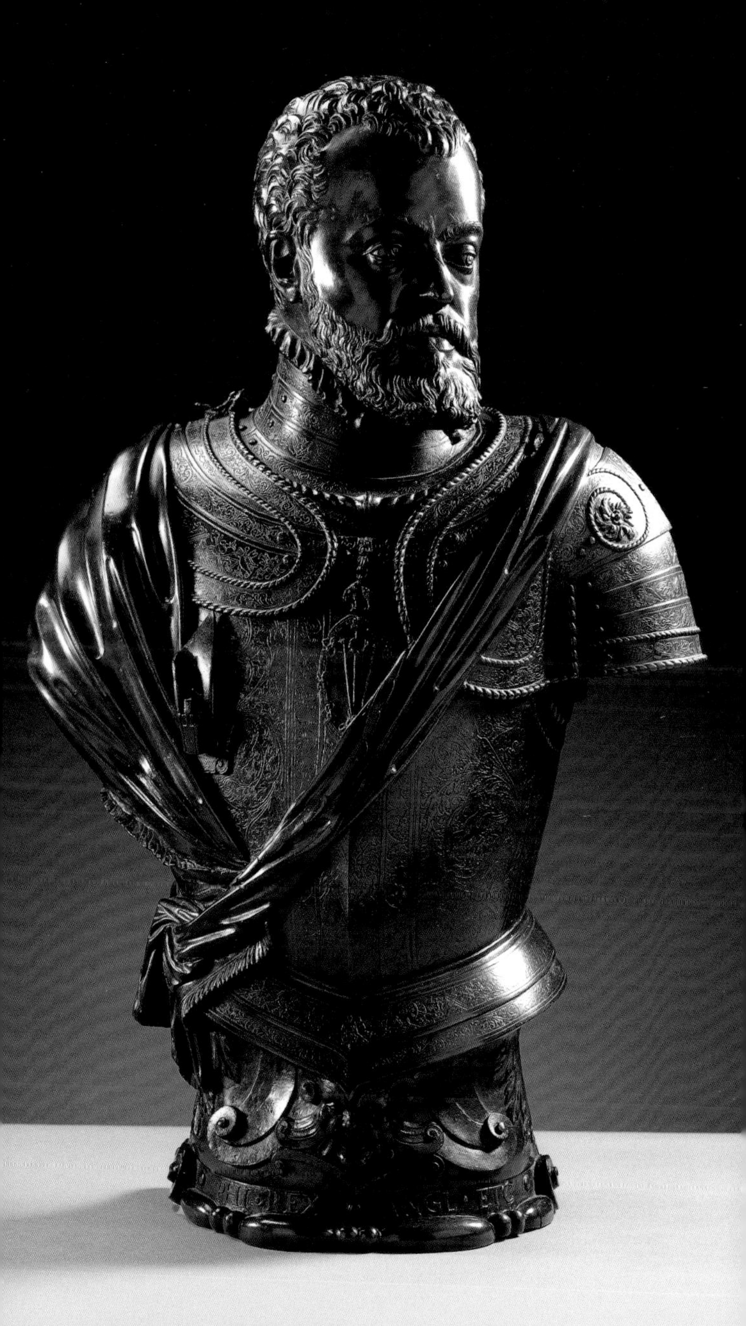

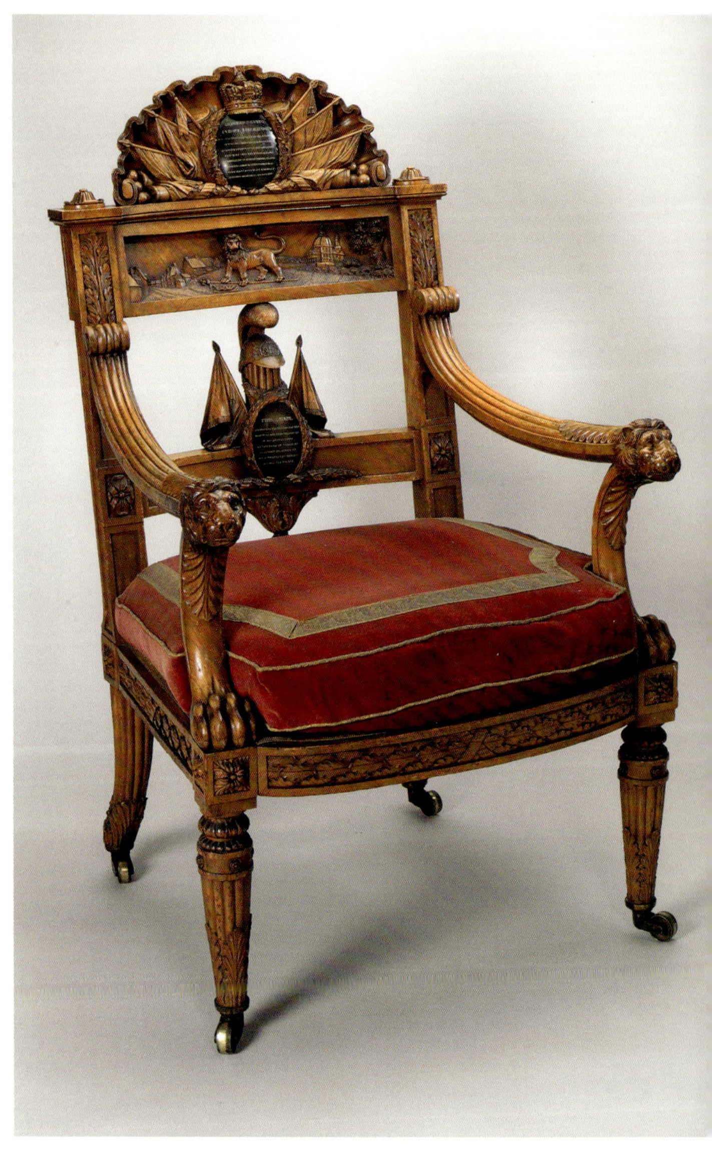

The Waterloo Elm Armchair

Thomas Chippendale the Younger

(1749–1822)

1820

The Queen's Guard Chamber at Windsor contains a variety of interesting relics commemorating the triumph of British arms across the centuries. Among the most unusual of these is this armchair made from the wood of the elm tree that marked the Duke of Wellington's command post at the Battle of Waterloo on 18 June 1815. Seated on his famous chestnut horse Copenhagen, next to the elm, the Duke directed his troops in their counter-attack on the Imperial Guard, and from this point oversaw the final crushing defeat of the armies of Napoleon Bonaparte.

By 1818 the elm tree – already much mutilated by souvenir hunters – had become such a magnet for tourists that the farmer on whose land it grew decided to fell it to protect his crops. The British antiquary John Children, who happened then to be visiting the site, purchased the felled tree. On his return to London, he commissioned Thomas Chippendale the Younger (son of the celebrated eighteenth-century cabinet-maker) to create this chair, which, complete with flattering dedicatory inscription, he presented to George IV in 1821. The tree supplied enough timber for several other pieces of commemorative furniture, including two similar but less elaborate armchairs for the Dukes of Wellington and Rutland.

Admiral Lord Nelson

Sir Francis Chantrey (1781–1841)

1835

The decisive defeat of the combined French and Spanish fleet off Cape Trafalgar in October 1805, and the death in action of the already celebrated British commander, Horatio Nelson (1758–1805), gave rise to a wave of commemorative projects, culminating in the national memorial in Trafalgar Square, completed in 1843.

Chantrey's powerful bust was commissioned as a more personal act of commemoration by William IV, who, as a young man, had served with Nelson and formed a lasting friendship. At their first meeting in 1782 he wrote of Nelson that 'there was something irresistibly pleasing in his address and conversation; and an enthusiasm when speaking on professional subjects that showed he was no common being'. The bust was ordered specifically for the centre of the Queen's Guard Chamber, and raised on a pedestal consisting of part of the foremast of Nelson's flagship *Victory*.

The austere style of the bust, with straight sides and back, was based on ancient Greek sculpture and often used for memorials in the nineteenth century. The portrait has great power and presence, achieved with the economy that was Chantrey's trademark. The intent gaze and matted hair mark the sitter as a man of vision and action, while his many orders and decorations are lightly but clearly drawn.

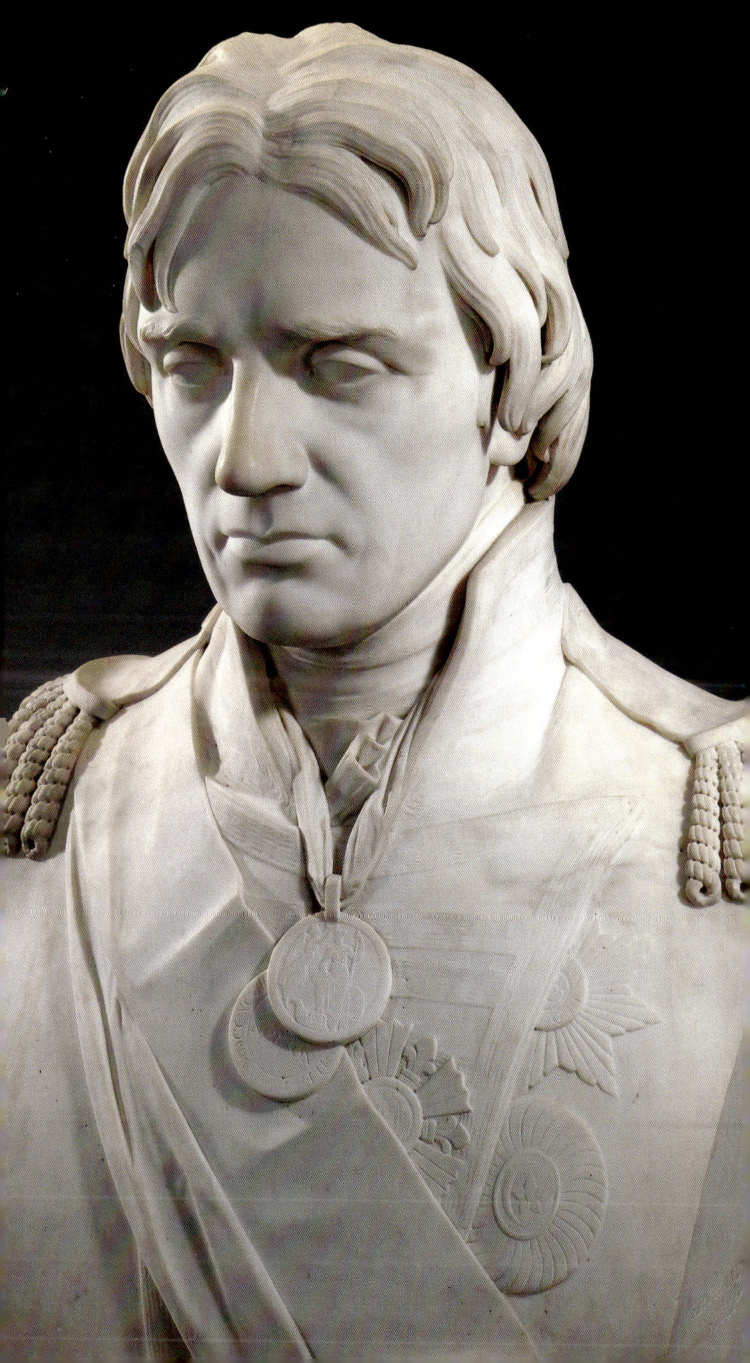

George II

Louis-François Roubiliac (1702–62)

c.1761

George II (1683–1760) was the last British monarch to lead an army in battle, and he is portrayed here as a resolute military commander. Armour of any kind was relatively unusual in portraiture at this date, and what is visible of the King's suit is notably old-fashioned. The same is true of the billowing knot in the end of the King's mantle, which may be a tribute to the Baroque genius of Bernini.

The French-born sculptor Louis-François Roubiliac trained in both Germany and France, and settled in England in the early 1730s. He came to dominate the fields of monumental sculpture and portrait busts, showing an equal command of the private, relatively simple and almost offhand style exemplified by his bust of Handel (page 131), and, as here, the full panoply and trappings of state portraiture.

George II was an unpromising subject and is said to have disliked sitting for portraits. This bust was commissioned by one of his greatest generals, Field Marshal Lord Ligonier (whose own bust by Roubiliac is also at Windsor), and it seems unlikely that the King sat for it. Despite this, the sculptor has repeatedly overcome the limitations of his material to distinguish each surface, whether the King's ageing skin or hair, the lace cravat or the polished steel of the armour; above all, nothing about the knotted mantle shows any sign of having been achieved with a chisel.

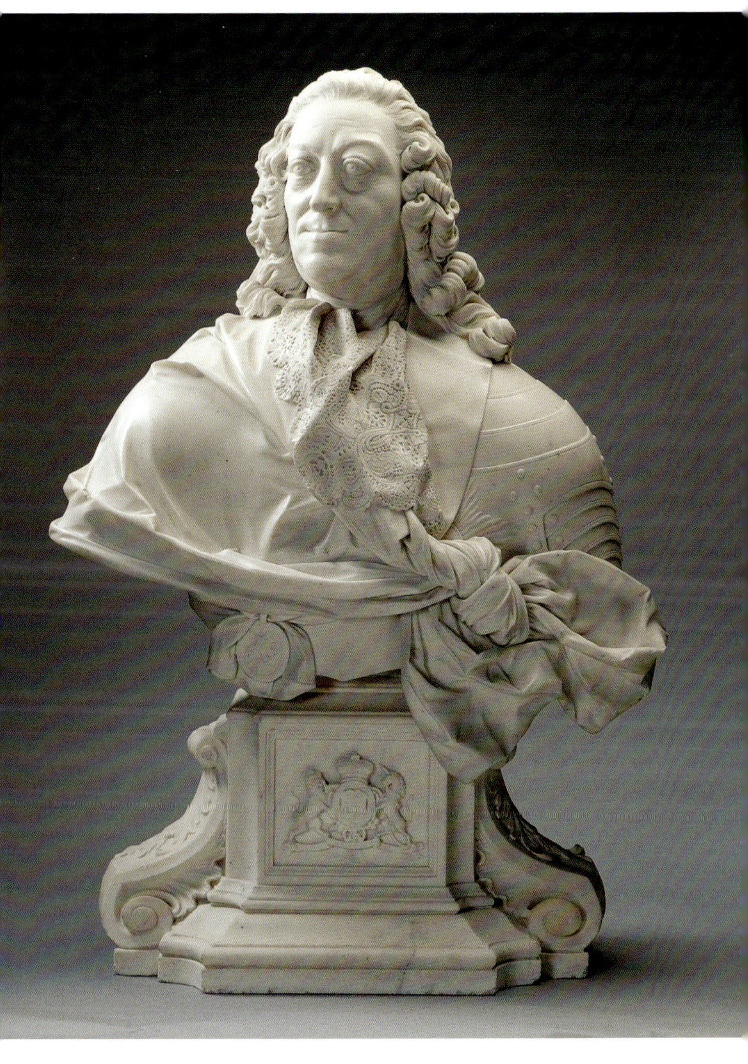

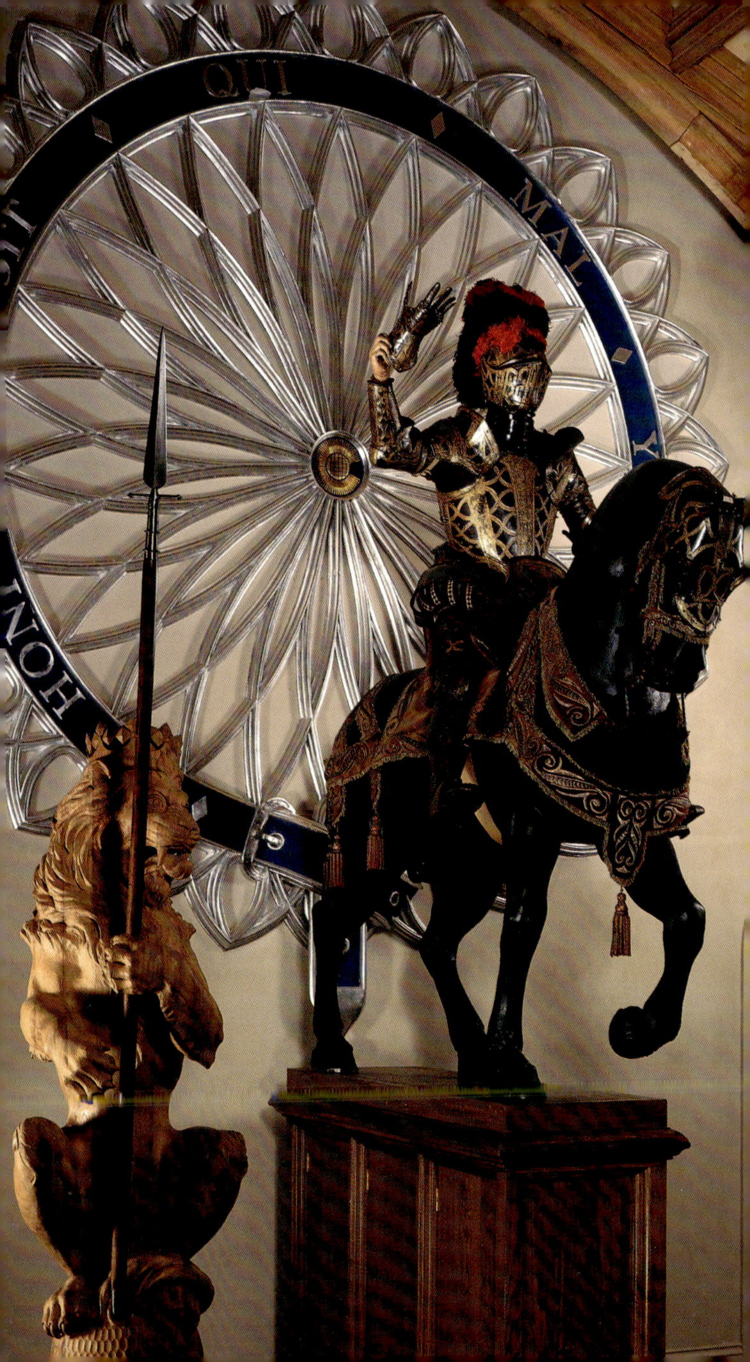
HONI
QUI
MAL
Y

Armour of the King's Champion

Greenwich workshop

1585

At coronations between 1066 and 1821 a ritual took place in which an armoured horseman issued a challenge to anyone prepared to dispute the new king's right to rule. Riding into Westminster Hall during the banquet that followed the coronation ceremony in the Abbey, the King's Champion held a gauntlet as if ready to throw it before any subject treacherous enough to deny the new sovereign's authority.

This armour formerly belonged to the Dymoke family of Scrivelsby in Lincolnshire, holders of the hereditary office of King's Champion, and it is thought to have been used at several coronations during the late seventeenth and early eighteenth centuries. Of blued steel, the armour is richly decorated with etched and gilded ornaments, incorporating the date 1585. It was originally made for Sir Christopher Hatton (1540–91), a favourite of Queen Elizabeth I, whom the Queen appointed Captain of her Bodyguard in 1572 and Lord Chancellor in 1587. Hatton ordered it from the Greenwich workshops as a gift to another of the Queen's favourites, Robert Dudley, Earl of Leicester (1532–88), but it seems to have been returned to his possession after Leicester's death. The armour was presented to King Edward VII by a group of his friends in 1901.

The Roof of St George's Hall

1994–6

The area now occupied by St George's Hall was first built for Edward III in the fourteenth century, with an elaborate and steeply pitched timber roof, and contained a great hall in the eastern half and a private chapel in the western. In the 1680s, Charles II remodelled the hall and chapel, replacing the timber roof with a painted ceiling. This, in turn, was removed in the 1820s when Jeffry Wyatville combined hall and chapel to form a single great hall as the new secular centre of the Order of the Garter. For this, Wyatville installed a shallow-pitched plaster roof, painted to look like oak.

Following the fire of 1992, which burnt out St George's Hall, the decision was taken to create a new roof of steeper pitch than the one it replaced, but of timber rather than plaster. The architect, Giles Downes, designed a structure consisting of 14 stepped arched trusses that echoed the great timber roof built by Edward III. Constructed of newly felled green oak from Sarnesfield in Herefordshire by the specialist firm Capps and Capps, it was designed and hand-finished in the medieval fashion, with pegged joints that allowed movement as the timber gradually dried out. The completed roof, the largest and most complex timber structure built in England since the sixteenth century, now supports the coats of arms of Knights of the Garter from the foundation of the Order in 1348, including blank shields for 'degraded' Knights, struck off for treason or other offences against the Crown.

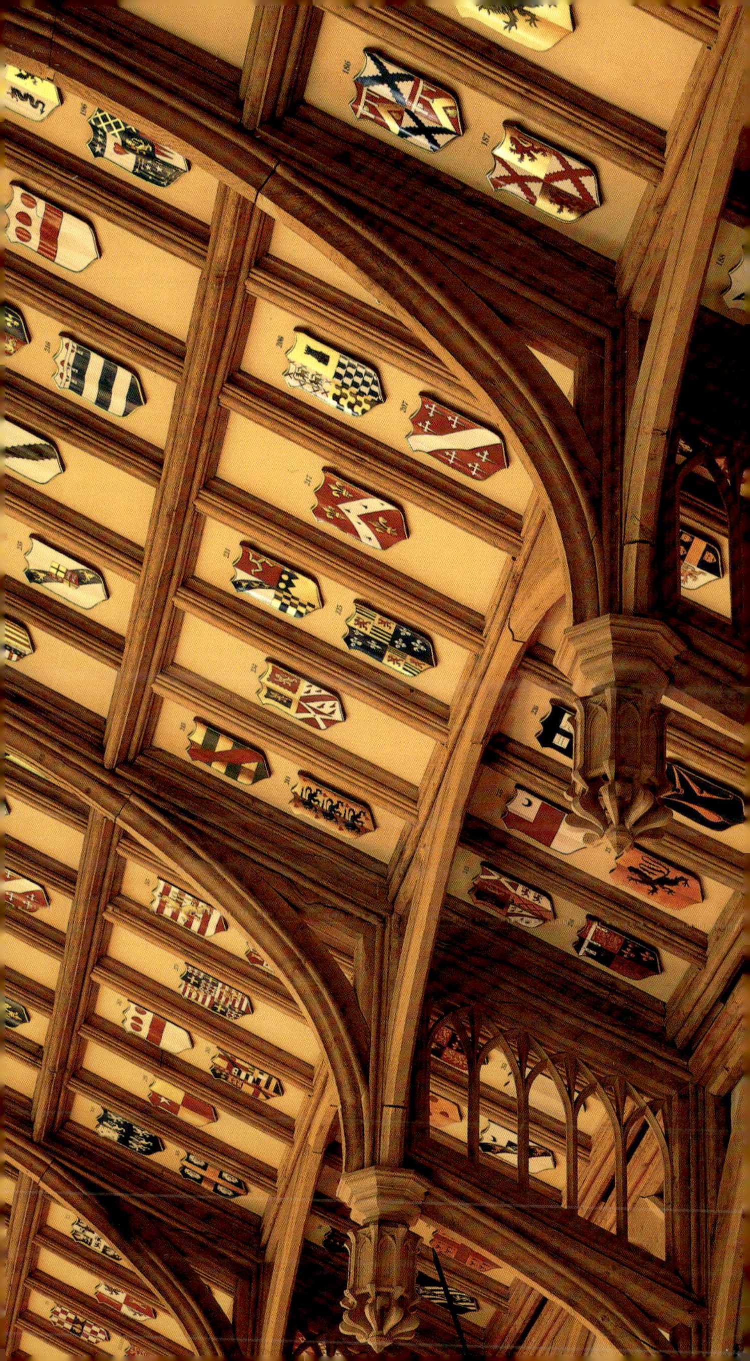

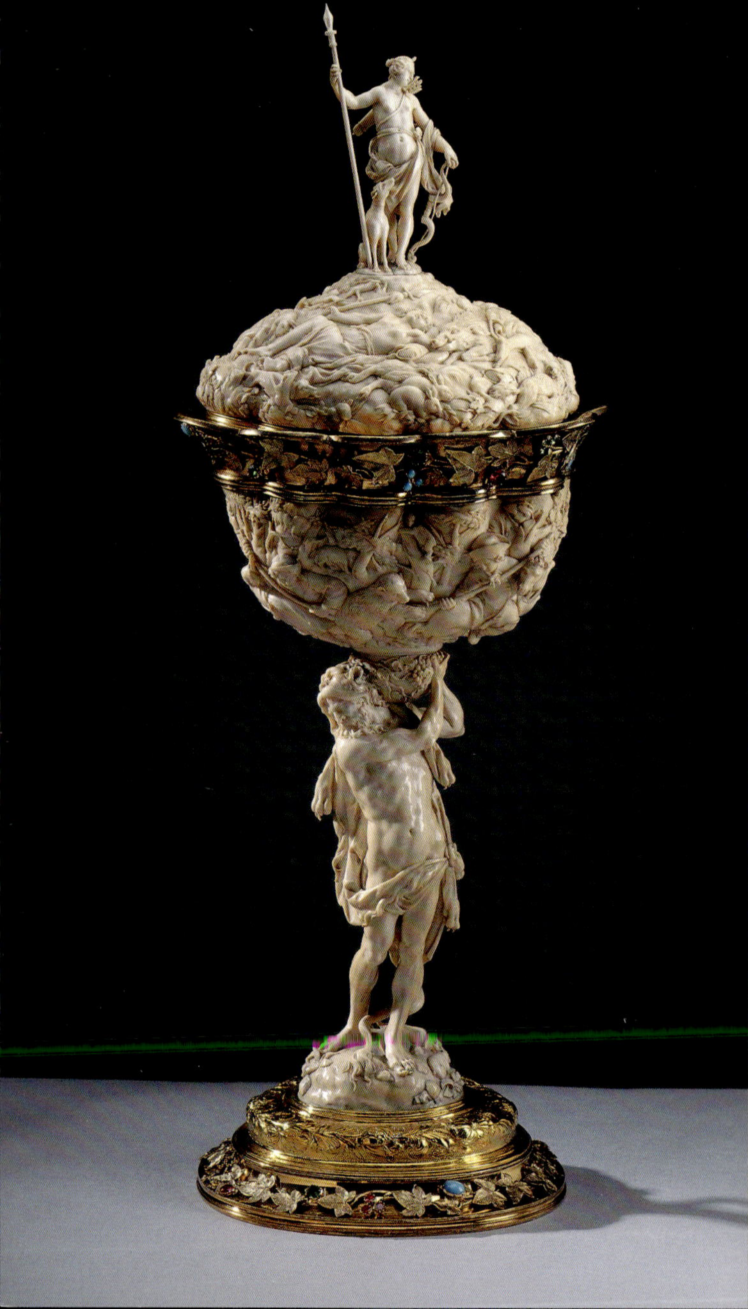

Ivory Cup and Cover

South German

*c.*1700 and 1824–5

In the first museums to be formed in modern Europe the most treasured objects were those that combined the wonders of nature, such as ivory, minerals and exotic shells, with artistic ingenuity. In this pre-eminent example, the mighty Hercules supports the bowl of the cup, which is carved with hunting scenes, while Diana, goddess of the hunt, presides over sleeping nymphs, a stag, a wild boar and a hare on the cover. Thus, while admiring the work of the carver, the viewer is also reminded of the prodigious, almost mythical creature that provided his material, the excitement of the chase and the deeds of the ancient gods.

The cup, which may be the work of the Bavarian carver Johann Georg Frisch (*fl.* 1689–1716), was first noted in this country in 1788 when it entered the vast collection of natural history and ethnography assembled at Leicester House in London by Sir Ashton Lever. It was purchased in 1806 by the great collector William Beckford, and proudly displayed in the centre of a long gallery at his country house, Fonthill Abbey in Wiltshire. At the subsequent sale of Fonthill the cup was purchased for George IV. Before it could form part of his extravagant displays of historic and contemporary plate, the royal goldsmiths Rundell, Bridge and Rundell were ordered to add 'a new silver chased rim…set with coloured stones to raise the cover' and a similar addition to the base.

Nautilus Cup

Nikolaus Schmidt (*c.*1550/55–1609)

*c.*1600

Like the German ivory cup and cover (on the previous pages), this piece was created to form part of a private display of precious curiosities, or *Kunstkammer* (chamber of art), and was never intended for practical use. The silver-mounted cup is formed from the translucent shell of an inkfish (*Nautilus pompilius* L.) found in the western Pacific. The nautilus was valued not only for its beauty but as a scientific curiosity: its many internal chambers, used for flotation, increase in size on a geometric scale. The outer layer of the shell has been stripped away to reveal the nacreous surface below, and the heel has been carved in the form of a helmet.

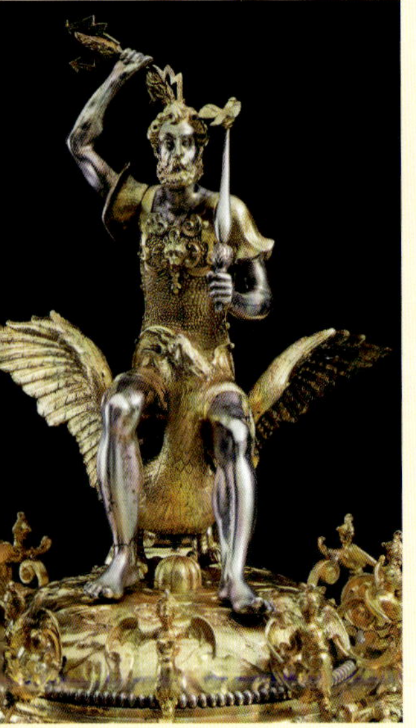

On the cover, Jupiter, holding a thunderbolt and a sceptre, is seated on an eagle, topped by a dove, to represent war and peace. The stem is formed as Neptune riding a hippocamp, or sea horse, and surrounded by other sea monsters and mermaids. In the classical tradition, Jupiter and Neptune were considered rulers of the air and the sea respectively.

The cup is one of the most celebrated works of the Nuremberg goldsmith Nikolaus Schmidt. It was purchased by George IV in 1822 at the sale of the contents of Wanstead House, Essex.

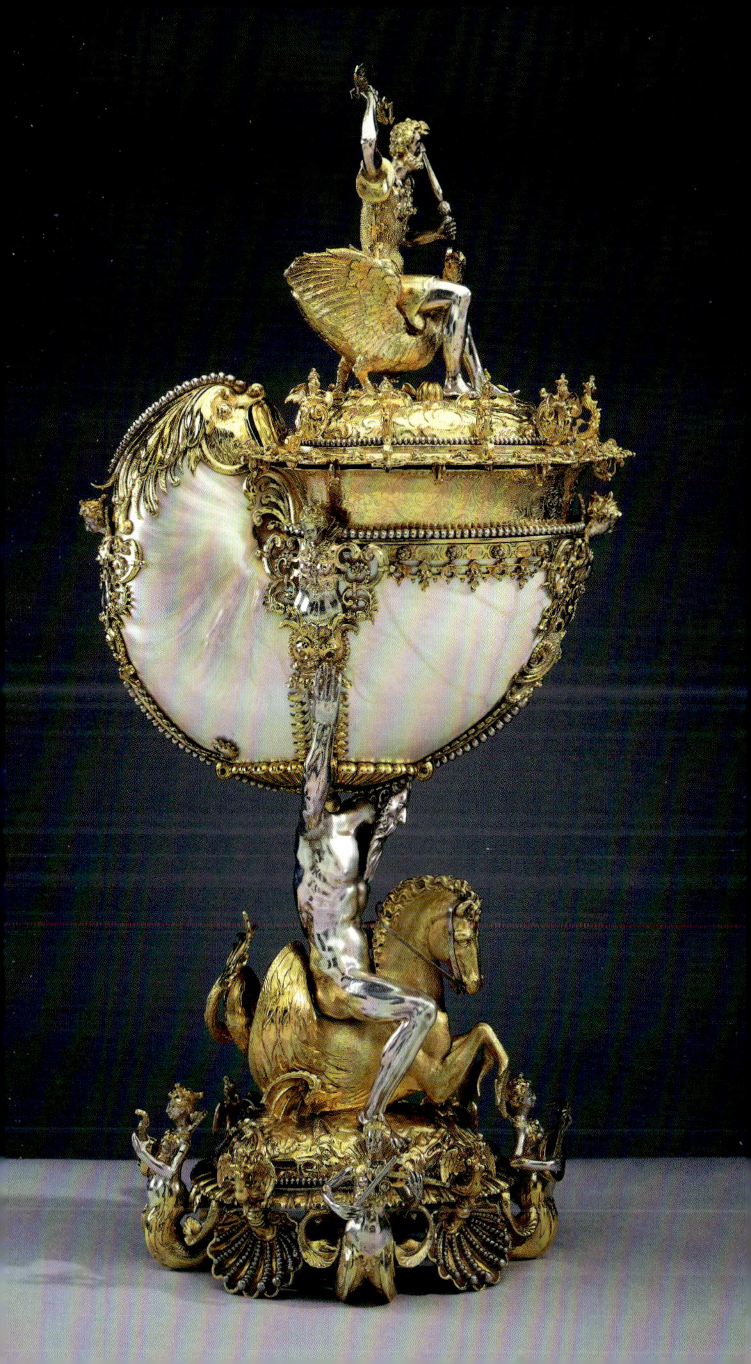

The 'Coronation Cup'

Rundell, Bridge and Rundell

1826

This jewelled, silver-gilt and enamelled standing cup is unusual among those collected by George IV for its religious imagery. It was designed by the champion of the revival of Gothic taste, A.W.N. Pugin (1812–52), at the age of 15, apparently after a meeting at the British Museum with a member of the firm of royal goldsmiths, Rundell, Bridge and Rundell. Pugin's sketches so impressed John Gawler Bridge that he asked him to work on some designs for the firm. Pugin was fascinated with medieval sources and this cup reflects Gothic architectural elements, such as the arcade of arches around the bowl, the line of angels, and the foot, based on fan-vaulting from a Gothic church.

The cup was misnamed the 'Coronation Cup' in an inventory of 1872, when it was thought to be a sacramental cup associated with the ceremony of the coronation. It is more likely that George IV commissioned it as an addition to his Gothic embellishments at Windsor Castle, begun in 1824. It bears a stylistic affinity with the sideboard designed by Pugin for the State Dining Room at Windsor. Pugin also designed chapel plate for St George's Chapel for Rundell, Bridge and Rundell, but this was never executed.

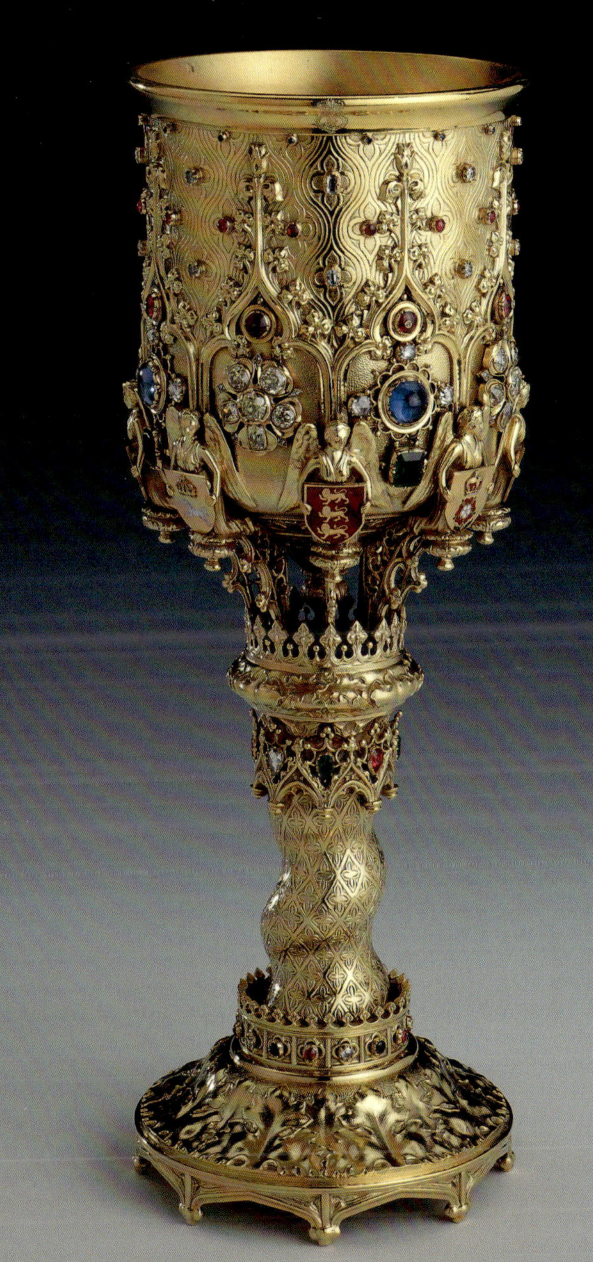

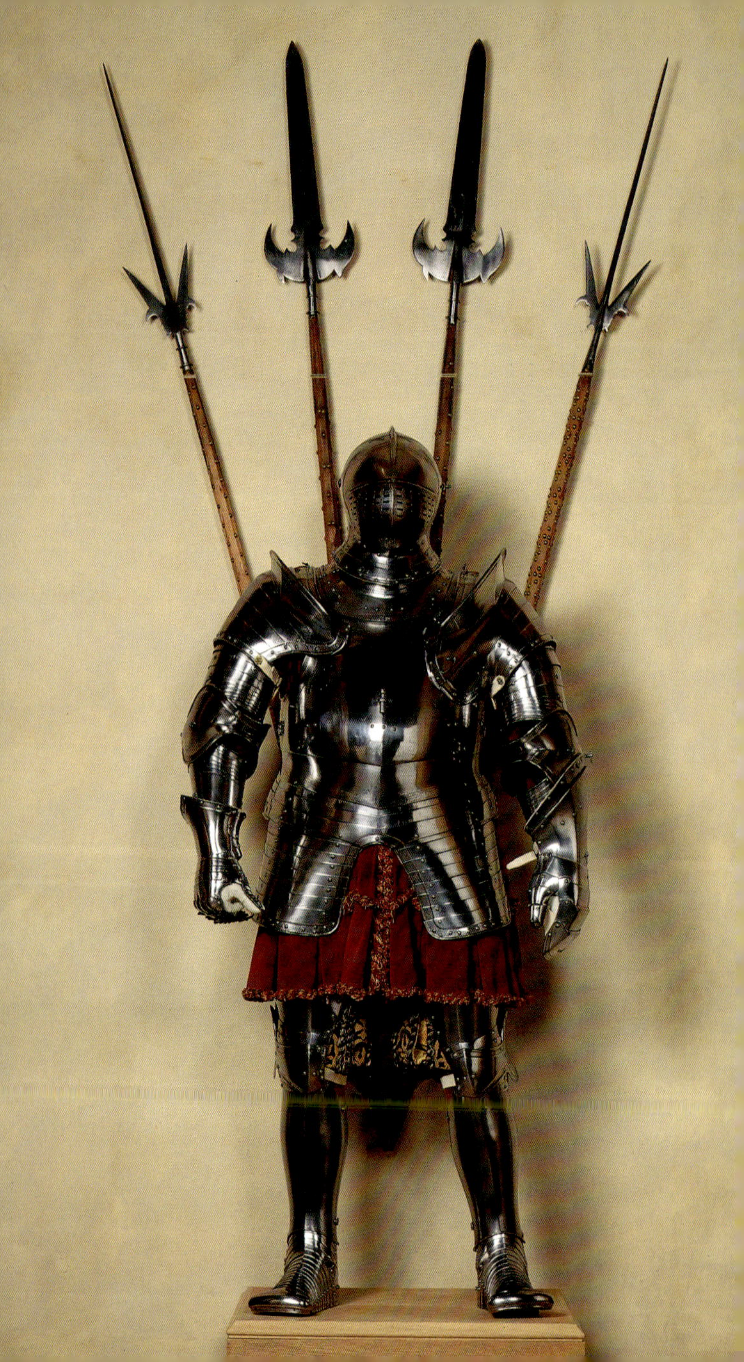

The Armour of Henry VIII

Greenwich workshop

c.1540

As a young man, Henry VIII (1491–1547) was outstandingly athletic and excelled in the arts of the tournament. His commanding presence was due in part to his great height (1.9 metres, or 6 feet 2 inches), which set him apart from most of his contemporaries. After a jousting accident in 1536 he grew corpulent, but four years later, at the age of 49, the King was reported to have found a new vigour, rising early and spending long hours each day in the saddle. This armour, which records his impressive girth at the time, was probably made for the jousts in celebration of the King's marriage to Anne of Cleves in January 1539/40. It was fashioned by the Master Workman Erasmus Kyrkenar, in the workshop founded by Henry at Greenwich in 1517.

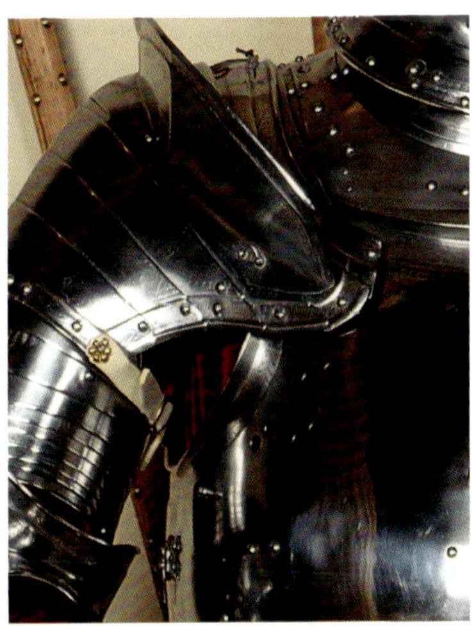

Like the later Greenwich armour of Henry, Prince of Wales (page 36), this suit has additional pieces – the grandguard, pasguard and manifer, for the tilt, which are secured by means of the central bolt. The six holes in the breastplate were for securing the King's lance-rest.

Silver-gilt Centrepiece

George Wickes (1698–1761)

1745, with later additions

The centrepiece, or epergne, was a relatively new addition to aristocratic dining in early Georgian England. The form developed in France and was intended to sit on the dining table throughout the meal, usually holding fruit, sweetmeats and candles. Detachable dishes and, as in this case, sugar casters were often added. The table would have been laid symmetrically so that each diner could reach every dish and help themselves.

This example, with its superb engraving and crest of feathers, was commissioned by Frederick, Prince of Wales, from his goldsmith, George Wickes. It may have been intended for the Prince's pavilion at the fashionable Vauxhall Gardens in London, where he entertained guests to supper. The design is based on a drawing by William Kent (1685–1748), although in execution it varies considerably. As the royal dining table became more crowded with massive plate, George IV had the centrepiece raised by the addition of the lion, unicorn and tritons, while the festoons and swags were added by John Bridge for Queen Victoria. The essential elements of the original design – the delicate trelliswork and elegant dishes – remain as a testament to Prince Frederick's taste.

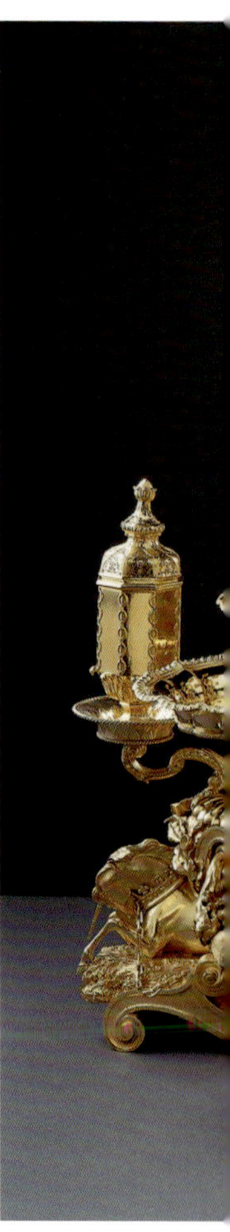

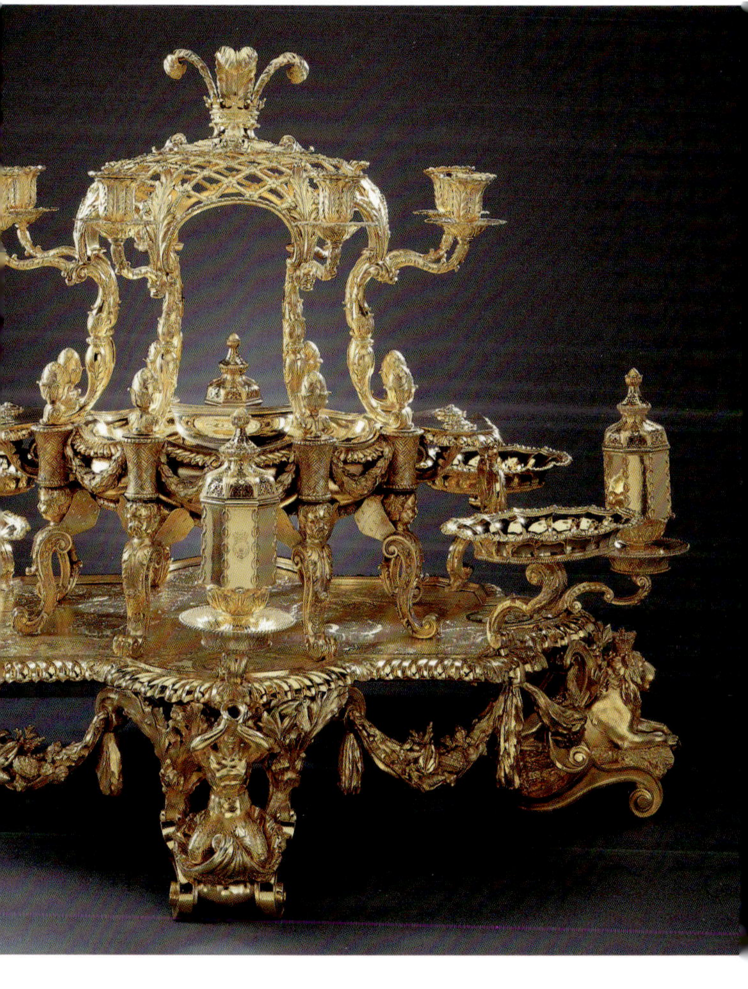

Floor of the Lantern Lobby

1995–7

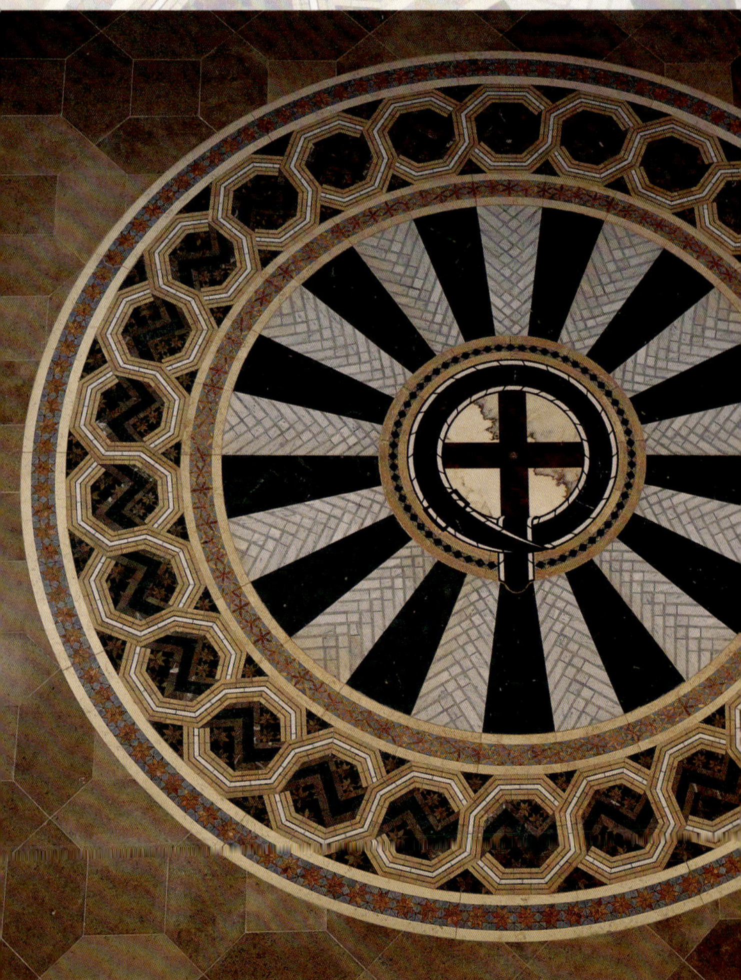

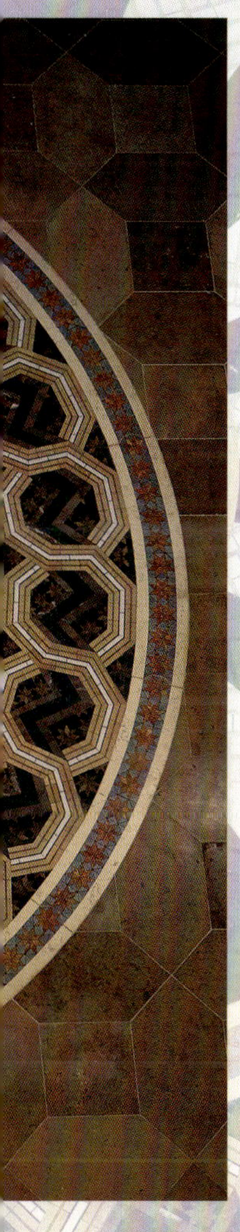

The fire of November 1992 began in Queen Victoria's Private Chapel, which adjoined the east end of St George's Hall. Although most of the original structure of the chapel was destroyed, it had never been considered an especially satisfactory space, and was in regular use as a passage between the Private and State Apartments.

At the suggestion of Prince Philip, a new, separate chapel was created on part of the old chapel site, while the main area was to be remodelled to provide a direct connection between the north and east sides of the Castle. Within this space, Giles Downes, the architect of the new scheme, created a decorative oak-framed and top-lit octagon in a modern Gothic idiom, incorporating a gallery and showcases for the display of gold plate. For the floor of the new space, Downes designed an intricately inlaid marble pavement of concentric bands, reflecting aspects of the Order of the Garter. The 26 linked octagons, for example, represent the number of the original Knights of the Garter, and at the centre is the Badge of the Order. Within the Badge is a silver disc inserted by The Prince of Wales on completion of the floor in 1997. The majority of the marbles used are English – including Duke's Red for the Cross of St George, supplied by the late Duke of Devonshire from a mine on the Chatsworth estate. The stones were cut and assembled by craftsmen from northern Italy.

Silver-gilt Sconce

Robert Smythier (*fl.* 1660 – *c.*1686)

1686

These sconces, or wall-lights, are among the most luxurious light fittings ever made. The central scene chased on each of the six sconces is the Judgement of Solomon, taken from the Old Testament. It shows two women, each of whom had had a child. One of these children had died and both mothers claimed the remaining child before Solomon, the King of Israel. Solomon ordered that a sword be brought and the child divided so that each woman could keep one-half. The true mother revealed herself by renouncing her claim so that the child's life would be spared. The baby was restored to her. This scene shows Solomon enthroned, with the suppliant women before him and the executioner on the right, raising a sword to divide the child. The story of the Judgement of Solomon became symbolic of justice and wisdom.

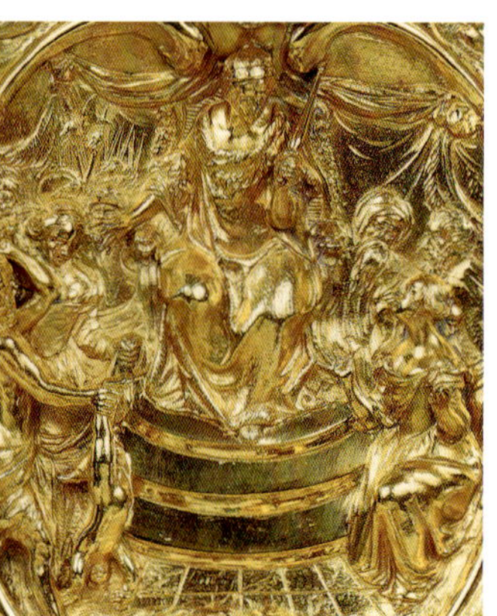

The sconces can be identified as the six which were delivered to the new Council Chamber at Whitehall Palace on 26 November 1686. The chamber formed part of the rebuilding of the Palace undertaken by Sir Christopher Wren for James II, and it was here that the King met the Ministers of his Privy Council. Sconces representing wisdom were therefore entirely appropriate to this setting. The crowned cipher of William and Mary was added in the following reign.

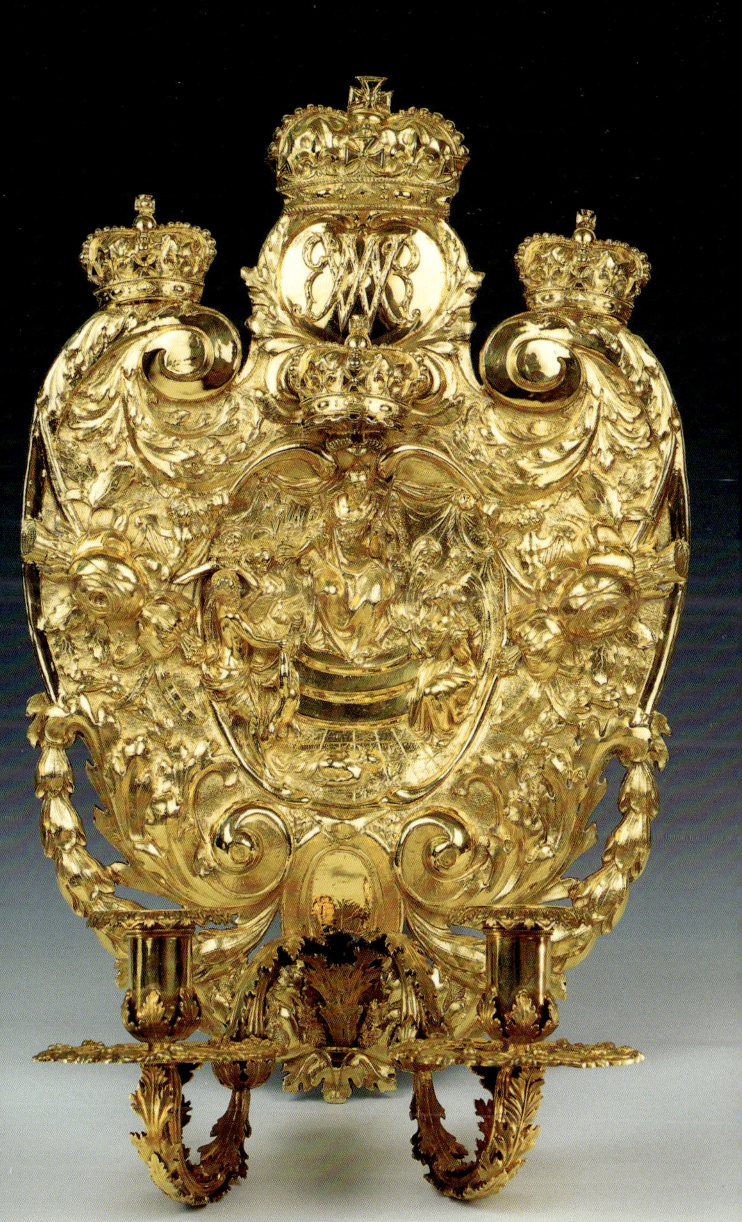

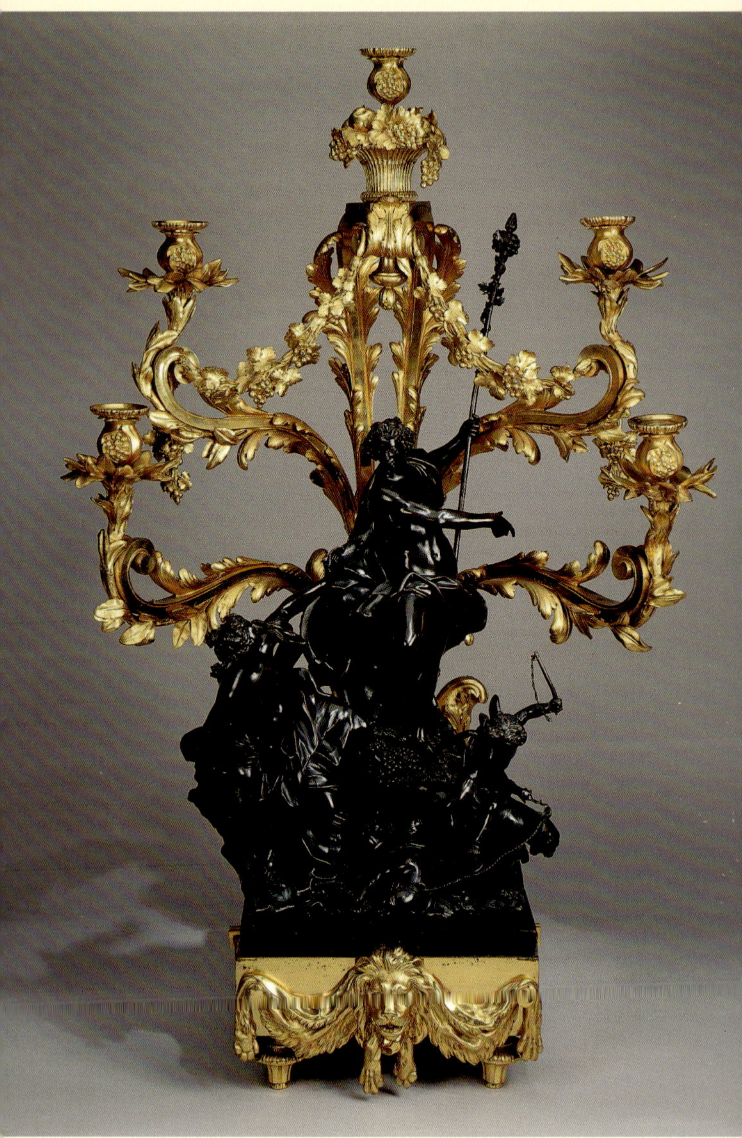

Gilt-bronze Candelabrum with a Bronze Group of 'Autumn'

attributed to Philippe Bertrand (1663–1724) candle-branches, Philippe Caffiéri (1714–74)

before 1716 and 1770

In this skilfully composed group, one of four representing the seasons, Bacchus, god of wine and the autumn harvest, rides in triumph on a chariot drawn by his panthers, which a winged cupid attempts to restrain as they feast on piles of grapes. The god has come to rescue Ariadne, the Cretan princess abandoned on the island of Naxos by Theseus. Ariadne turns imploringly towards the godly apparition.

It is not known for whom the four groups were originally made, and it was only after they entered the famous collection of the Comte d'Orsay in Paris in 1769 that they were fitted with elaborate and superbly finished gilt-bronze candle-branches by the outstanding sculptor and chaser of bronzes, Philippe Caffiéri. The bronze groups are in the style of Philippe Bertrand, a versatile sculptor much employed by Louis XIV in the chapel and garden at Versailles.

The four candelabra groups were purchased for Windsor Castle by George IV in 1825, for the large sum of £928, from the collection of George Watson Taylor.

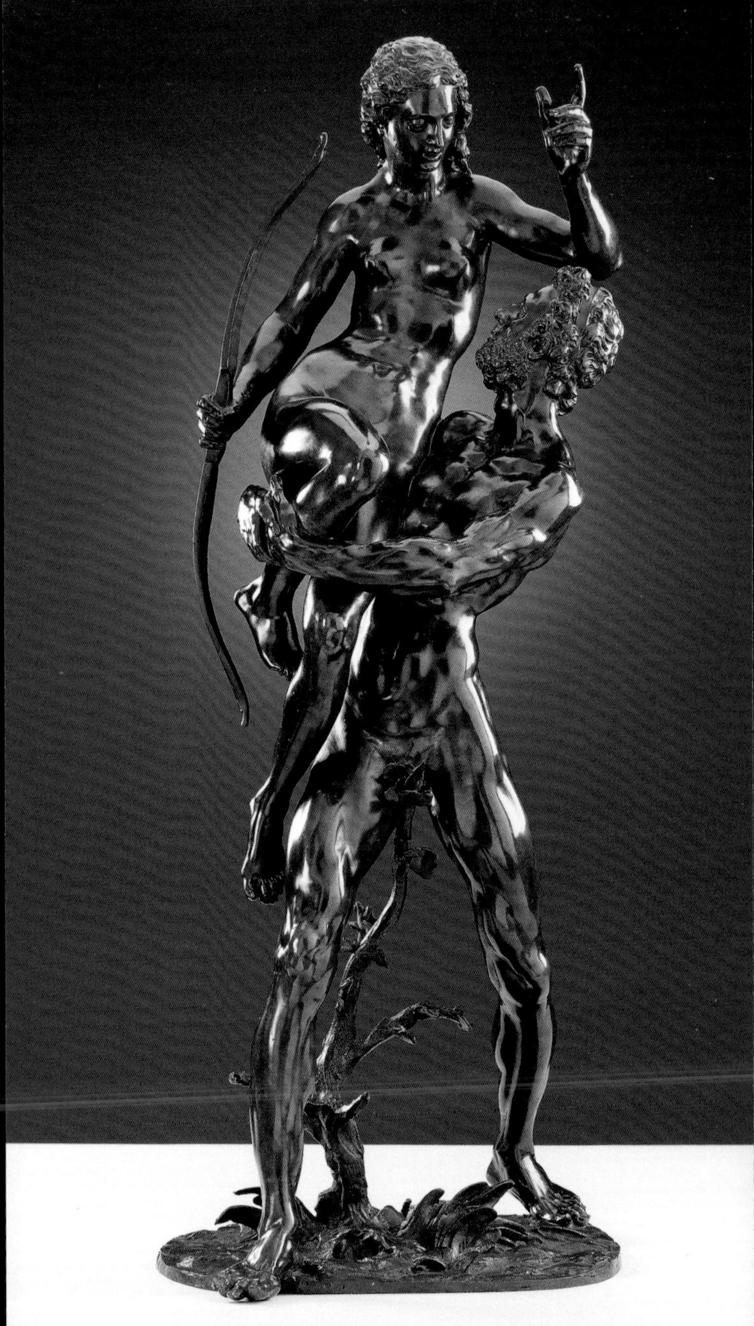

Theseus and Antiope(?)

Adriaen de Vries (1556–1626)

c.1600–1601

Adriaen de Vries, who was born at The Hague, trained in the studio of Giambologna in Florence, where he learnt to compose towering groups of several figures, intended to be viewed with equal satisfaction from any angle. His own contribution to the development of this type of group was the balletic quality of 'lift' that is so evident in this masterpiece; and while the structural strength of bronze gives the sculptor far more freedom in this direction than when he uses marble, de Vries exploits this freedom to an almost playful extent, limiting the male figure's contact with the base to the ball of one foot and the heel of the other. In order to support his clay models he wove a complicated wire armature which remains embedded inside the cast bronze.

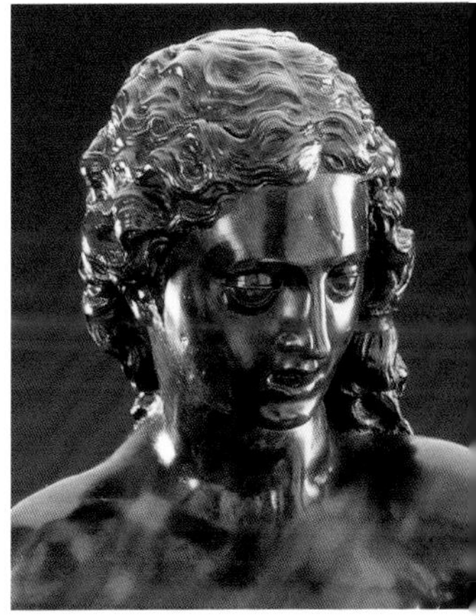

The identity of the figures has never been certain, but they are now thought to represent Theseus, legendary King of Athens, and his bride Antiope. Theseus was celebrated for his bravery in a series of struggles with monsters, including the Cretan Minotaur. He joined Hercules in the battle against the Amazons and was rewarded with the hand of Antiope, sister of the Amazon Queen. The bronze was probably acquired by George IV, who also purchased de Vries's relief of Rudolf II (pages 50–51).

Axminster Carpet

1851

This exceptional carpet was made by Blackmore Brothers of Wilton, acting on behalf of the West End carpet suppliers Watson and Bell, for the Green Drawing Room at Windsor. The designer was Prince Albert's artistic adviser, Ludwig Gruner of Dresden, who charged just over £80 for his three months' work. Although produced at Wilton, it is actually hand-knotted in the Axminster fashion, and at a greater density than usual (64 knots to every 6.5 square centimetres, or 1 square inch), no doubt accounting for the substantial bill of almost £730. When completed, it was shown in a specially constructed setting at the 1851 Great Exhibition, where it attracted considerable attention. In the *Illustrated Catalogue* it was praised for its 'immense size and brilliant, yet not gaudy colouring'.

Designed to fit the elongated T-shape of the Green Drawing Room, the central panel has a large wreath of flowers, flanked by smaller panels containing roundels with the national emblems, and borders centred by lozenges enclosing the V & A monogram. It replaced the original carpet, which had been designed by the French artist J.-J. Boileau and woven by Whitty of Axminster in 1828. One hundred and forty-one years after the new carpet was made, it survived the devastating Windsor fire of November 1992 with minimal damage, thanks to the protective covering that had been installed and the depth and strength of the pile. Some slight scorch-marks and staining are visible at the northern end, caused by the burning timbers that fell onto it from the floor above.

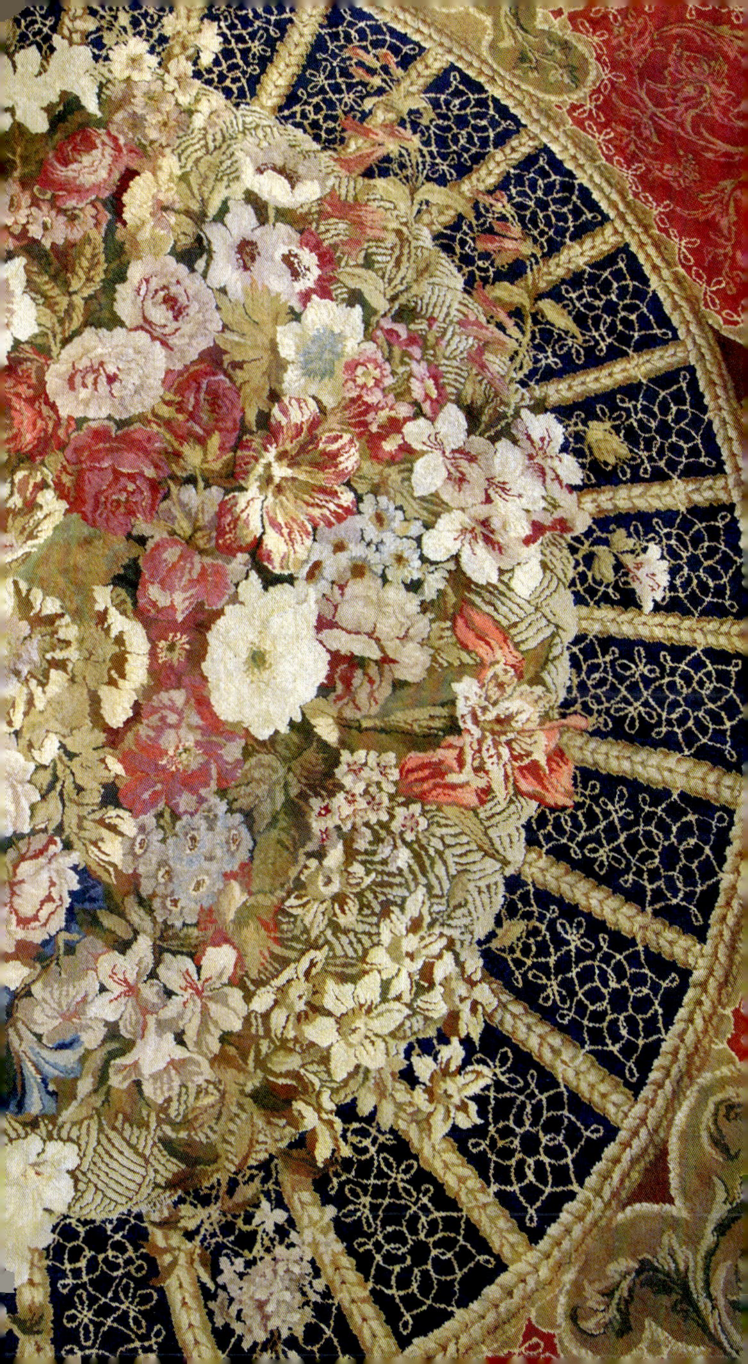

Princess Sophia

Sir Thomas Lawrence (1769–1830)

c.1825

Princess Sophia (1777–1848) was George IV's favourite sister. He commissioned this portrait, together with that of their sister, Princess Mary, to hang in the Green Drawing Room. Sophia, the fifth daughter of George III and Queen Charlotte, was not physically strong, suffering from repeated bouts of ill health and becoming blind towards the end of her life.

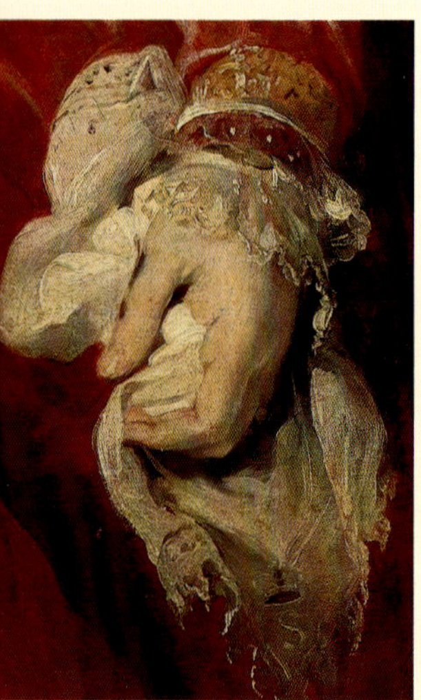

Painted when the Princess was nearly 50, it is clear that Lawrence took a sympathetic view of his sitter. The Princess adopts a pose of languor, but the vibrant red of her dress and the youthful pallor of her skin serve to dispel the image of Princess Sophia as an invalid. Subtle indication of her frailty is perhaps achieved by the handkerchief clutched in her left hand and the eyeglass tucked into her waist.

Although George III had appointed Lawrence Principal Painter in 1792, it was under George IV's patronage that his reputation flourished. The miniature of George IV that hangs from Princess Sophia's left shoulder perhaps acknowledges Lawrence's gratitude towards his patron, as well as indicating the mutual affection between brother and sister.

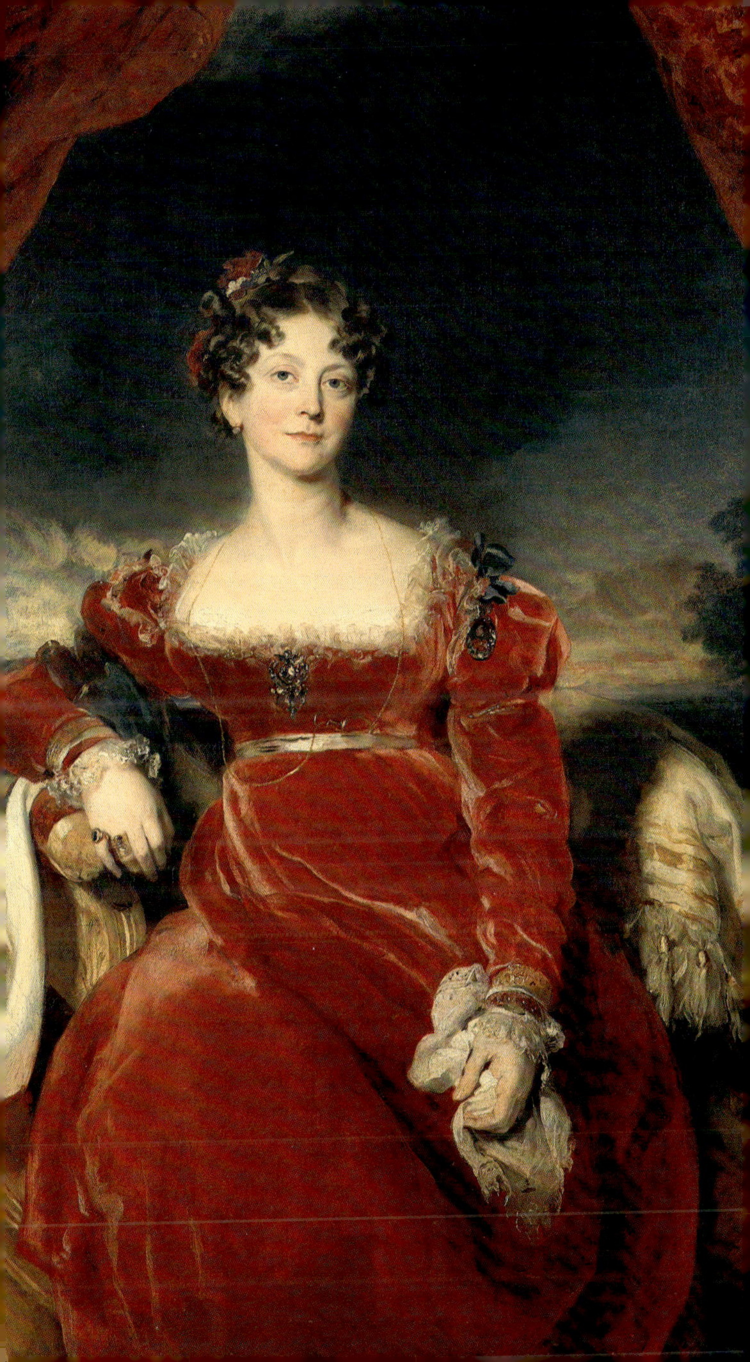

The Louis XVI Service

Sèvres porcelain factory

1783–93

As the proprietor of the Sèvres porcelain factory, Louis XVI (reigned 1774–91) was entitled to the pick of the factory's luxurious productions. However, nothing produced at the factory in the eighteenth century compared in quality to this dinner and dessert service, which was begun in 1783. The King was intimately involved in its production, drawing up the schedule in his own hand. The specification was so exacting and the costs so high that its completion was intended to take 23 years. In the event, the King's execution after only ten years brought production to a halt, and the Revolutionary authorities eventually offered the service for sale. It was acquired in two stages by George IV in 1811.

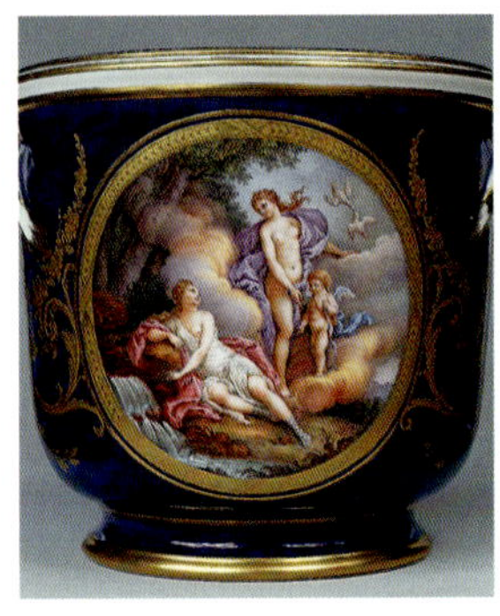

It is the quality of the painted and gilded decoration that distinguishes this service from any other, and accounts for the fact that each plate cost 13 times as much to make as any equivalent Sèvres plate of a standard pattern. The enamelled reserves represent scenes from mythology and history, and were copied from the factory's collection of engravings by eight of the best Sèvres artists, while the gilding is tooled with exceptional subtlety in order to exploit the candlelit conditions in which the service would have been admired. Many of the scenes are of a dramatic and often violent kind, with vengeful gods and goddesses or mythical heroes engaged in acts of abduction or destruction, while a significant proportion include languorous female nudes. Although 60 plain-centred plates were included in the order, it is unlikely that the service was ever used. It serves instead as a sort of miniature picture gallery, to be displayed in cabinets around the walls of a room and occasionally studied at close quarters in the hand.

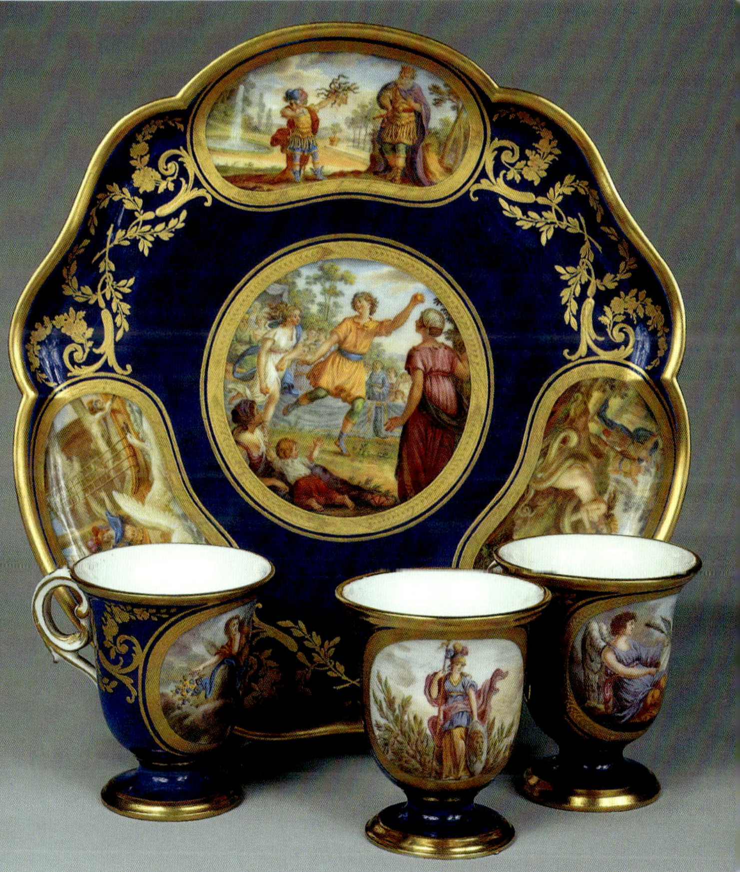

Chimneypiece

Benjamin Vulliamy (1747–1811) and Benjamin Lewis Vulliamy (1780–1854)

1807

Towards the end of the eighteenth century, the dynasty of London clock-makers founded by Justin Vulliamy in the 1740s began to diversify into the production of bronze ornaments, a field in which the patronage of George IV provided much business. The manufacture of chimneypieces and fire surrounds was a natural progression for makers of mantel clocks and candelabra, and in 1806–7 the firm supplied seven for the rapidly evolving interiors of Carlton House.

This example is one of a pair of 'large and magnificent' chimneypieces (the other is in the Green Drawing Room) originally installed in the Crimson Drawing Room at Carlton House (for the prodigious sum of £2,002), and brought to Windsor in 1826 for re-use in George IV's new apartments. They incorporate bronze figures of satyrs, each of whom cradles two male infants in his arms, 'presenting them', in the words of an early description of Carlton House, 'to the comforts of the fire'. These figures may have been inspired by the well-known ancient group of Hercules with the infant Telephus (sometimes called Silenus and Bacchus). For the design of the finely chased and gilded frieze and the panels at either end, the Vulliamys turned to engravings of antiquities and the more recent work of Italian neoclassical designers. No fewer than 19 different tradesmen were involved in manufacturing the chimneypieces.

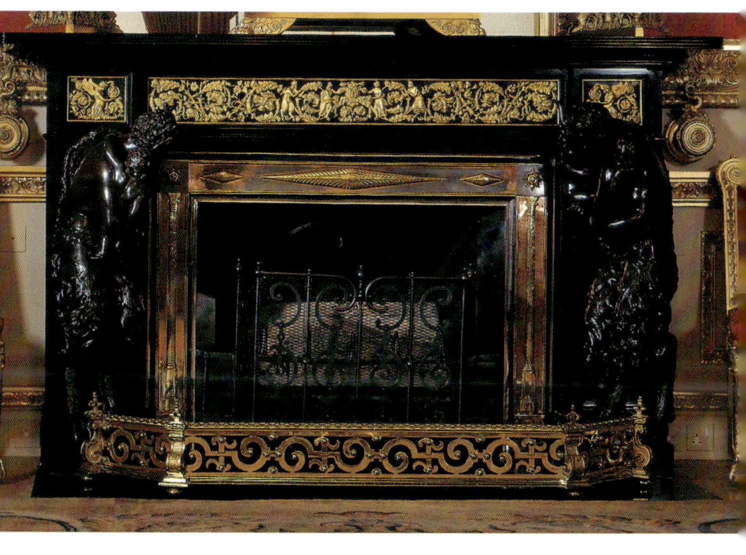

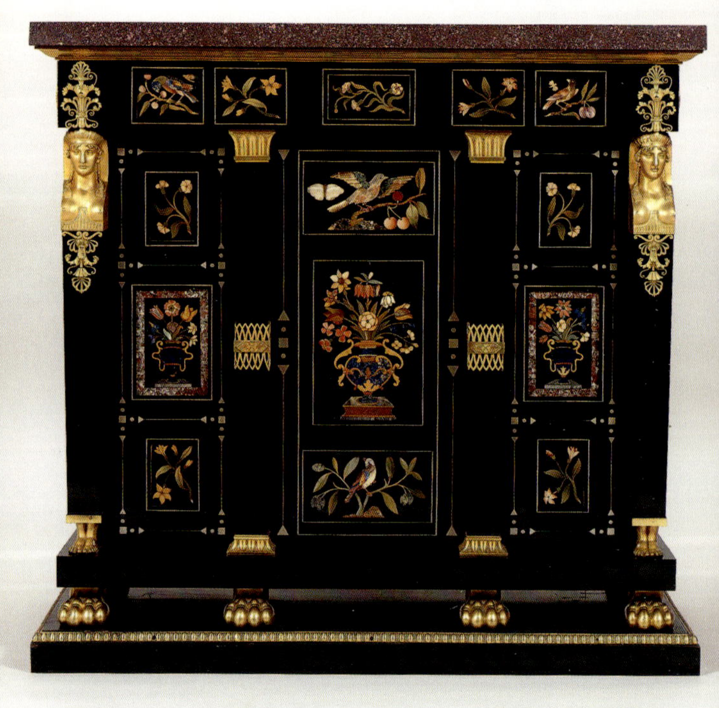

Pair of Cabinets

Martin-Eloy Lignereux (1752–1809)

1803

These elegant and sophisticated French cabinets arrived in the Royal Collection thanks to the short-lived peace between France and Britain signalled by the Treaty of Amiens in 1802. Before and after this date, until the victory of Waterloo in 1815, France – under the iron rule of Napoleon Bonaparte – was effectively closed to British travellers, and trading links were substantially curtailed. During the brief lull in hostilities, George IV's intimate friend Sir Harry Fetherstonhaugh, the owner of Uppark House on the South Downs, travelled to Paris and, while visiting the fashionable dealer-decorator and furniture-maker M.-E. Lignereux in the rue Vivienne, placed an order for a number of objects, including these cabinets, on behalf of the Prince.

Sir Harry would certainly have known that Lignereux's intended combination of fine gilt bronzes in the newly fashionable Egyptian style, Florentine *pietra dura* panels (both inlaid and carved in relief) and rich porphyry tops, all set off by glossy ebony veneers, was of exactly the kind to appeal to the Prince's taste for rich and ornamental furniture. Lignereux, who was evidently very proud of his work and no doubt hoped for further orders, described the cabinets in a letter to the Prince as 'made with very particular perfection and extraordinary care'. When the King moved to Windsor in the late 1820s, the cabinets were selected first for his new bedroom, and subsequently for the Crimson Drawing Room.

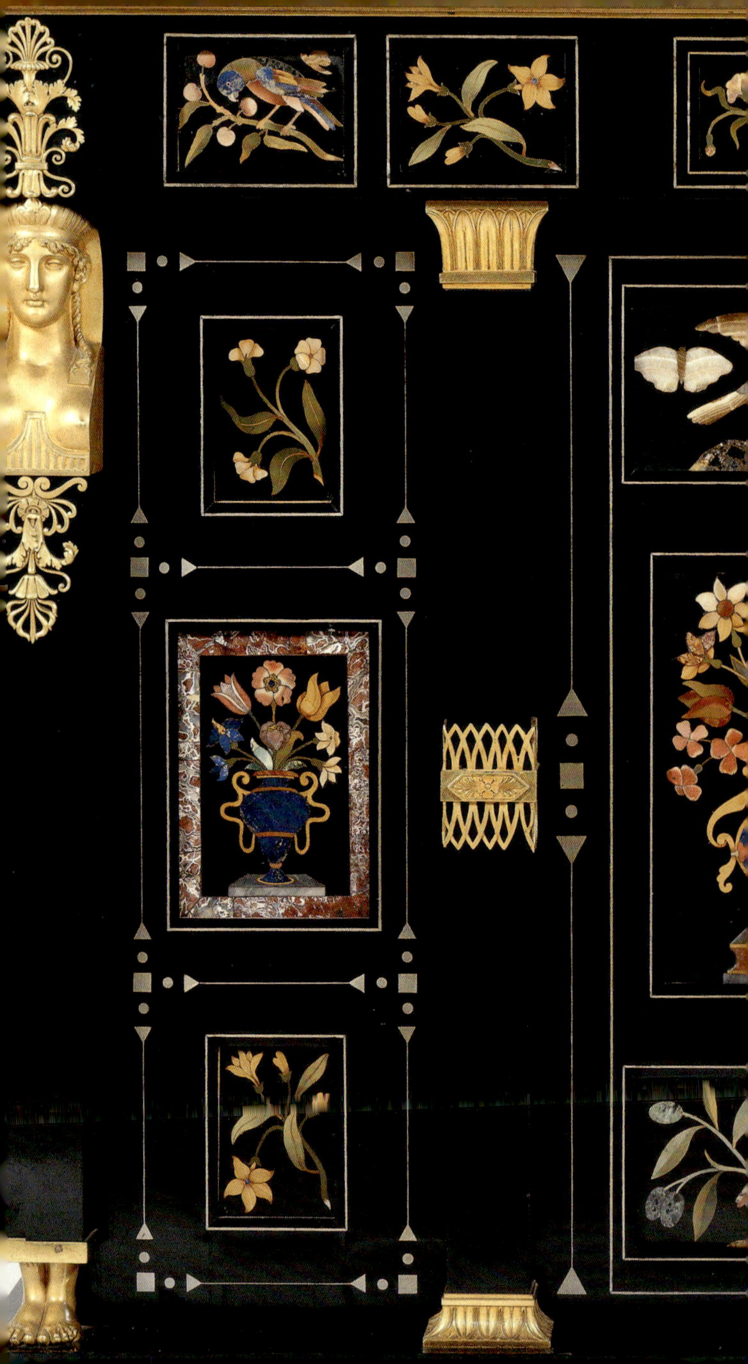

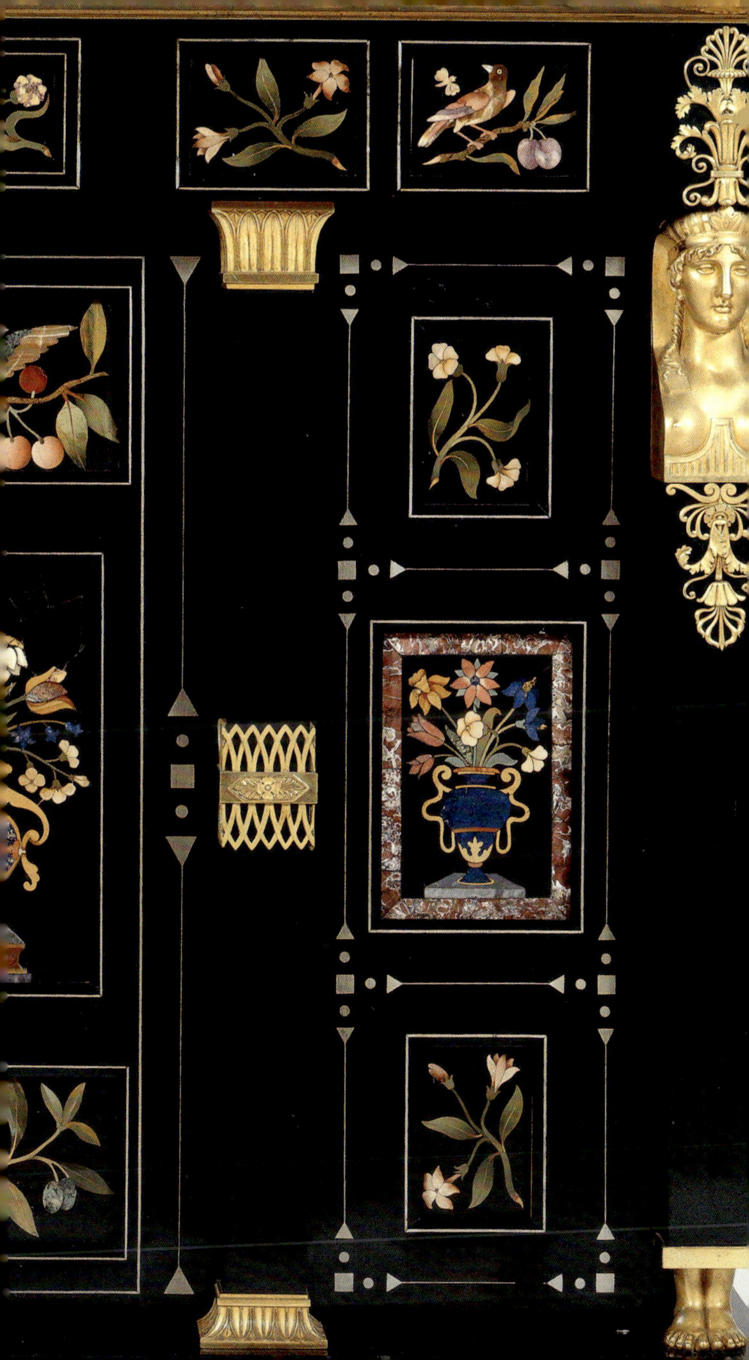

'Artium Genio' Clock

Pierre-Philippe Thomire (1751–1843)

1813

Clocks illustrating classical or mythological subjects by means of sculpture were fashionable throughout the second half of the eighteenth century and well into the nineteenth. In France the leading bronze-maker of the Empire period, Pierre-Philippe Thomire, specialised in clocks of this type, where the timekeeping element often appears secondary to the allegorical content of the case. In some instances, as in this clock, the mechanism was of distinctly inferior quality. George IV's clock-maker, Benjamin Lewis Vulliamy (1780–1854), attempted to service it a number of times after its arrival at Carlton House in 1813, finally giving up and replacing it with one of his own manufacture in 1822. The quality of the case, however, is beyond doubt: the laureate, winged figure representing the Genius of the Arts, his shield emblazoned with a figure of Fame on a ground of lapis lazuli, contemplates the scattered emblems of the arts of sculpture, painting and music; and the base, panelled with lapis lazuli, is mounted at the centre with a plume of feathers, perhaps alluding to the princely purchaser. As Prince of Wales, Regent and King, George IV was a substantial client of Thomire's firm, so such an allusion is not altogether unlikely.

The clock was joined at Carlton House by a pair of candelabra, also by Thomire, in 1817, and the garniture was eventually transferred to the Crimson Drawing Room at Windsor Castle in [illegible].

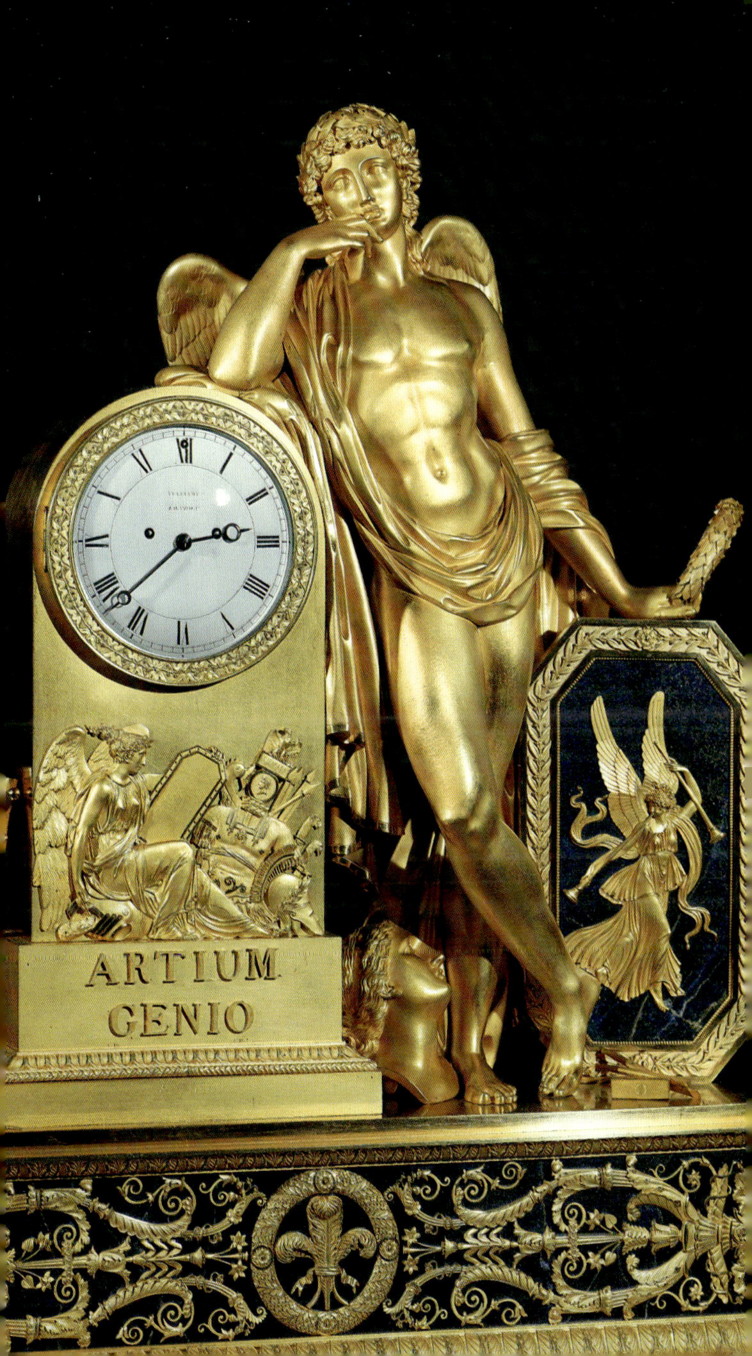
ARTIUM
GENIO

Pair of Sofa Tables

Morel and Seddon

*c.*1828

When George IV was planning his new suite of apartments on the east front of the Castle in the 1820s, he intended the Crimson Drawing Room as his principal reception room. The decorations were accordingly among the most lavish of the new work. Some of the furniture and fittings were to be transferred from the room of the same name at Carlton House, the King's former London residence, demolished in 1826; but a quantity of new furniture, which included this pair of

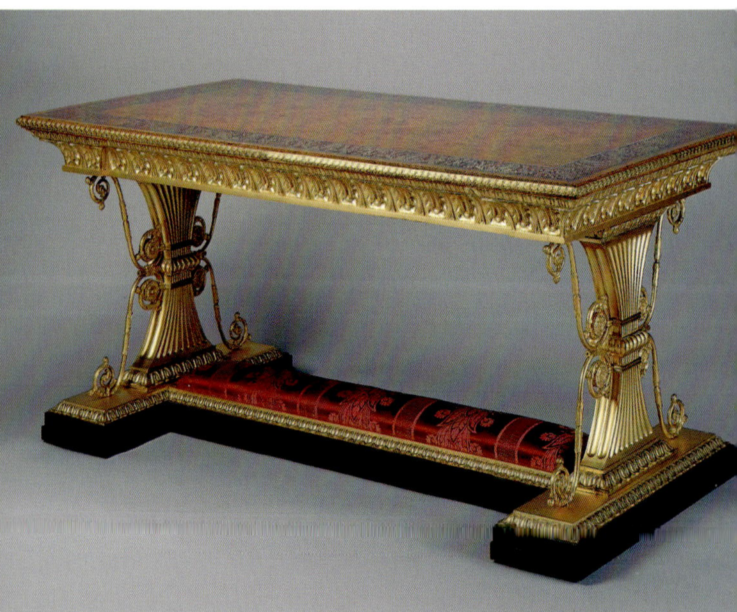

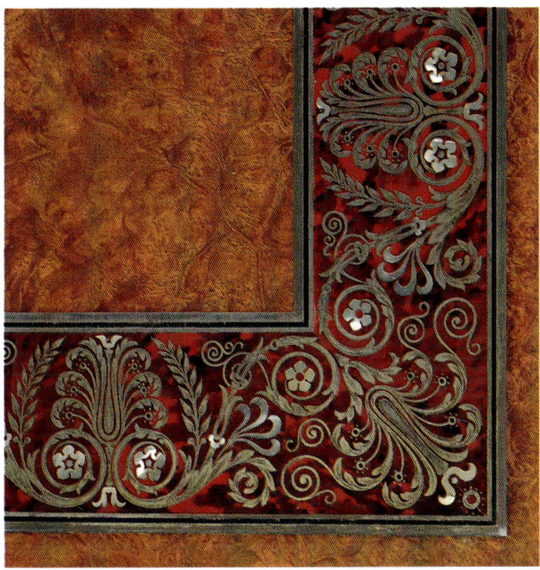

tables, was also required. This was to be supplied by the firm of Morel and Seddon of Aldersgate Street in the City of London.

The rich late Empire style selected by the King, popular in France in the early 1820s, was developed for Windsor by the Parisian cabinet-maker F.-H.-G. Jacob-Desmalter, invited to England specifically to help Morel and Seddon with the design of new furniture. The sofa table is a fine example of this collaboration: the elegant gilt-bronze and giltwood pedestals support a top of richly figured amboyna, the border inlaid with brass, pewter and mother-of-pearl on a ground of red-stained tortoiseshell. When in use for writing or reading, the user's feet rested on the well-padded rail, which was covered in the same patterned silk as the walls. The two tables, together with a set of three card tables, cost the substantial sum of £1,728.

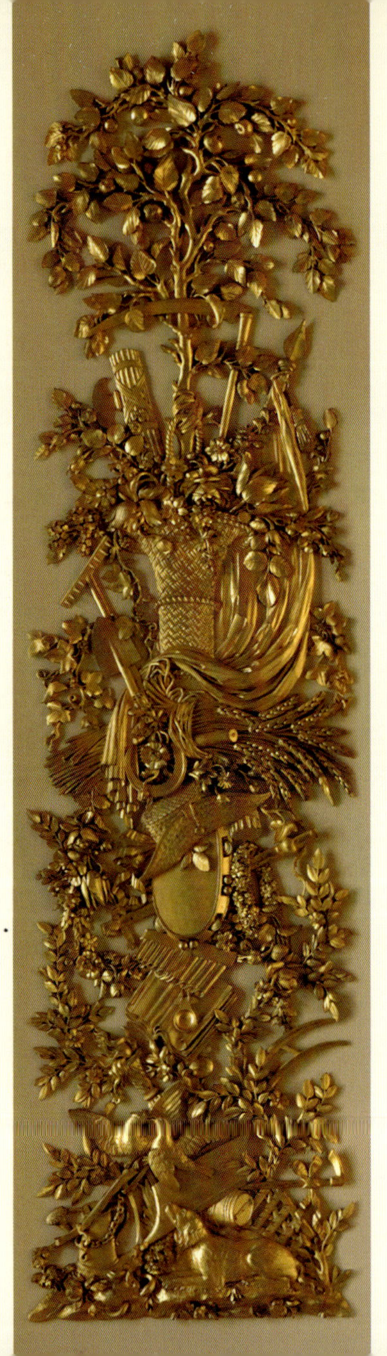

Giltwood Trophy

Edward Wyatt (1757–1833)

1811–16

The carver and gilder Edward Wyatt, cousin of George IV's architect Jeffry Wyatville, supplied many of the ornamental carvings in the sumptuous interiors of the King's metropolitan palace, Carlton House, and in so doing contributed dramatically to the all-pervading sense of luxury and extravagance for which the house was a byword. Between 1811 and 1816, Wyatt supplied a series of 'emblematical pannels' for the doors of three of the principal rooms on the garden front of Carlton House: the Blue Velvet Room, the Ante Room and the Old Throne Room. Carved in the most minute and jewel-like detail, and burnished to look more like gilt bronze than giltwood, they illustrate such themes as architecture, painting, music, agriculture, commerce and navigation. Nothing quite like them is to be found in any other English house of this date.

When Carlton House was demolished in 1826, many of the finest of the architectural fittings, including the doors with their carved panels, were removed for re-use in the principal rooms of George IV's new apartments at Windsor – the Crimson, Green and White Drawing Rooms – constructed by Jeffry Wyatville within the east range of the Castle in 1824–8.

Queen Elizabeth in Coronation Robes

Sir Gerald Festus Kelly (1879–1972)

1938–45

Kelly was initially commissioned to paint the state portraits of King George VI and Queen Elizabeth in 1938. He started immediately and had almost finished by the outbreak of the Second World War in 1939. The paintings were moved from his studio in London to Windsor Castle, where Kelly spent the next five years completing his commission. The Castle provided a refuge not only for Kelly, but also for the young Princesses Elizabeth and Margaret Rose, who were sent to the safety of Windsor for the duration of the war, while their parents remained at Buckingham Palace.

Queen Elizabeth (1900–2002) is depicted wearing her coronation robes, which incorporate an elaborate scheme of embroidered national and imperial emblems. Kelly enjoyed his sittings with the Queen and said of her, 'It is hard to suggest the admiration and affection which grew all around her. From wherever one looked at her, she looked nice: her face, her voice, her smile, her skin, her colouring – everything was right.'

The backdrop of this painting was originally intended to depict the doors of the Crimson Drawing Room. Kelly later changed his mind and asked his friend Sir Edwin Lutyens to design a model for the background, based on the Viceroy's House in Delhi, which makes the painting appear more spacious and stately.

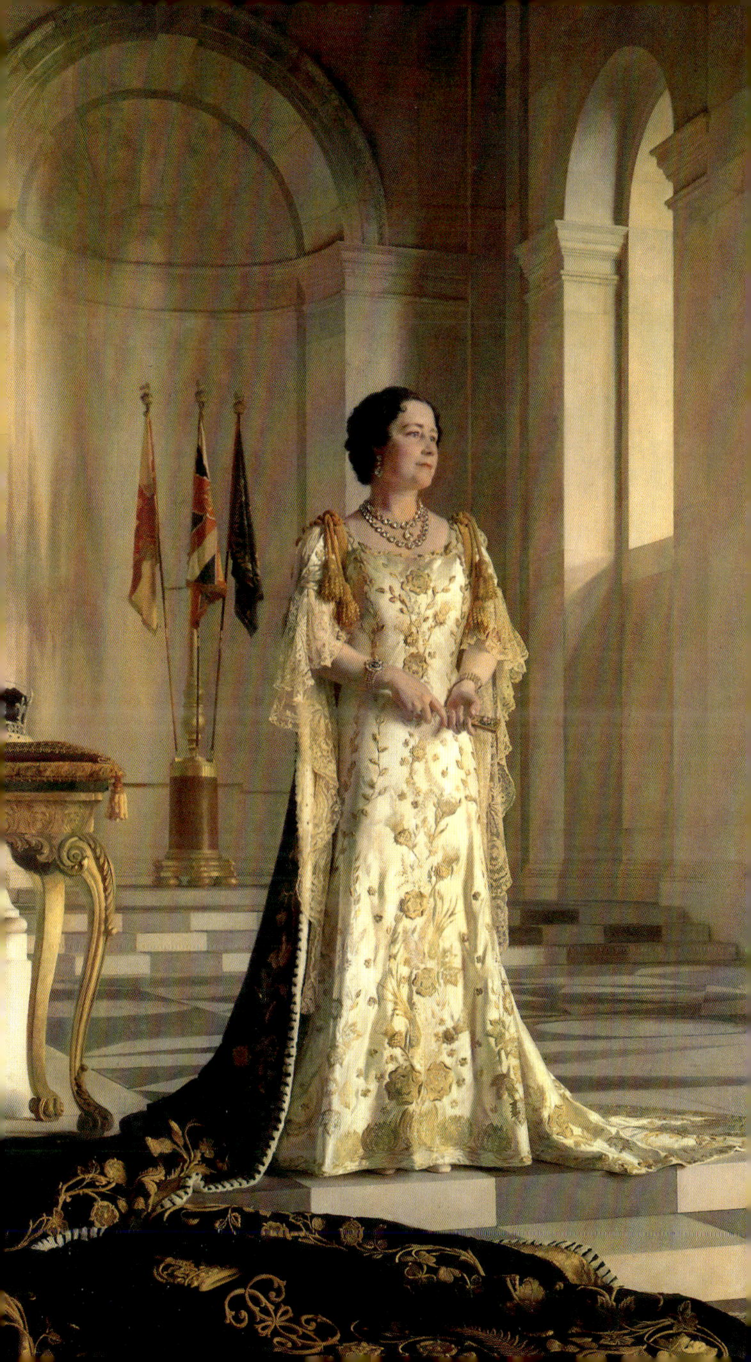

St Petersburg Porcelain Vase

Imperial Manufactory

1844

Monumental vases of this type were produced in the nineteenth century by a number of European factories, most notably those at Sèvres, Berlin and St Petersburg. They were often used as diplomatic presents between rulers, thereby providing a useful advertisement for the skills and achievements of the factory concerned. Such vases, which were mostly in the form of the ancient marble Medici Vase, were almost always on a large scale, used lavish quantities of gilding and gilt bronze, and were frequently decorated with panoramic views of important buildings or landscapes.

This vase was made to the order of Tsar Nicholas I at the Imperial Manufactory at St Petersburg, founded by Tsarina Elizabeth in 1744, and was intended as a gift to Queen Victoria following the Tsar's State Visit to London in June 1844. It is decorated on either side with views of two of the imperial palaces, Tsarskoe Selo and Peterhof, both on the outskirts of St Petersburg. When it arrived at Windsor in December 1844, the Queen placed it in the bay window of the Green Drawing Room. King Edward VII sent it to Osborne House on the Isle of Wight, but following the restoration of the Castle after the fire of 1992 it was returned to Windsor, and now stands in the State Dining Room.

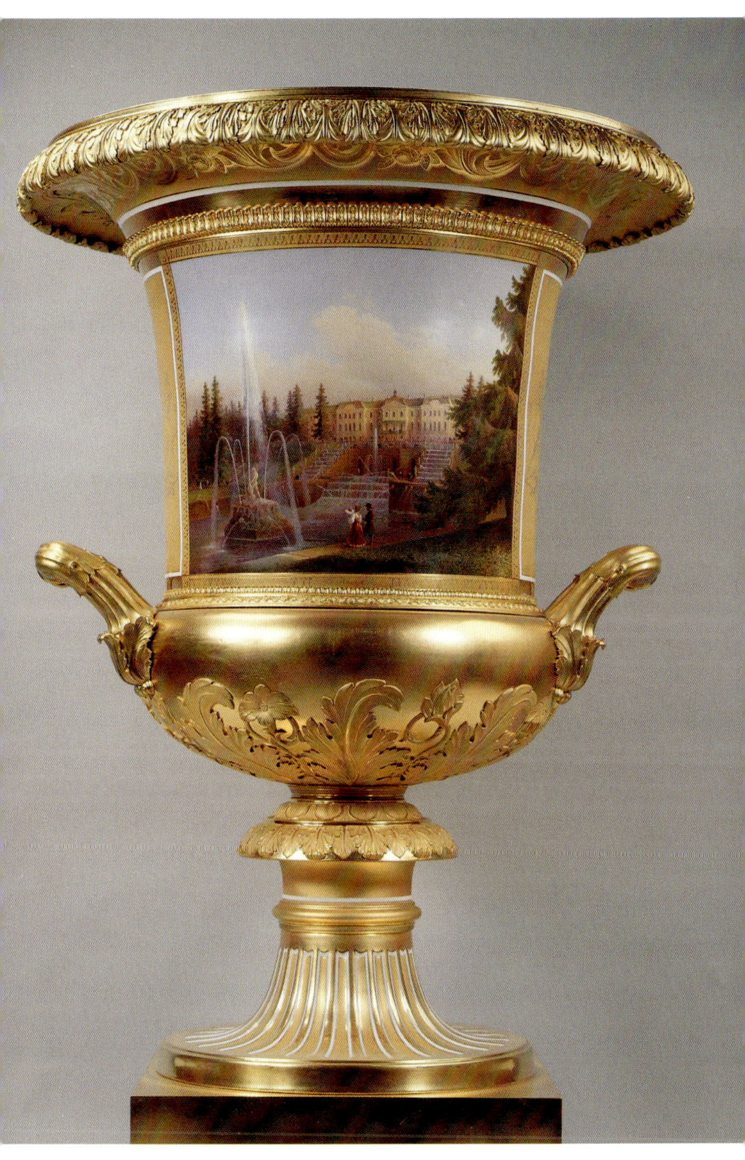

Gilt-bronze Gothic Chandelier

Hancock and Rixon

1828

The design of the Gothic furniture and fittings made as part of George IV's extensive remodelling of Windsor Castle in the 1820s was entrusted to the French émigré architect and designer Auguste-Charles Pugin. He worked for the firm of Morel and Seddon, who were in overall charge of the supply of all the new furniture and furnishings for this project. To assist him, he employed his highly precocious 15-year-old son, Augustus Welby Northmore Pugin, better known as the collaborator of Sir Charles Barry in the design and building of the new Palace of Westminster.

The younger Pugin took over some of his father's designs for Windsor and gave them a more robust and inventive Gothic feel. This understanding of Gothic form and detail is very apparent in the case of the chandelier, which was ordered from the lamp-makers Hancock and Rixon in January 1828 and delivered for the Octagon Room in December of that year. Queen Victoria rehung it in the Private Chapel, where it remained until the fire of 1992. Shattered into many pieces and buried under 3 metres (10 feet) of rubble, it was restored over a three-year period and rehung in its original position in 1997.

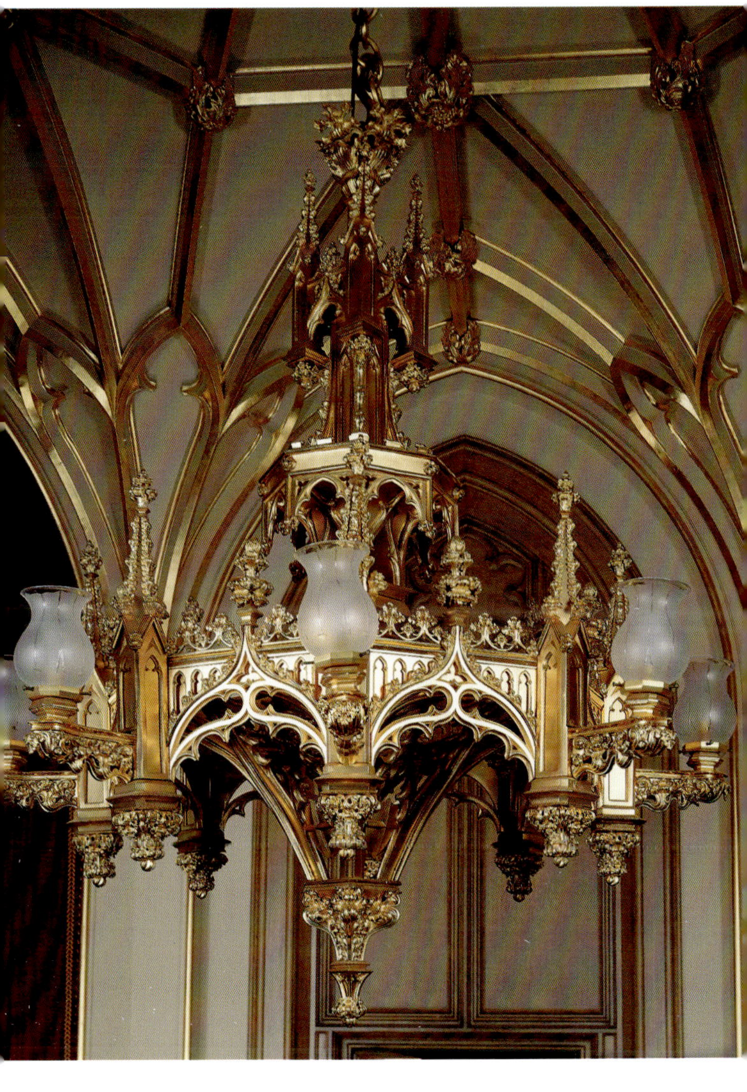

The Manchester Service

Sèvres porcelain factory

1760–83

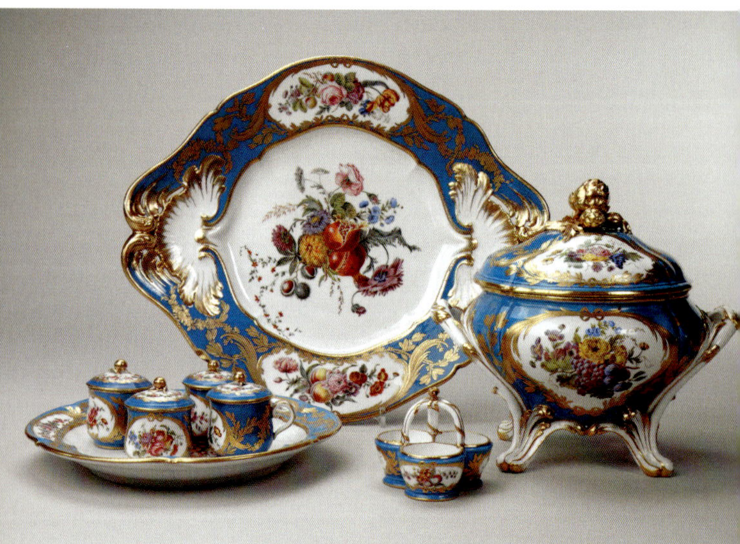

Most of the outstanding pieces of Sèvres porcelain on display at Windsor were purchased by George IV in the course of his 50-year career as a collector, almost all of them having formerly been in French aristocratic or royal hands before the Revolution of 1789. This magnificent dinner and dessert service, with richly gilded *bleu céleste* grounds, is a notable exception, since its original owner was English.

The service was presented by Louis XVI in 1783 to Elizabeth, Duchess of Manchester, in recognition of the work of her husband, the 4th Duke (1733–88) and British

Ambassador to the Court of Versailles, in bringing about the treaty that concluded the War of American Independence. The Duke himself received a diamond-encrusted gold box, set with a portrait of the French King.

The service, which comprises 283 pieces, was purchased by George IV from the Duchess of Manchester in 1802 for £882. The Duchess seems to have retained the 106 pieces of biscuit porcelain sculpture for table decoration which had been part of the original gift. The individual pieces range in date of production from 1760 to 1783, the majority falling within the last seven years of that range. The shapes and decorative style of the service date from the earliest years of the Sèvres factory, but remained current for almost 30 years.

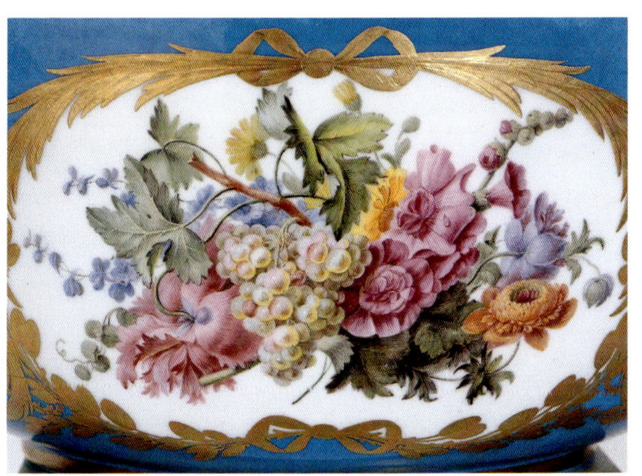

Malachite Vase
Peterhof lapidary workshop
1836

Malachite, the distinctive bright-green material (technically, the mineral hydrated copper carbonate) with which this enormous vase is veneered, was first extracted from mines belonging to the Demidov family in the Ural Mountains of central Russia in the eighteenth century. The fashion for malachite objects reached its height in the early nineteenth century, and in the reign of Tsar Nicholas I (1825–55) the working of this strongly marked substance became one of the main specialities and most admired achievements of the imperial lapidary workshops of Peterhof, Ekaterinburg and Kolyvan. Its brittle nature meant that for larger objects malachite could only be used as a veneer. The skill of the lapidaries lay in piecing together the veneers to make the most striking but natural-looking patterns.

The Windsor vase, which was made at the Peterhof workshop at a cost of 40,000 roubles, originally for display in the Hermitage, arrived at Windsor in 1839. Nominally it came as a personal gesture of thanks from Nicholas I to Queen Victoria, for the way in which his son and heir, the future Alexander II, had been received in England earlier in the year; but its secondary purpose was undoubtedly to assist the process of courting Britain's support for Russia's plans for the future of Turkey.

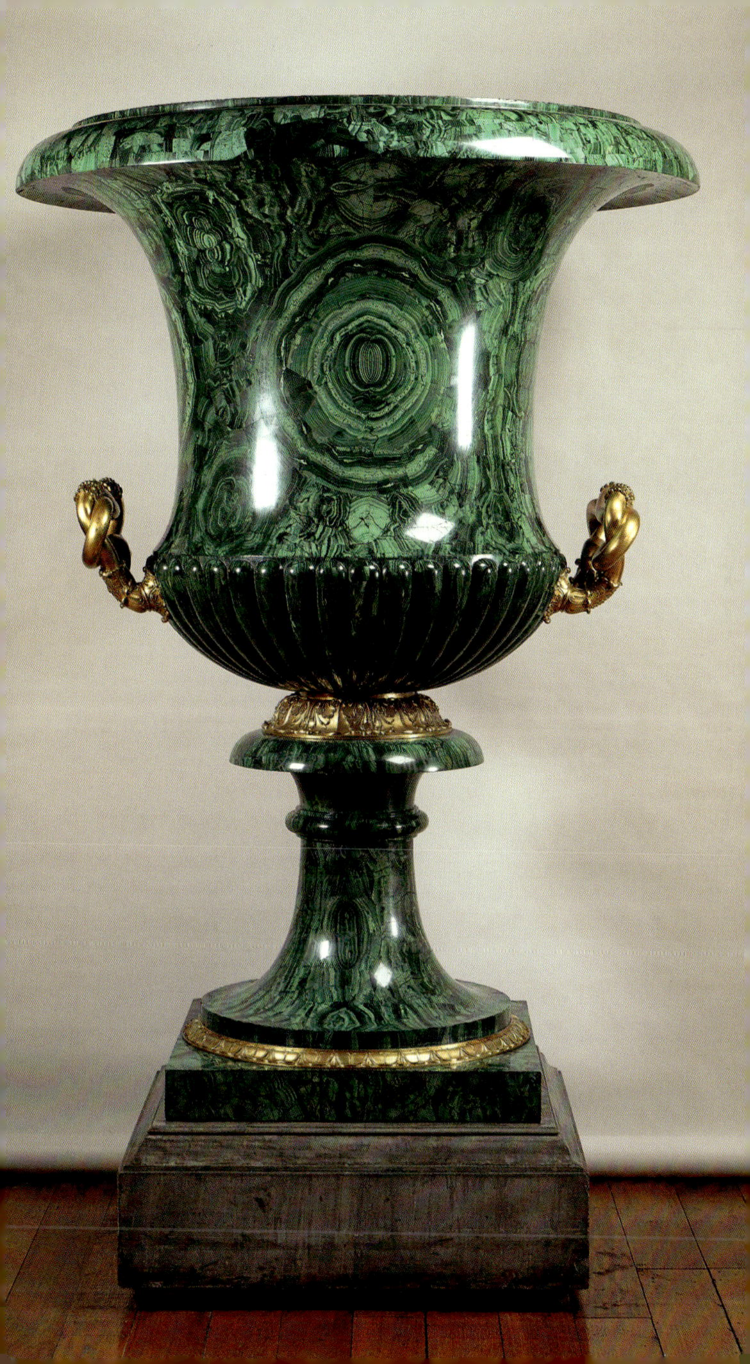

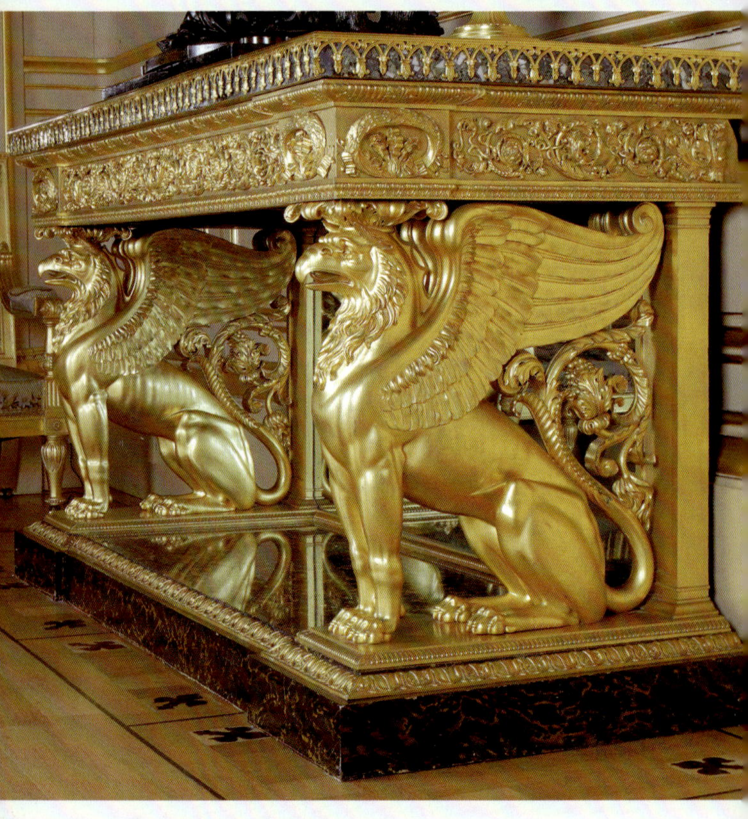

Pair of Giltwood Tables
Tatham, Bailey and Sanders
1814

The furniture-making partnership of Thomas Tatham, Edward Bailey and Richard Sanders worked extensively for George IV at Carlton House in the early nineteenth century, providing a vast array of gilded, upholstered and veneered furniture in the neoclassical style. This magnificent pair, with green scagliola (imitation marble) tops, was provided for one of the most sumptuous rooms at Carlton House, the Crimson Drawing Room, furnished by the partners between 1808 and 1814. They were made to fit the piers of the window wall, where they supported a display of vases and bronze groups.

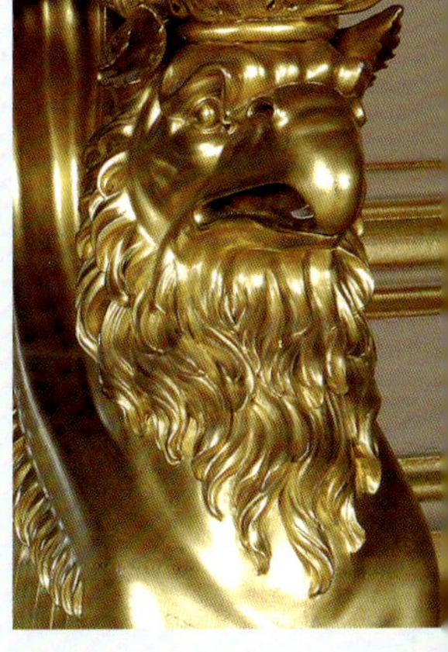

It may be that the distinctive design of the winged griffins was inspired by a drawing of an antique fragment recorded by Charles Heathcote Tatham, brother of Thomas, who had travelled extensively in Italy, recording classical antiquities: one of these drawings (published in 1799), for an 'Antique fragment of a table foot' in the Vatican, resembles the griffins supporting the table-tops quite closely. The richly carved frieze was originally backed with crimson velvet, to match the setting at Carlton House; and above the griffin heads are ribbon-ties carved in the form of the Prince of Wales's feathers. When Carlton House was dismantled in 1826, these tables were sent to Windsor, where they were placed in the new Grand Corridor and later moved to the Grand Reception Room.

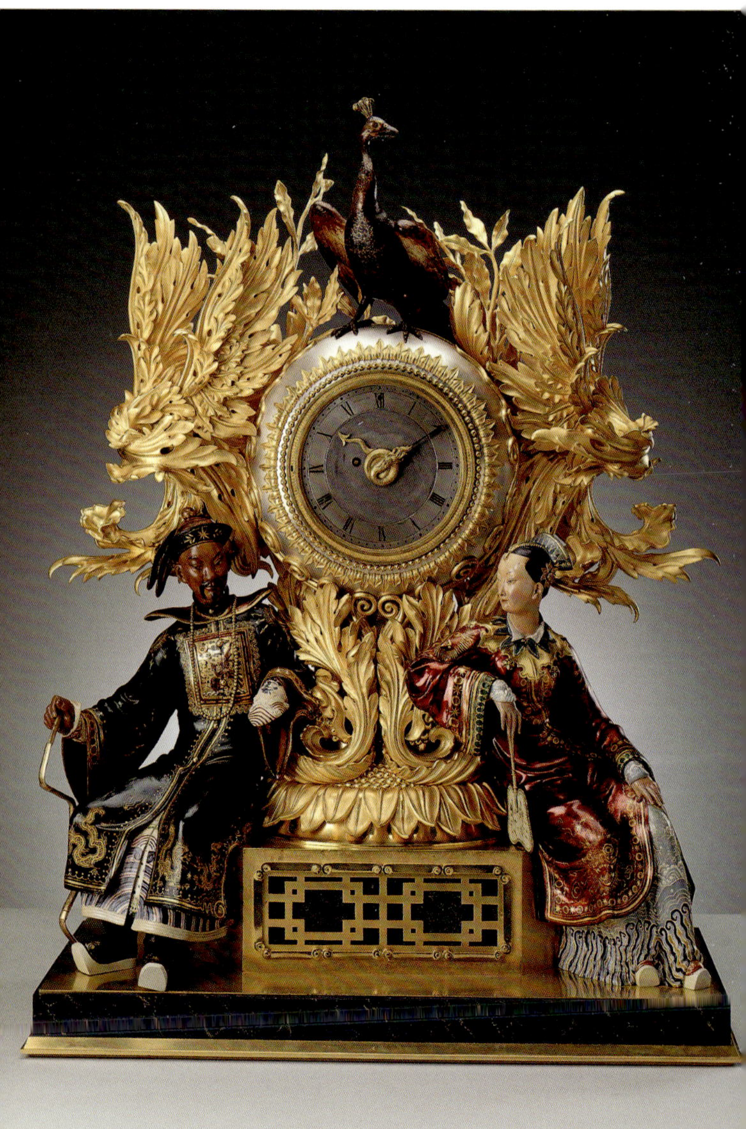

The Peacock Clock

Benjamin Lewis Vulliamy (1780–1854)

1819

Brighton Pavilion, for which this clock was made, was without doubt one of the most extraordinary and exotic buildings of its age. It was enlarged and altered over a 40-year period from the early 1780s, and the final phase of building and decoration, from 1815 to 1822, was the work of John Nash, George IV's favourite architect. Nash gave the exterior of the Pavilion its largely 'Indian' aspect, while the firm of Crace and the designer Robert Jones transformed the interiors into a fantastic and vividly colourful vision of Cathay.

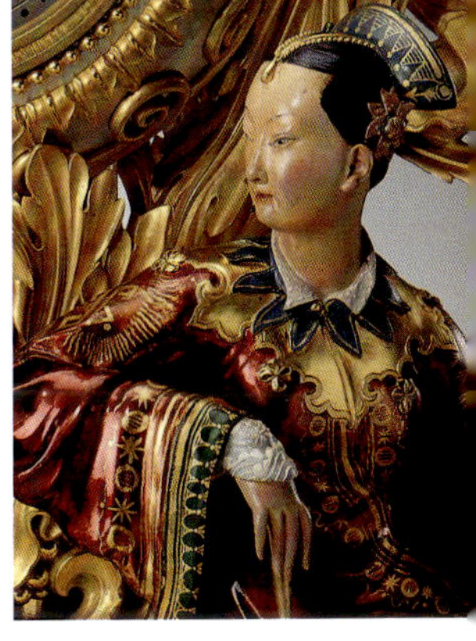

In the barbaric splendour of the Banqueting Room, designed by Jones, where dragons and Chinese figures abound, this clock and a matching barometer stood on the chimneypieces at either end. They were manufactured to Jones's design by George IV's versatile and gifted metalsmith and clock-maker, Benjamin Lewis Vulliamy. Each case is surmounted by a peacock supported on elaborate gilt foliage, seemingly in the form of winged creatures. Below, at either side, sit courtly Chinese figures wearing richly coloured robes, resting on a base veneered with lapis lazuli. The total cost for clock and barometer came to the large sum of £1,308. Both were moved to Windsor by Queen Victoria after the sale of the Pavilion in 1849.

Louis XV

Jean-Baptiste Le Moyne (1704–78)

1776

This bronze group is all that remains of a grandiose plan presented to Louis XV in 1757 to redevelop the centre of the city of Rouen in Normandy to accommodate a new square, the Place Royale. Rouen was one of a number of provincial capitals where civic improvements and statues in honour of the King were planned during the 1750s. The architect of the Rouen scheme, Antoine-Mathieu Charpentier, collaborated with the sculptor Le Moyne in the design of the monument, which recalls the tradition of the ancient Gauls who raised their chieftains aloft on a shield. The decision to depict the King in modern armour rather than disguised as a Greek or Roman hero was widely praised. Although the sculptor's model was accepted by the King, his death in 1774 brought the project to a halt. His successor and grandson Louis XVI ordered that the model should be preserved, and the founder, J.C. Delarche, made at least two bronze casts. This one, which was purchased by George IV in 1813, was probably the cast made specifically for Louis XVI.

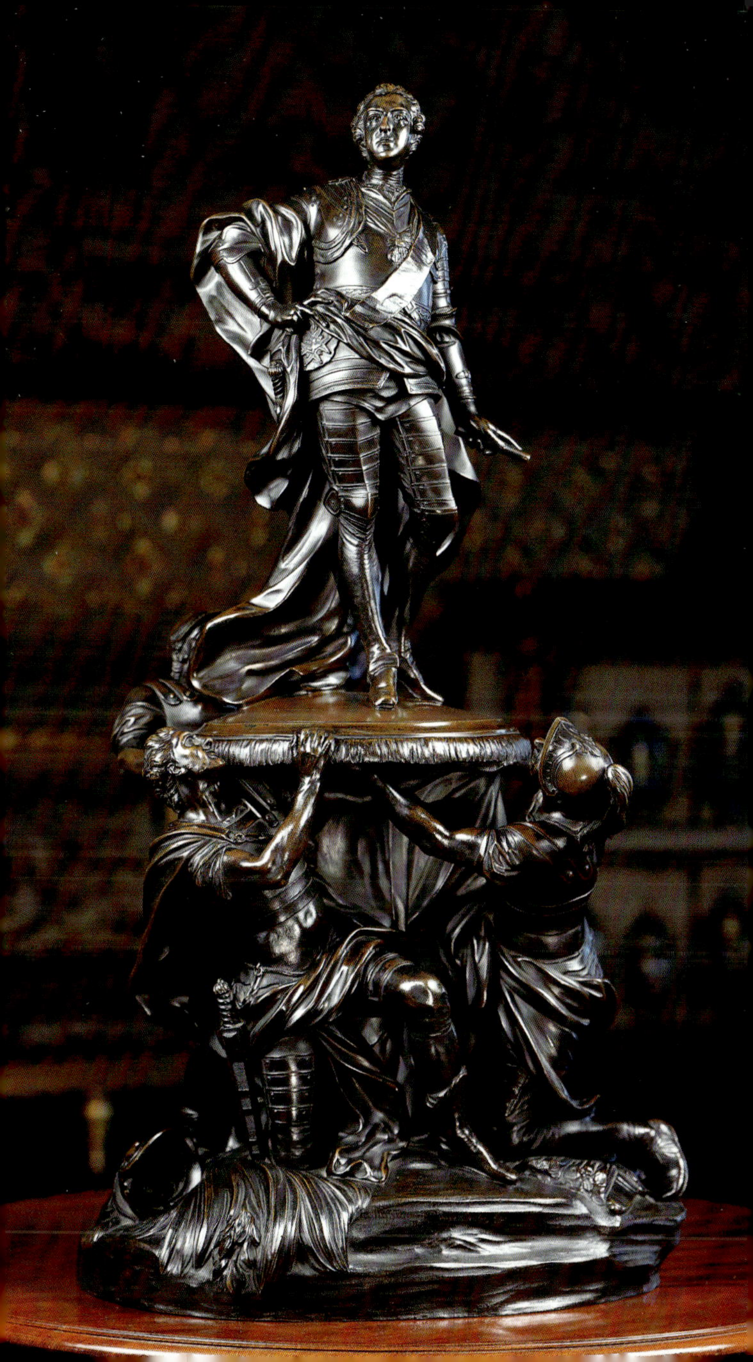

The Arch of Constantine

Giovacchino Belli (1756–1822) and Pietro Belli (1780–1828)

1808–15

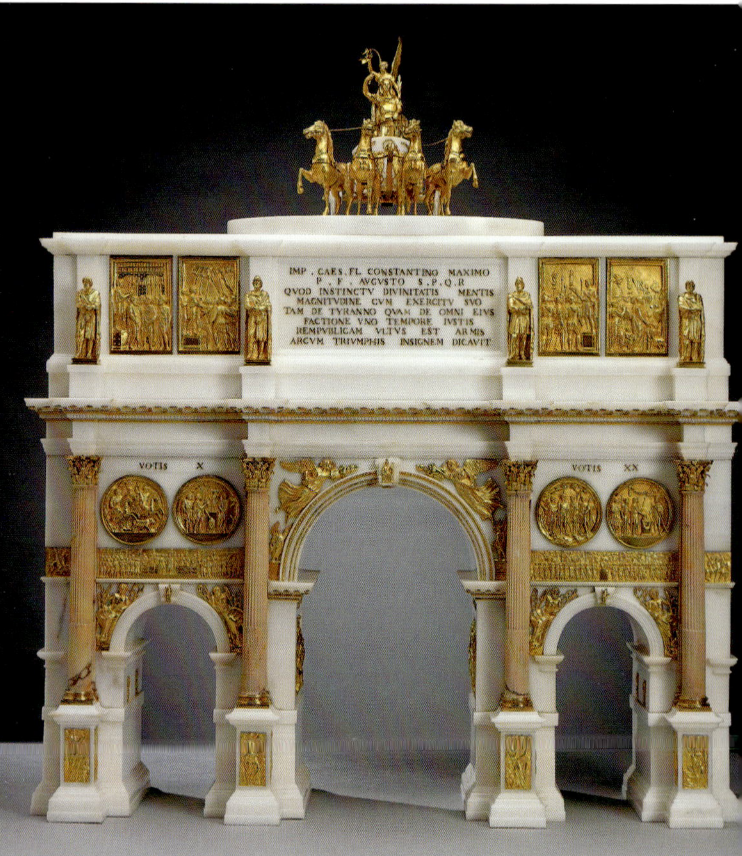

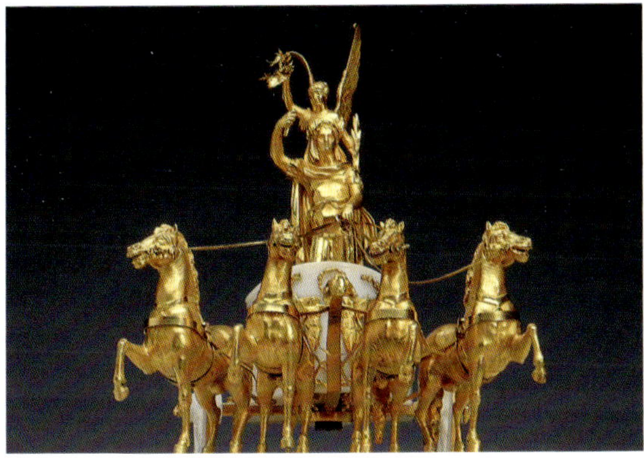

The three triumphal arches erected by the Emperors Titus, Septimius Severus and Constantine in the Forum at Rome have long been among the most famous of all ancient monuments. During the eighteenth and early nineteenth centuries they were admired by Grand Tourists, and studied, painted and drawn by artists and architects. Full-scale versions were built in many European capitals, including London and Paris, and small models were made as souvenirs for the libraries and cabinets of collectors.

This is one of three marble models of especially luxurious quality, made by the Roman silversmiths Giovacchino Belli and his son Pietro, under the auspices of the Academy of St Luke. Although the ancient arches themselves were in a ruinous and adapted state, the models reconstruct their original appearance. Seven years in the making, they incorporate hundreds of gilt-bronze plaquettes and mouldings, applied with what the sculptor Antonio Canova called 'genius, accuracy and infinite precision'. Probably designed originally with Napoleon in mind, the arches were brought to London after his defeat in 1815 and purchased by the Prince Regent for his library at Carlton House.

Queen Elizabeth II in Coronation Robes

Sir Herbert James Gunn (1893–1964)

1953–4

The state portrait of The Queen (b.1926) was commissioned to commemorate Her Majesty's Coronation, which took place on 2 June 1953. Wearing her coronation dress and the purple Robe of Estate, The Queen stands in the Throne Room at Buckingham Palace. Her robe falls over the throne specially made for the occasion and the Imperial State Crown and the sceptre are placed on the table beside her. The Queen wears the Diamond Diadem made for George IV, Queen Victoria's collet diamond necklace and diamond drop earrings, and the Collar and Badge of the Order of the Garter.

Her Majesty's dress, made of white satin, was designed by Sir Norman Hartnell, The Queen's principal dressmaker. The embroidery design incorporates national and Commonwealth emblems executed in seed pearls, crystals, coloured silks and gold and silver thread. The decoration on the robe comprises a border of wheat ears and olive branches, symbolising peace and plenty. It was embroidered by the Royal School of Needlework, who worked for a total of 3,500 hours between March and May 1953.

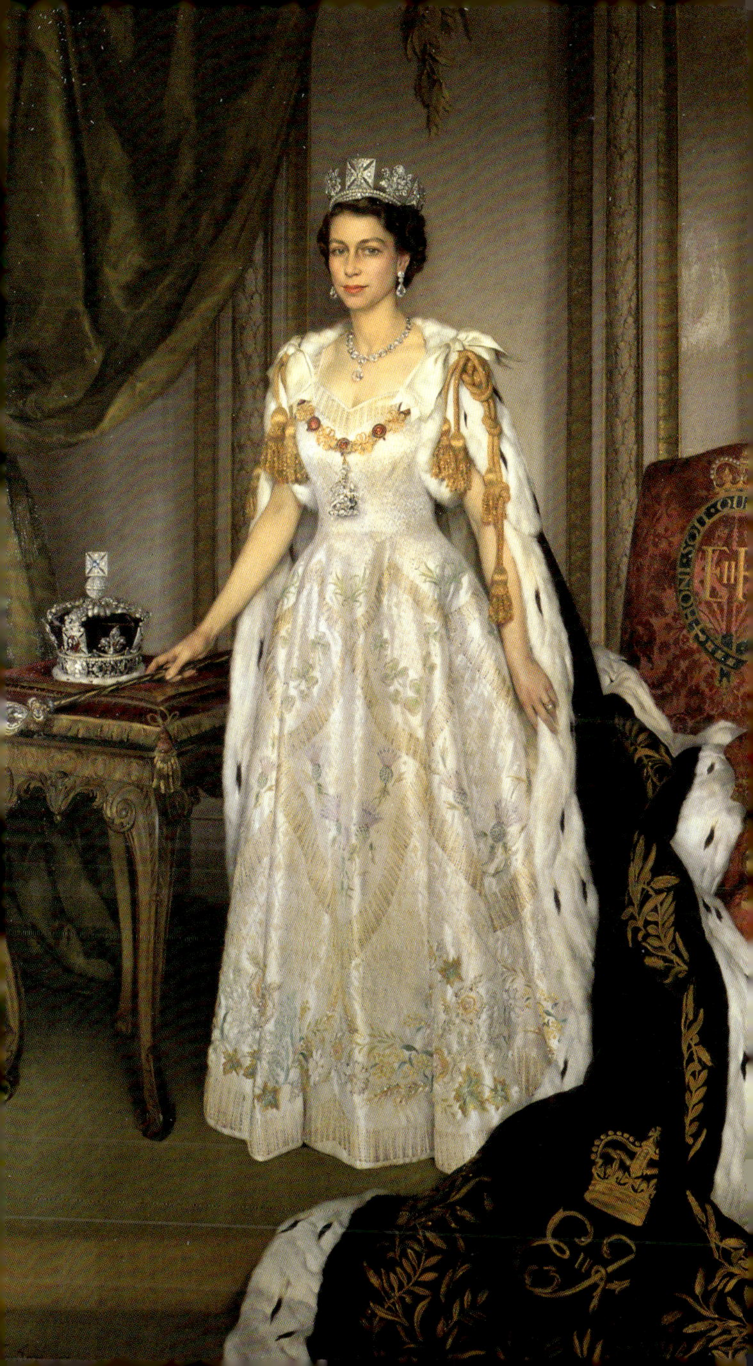

Ivory Throne
Southern India
c.1850

This magnificent throne was presented to Queen Victoria in 1851 by Maharajah Martanda Varma IV, the ruler of Travancore in southern India. The gift was intended to advertise the specialist skills of the ivory carvers of Travancore, and to this end it was displayed as the centrepiece of the Indian Court at the Great Exhibition in Hyde Park, opened by the Queen in May 1851. Its finest moment came when it was used by Prince Albert at the closing ceremony of the exhibition in October.

Basically of European form, the throne has a wooden frame, held together by a series of bolts with foliate gilt-bronze knobs. The decoration, which is highly elaborate, consists of panels of elephant ivory carved in low relief, partly in the European style, with lions, unicorns, dragons, putti and angels set among foliage. The cresting, carved with the conch shell emblem of Travancore, and supported by two mythic lions with elephant trunks, was originally set with jewelled ornaments, now detached. When Queen Victoria was proclaimed Empress of India in 1877, she was photographed seated on this throne, and until her death in 1901 it was placed under the canopy in the Garter Throne Room. It has recently been returned to this position.

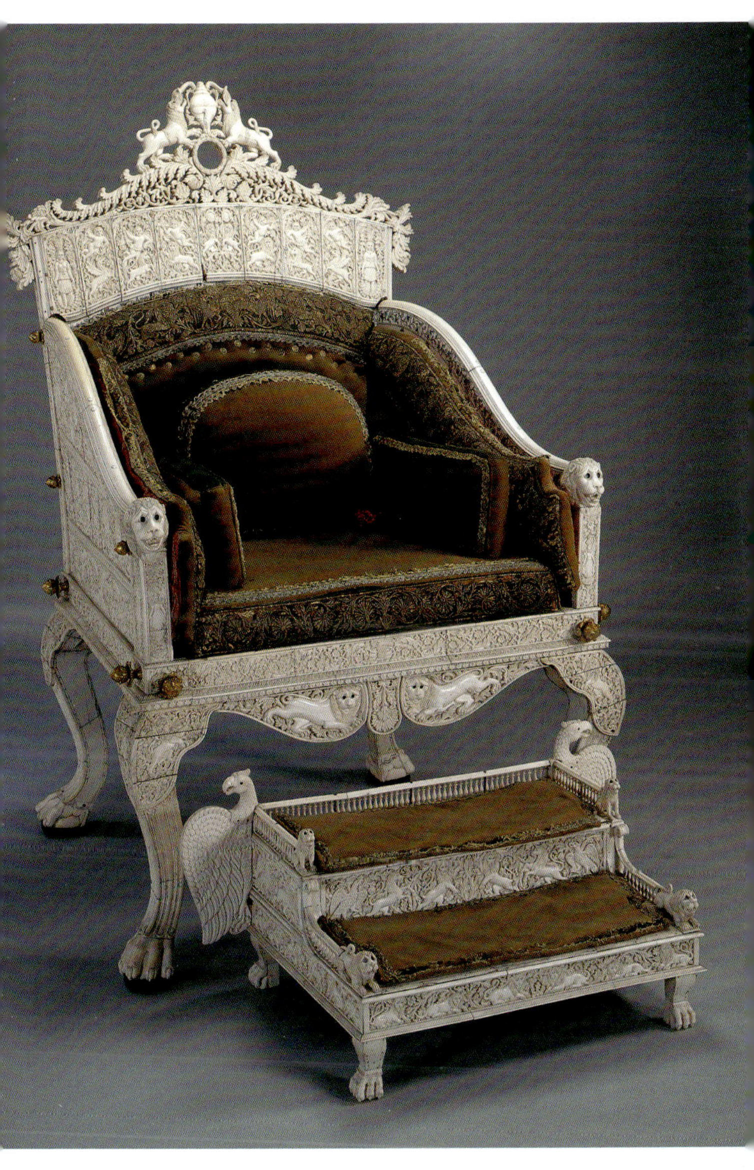

Further Information about the Royal Collection

This book is intended to introduce the reader to some of the most interesting items to be seen at Windsor Castle. There are many other publications which give further information about different aspects of the Royal Collection. Details of some of them are provided on the pages that follow. If you would like to receive a catalogue of current publications, please write to the address below, or visit our website at www.royalcollection.org.uk

Royal Collection Enterprises Ltd
St James's Palace
London SW1A 1JR

For tickets or more information on the opening of the State Apartments at Windsor Castle, please contact:

Ticket Sales and Information Office
Buckingham Palace
London SW1A 1AA

Credit card booking line: (+44) (0)20 7766 7304
Group bookings: (+44) (0)20 7766 7321
Fax: (+44) (0)20 7930 9625
Email: bookinginfo@royalcollection.org.uk
groupbookings@royalcollection.org.uk

Further reading

H.M. Colvin (ed.), *The History of the King's Works, I–VI*, London 1963–82.

D. Linstrum, *Sir Jeffry Wyatville: Architect to the King*, Oxford 1972.

D. Millar, *The Victorian Watercolours and Drawings in the Collection of HM The Queen*, London 1995.

O. Millar, *Tudor Stuart and Early Georgian Pictures in the Royal Collection*, London 1963.

O. Millar, *Later Georgian Pictures in the Royal Collection*, London 1969.

O. Millar, *The Victorian Pictures in the Collection of HM The Queen*, Cambridge 1992.

Adam Nicolson, *Restoration: The Rebuilding of Windsor Castle*, London 1997.

W.H. Pyne, *The History of the Royal Residences*, London 1819.

H. Roberts, *For The King's Pleasure: The Furnishing & Decoration of George IV's Apartments at Windsor Castle*, London 2001.

J. Roberts, *Views of Windsor: Watercolours by Thomas and Paul Sandby*, London 1995.

J. Roberts, *Royal Landscape: The Gardens and Parks of Windsor*, New Haven and London 1997.

J.M. Robinson, *Windsor Castle: A Short History*, London 1996.

W.H. St. John Hope, *Windsor Castle: An Architectural History*, London 1913.

Exhibition catalogues

London, The Queen's Gallery, Buckingham Palace, *Sèvres Porcelain from the Royal Collection*, 1979–80.

London, The National Gallery, *The Queen's Pictures. Royal Collectors Through the Centuries*, 1991.

London, The Queen's Gallery, Buckingham Palace, *Carlton House: The Past Glories of George IV's Palace*, 1991–2.

London, The Queen's Gallery, Buckingham Palace, *The Quest for Albion. Monarchy and the Patronage of British Painting*, 1998.

Cardiff, The National Museum and Gallery, *Princes as Patrons*, 1998.

London, The Queen's Gallery, Buckingham Palace, *Royal Treasures*, 2002–3.

London, The Queen's Gallery, Buckingham Palace, *George III & Queen Charlotte: Patronage, Collecting and Court Taste*, 2004.

Edinburgh, The Queen's Gallery, Palace of Holyroodhouse, *Holbein to Hockney: Drawings from the Royal Collection*, 2004.

London, The Queen's Gallery, Buckingham Palace, *Renaissance & Baroque: The Art of Italy in the Royal Collection*, 2007.

Text written by Hugh Roberts and Jonathan Marsden, with Alexandra Buck, Martin Clayton, Kathryn Jones, Leonora Martin and David Oakey.

Index

Page numbers in **bold** refer to illustrations.

First published 2008 by Royal Collection Enterprises Ltd
St James's Palace, London SW1A 1JR

ISBN 978-1-905686-02-5

158980

British Library Cataloguing in Publication Data:
A catalogue record of this book is available from the British Library.

Production by Debbie Wayment
Designed by Mick Keates
Editorial and Project Management by Alison Thomas
Printed in Singapore by C.S. Graphics Pte Ltd.

COVER ILLUSTRATIONS

Main illustration: Gold Tiger's Head (p.40)
Inset illustrations (top to bottom): Tatham, Bailey and Sanders, Pair of Giltwood Tables (p.206); Anthony Van Dyck, *The Five Eldest Children of Charles I* (p.126); The Armour of Henry, Prince of Wales (p.36); Leonardo da Vinci, *A Masquerader* (p.24); Brameld Brothers, The Rockingham Service (p.30)
Back: Sir Herbert James Gunn, *Queen Elizabeth II in Coronation Robes* (p.214)
Title page illustration: Leonard Knyff, *Windsor Castle* (p.96)

PHOTOGRAPHIC CREDITS

Page 10 ©Peter Packer; *Pages 12–13* ©John Freeman; *Page 15* ©Peter [illegible]; *Page* [illegible] ©The Dean and Canons of St George's Chapel, *Page 18* ©G. Newbery; *Page 19* ©David Cripps; *Page 35* ©Peter Smith; *Pages 38–39* ©Mark Fiennes; *Page 124* ©John Freeman; *Page 138* ©Mark Fiennes; *Page 156* ©Mark Fiennes; *Page 159* ©Mark Fiennes; *Page 170* ©Mark Fiennes